# The Voyage of Storm Petrel
## Book Two

# The Voyage of Storm Petrel

**Gambia and Europe Alone in a Boat**

Clarissa Vincent

Published by: girl in a gale books.
Copyright © 2012 Clarissa Vincent
All rights reserved. No part of this book may be reproduced in whole or in part (other than for purposes of review), nor may any part of this book be stored in an information retrieval system without written permission from the publisher.
A catalogue record for this book is available from the British library.
Typesetting and design by Clarissa Vincent
Photographs Copyright ©2012 Clarissa Vincent
Illustration - Maps - Copyright ©2012 Becky Gilbey

# The Voyage of Storm Petrel
### Book Two
## Gambia and Europe alone in a boat

## Acknowledgements

The inspiration to set sail on a long voyage was Anne and Neville on a newly built Wharram Tiki catamaran called Peace Four, in Bristol Marina. They left for Spain within days of the start of the voyage of Storm Petrel and nurtured me, like a mother gull, all the way to Portugal. To Kresza who loved bashing around the North Sea, France and Belgium in bobble hats and duffel coats with me and my dream of one day sailing to Spain. Often alone I'd imagine conversations with Kresza and laugh at the rawness and vulnerability of being far from land in a small boat. Thanks to Becky Gilbey for her gorgeously sensual illustrations - Maps. To my Mum and Dad for their unfailing support and worry while I was out on the wide grey sea of life. Thanks to Felix Grant for constantly encouraging me to do whatever I wanted to do.

Warm respect to shipmate Buba Samateh of Kemoto, The Gambia, who taught me the River Gambia ways and then helped sail 1500 kilometres back from west Africa to the Canaries, a hard slog of 27 days against the prevailing Atlantic Ocean winds and currents.

A special mention of my cairn terrier, 'Loba', who joined the voyage in the Canaries. She led me away from the Atlantic Ocean, towards the inland waterways of France. Now I'm a sailor home from the sea, in Woodbridge, Suffolk and Loba continues to be my constant companion.

## Forward

The free spirit, Clarissa Vincent.

I've known Clarissa for several years, through hundreds of email communications, and have not only learned to love her as a sister but admire her courage and energy. Google her name and she pops up everywhere. You'll discover her blog and music (she plays sax and guitar, on her own and with a group) via her YouTube presence. You'll find her on social networking sites, and somewhere along the line you'll learn of her ability to repair or improvise just about anything.

Best of all, she has allowed us to vicariously experience her sailing adventures through her book, "The Voyage of Storm Petrel". She followed her dream of sailing alone out of Bristol, UK to several destination points, found a best friend (Loba), and boldly extended her voyage to include Gambia, Africa. And if that weren't enough activity to make most of us gape in awe, she has acquired a motorcycle and is now legally licensed to pilot it to new adventures. Clarissa is an amazing person of diverse talent, a true inspiration to fulfil our dreams, live our lives and enjoy them to the fullest, just as we should.

Gayle Reynolds

# Chapters

1. Dakar                                     1

2. Mind out your tea's getting hot!      54

3. Loba Joins the Voyage             127

4. A Braver Coast: The Costa Brava    169

5. The French Inland Waterways       209

# Chapter 1

# Dakar

## Ten Kilometres Before Arrival at Dakar

"Bonjour madam, avez vous du pain?" The Senegalese fishing boat went away with my gift of a packet of pumpernickel bread, leaving a hot afternoon a few kilometres from the city of Dakar. I was 11 days out of the Canary Islands, having sailed past the coasts of Morocco, the Sahara Desert and Mauritania, to arrive off Senegal in West Africa.

During the evening I drifted and paddled around the headland until at midnight a slight breeze got Storm Petrel trickling along towards Hann Plage, a beach marked on the chart. The Dakar Yacht Club promised a sheltered anchorage and a meeting place for sailors from all seas.

I anchored and slept. In the morning I looked out at a new land feeling elated to have made the choice to come. My first night's sleep at anchor in the calm bay was not blissful, as expected after the eleven day voyage, it was deathlike. I awoke feeling rigor mortised rather than rested and my back ached. It was Sunday so I remained aboard waiting for Monday when I could clear–in with the port authorities – I was also reluctant to actually venture ashore as, through binoculars, I scanned a dense mass of humanity sprawling together on the beach, all robed and wearing head scarves or little round hats, which was all a bit shocking. I was seeing Hann fish market and later when my initial culture shock reduced I was to stroll freely amongst this stinking market place which was also full of laughter and people being alive to one another.

A hilarious moment in Hann market involved two fish wives posing for me to take pictures, one of them turning around and offering her behind to the camera. There were persistent attempts by youngish men to accompany me and try to tell me what would make a good photograph but of course they were trying to guide me with a view to getting some money for the service. I learned to move around alone and politely dismiss all befrienders. An older man was perturbed by the camera and he told me that many people on the beach felt uncomfortable about being photographed, so I wandered through the crowds, stepping over warps attached to pirogues and fending off the stares, the laughter, the curiosity towards this white person, with my camera held more discreetly in my hand. Gradually I felt I was learning to be more self-assured, giving a little time to questions and comments here, taking leave of cheeky kids there, treating lightly the occasional humiliation of being a stranger in a strange land.

There was a beach with the CVD compound, a large fish market and a fleet of pirogues. Pirogues were open wooden fishing boats, with a hole cut in the aft keel to take the leg of an outboard motor, they ranged in length from 4–15m and I was riveted by the sight of the big pirogues grounded near the beach for discharging fish, swaying gently to the swell and canted over like a toy. Pirogue construction was done by eye – nothing written down – using sawn hardwood beams and planks. A large pirogue must have weighed many tons with such massive hardwood scantlings. Beams ran across the whole internal length, like a wooden bridge structure and the ten to fourteen crew clambered over and among the cross beams to work and sleep. In a large round ceramic pot, or a heap of sand, a fire was lit at night to cook food and for light. Wooden boxes fitted between the cross frames, filled the spaces like plugs, a kind of container hold. Salt and ice, curiously, mixed together, preserved the catch for up to two weeks as these boats occasionally fished all the way down to Sierra Leon and when the boats were hauled ashore for maintenance the boxes were lifted out onto the beach for the crew to use as living shelters while they waited to go fishing again. A trip down to Sierra Leone would last ten days – three days going; three fishing; and three back – with one day for all the other things which happen at sea, such as fouled nets, engine breakdown or collision with cruising yachts. Hundreds of pirogues lay resting in the silver sand above the tide line of deep green seaweed, some in repair and others finally rotting. Black kites, palm vultures and white waist–coated pied crows floated on the seemingly unceasing trade winds.

The CVD (Cercle de Voile de Dakar – Dakar yacht club) was a tranquil, tree shaded compound, a bar, a kitchen, sail workshop, showers, hand washing sinks and washer women, on site mechanic and other resources. Hammocks swung lazily between trees, beneath the liquid calls of tropical birds. The nasal whirring of a single hornbill (Bucerotidae) sounded like a group of four or five birds calling together. Lizards clung to sun drenched walls along the beach called Hann Plage and scuttled back, bobbing their heads into the narrative time and time again and so I apologise for mentioning them every time I saw them, but I always loved seeing lizards.

A more or less middle class suburb of Dakar existed back from the beach. Garden walls reached from the distinctly Moorish styled, pied–a–mer villas, into the sand, where big lizards lived. From an equestrian centre, aloofly poised French girls and steely set men, emerged on horses to ride along the less crowded reaches of beach in full dressage. Occasionally a romantic broke with form to thunder along the edge of the waves, wearing nothing but a pony tail, rolled up trousers and t–shirt. One day a horse and rider waded into the sea, up to the horses belly and stood for ten minutes facing out to sea. I wondered whether the horse looked at the ocean as an endless expanse of belly deep water because it had never walked further than belly deep, like a flat earth view of the sea. Further along towards the fish market a black, stinking, open sewer snaked out over the beach to slither into the sea. Women carrying plastic bowls filled with beans, rice, fresh water, trays of fish or cosmetics to sell, paused at the black obstacle to pick there way across where it divided in two, or to tread across a bridge of driftwood.

The fish market happened each day with the arrival of dozens of pirogues, tilting and swivelling in the shallows. The market was a mass of buyers and sellers. Carriers waded to and from the grounded boats and the crowded beach. Mooring warps lifted and dropped with the strain of the slowly heaving pirogues, which appeared like giant seed pods. The market solidified into stalls and covered hovels.

Café touba was a local, strong, herb flavoured coffee which was drunk sitting on nailed up benches, around a low table set inside a structure of wood, corrugated sheet and wispy thin, printed materials. Through these sun bleached veils the scene took on a grainy, filmic look. Faces appeared around the curtains, to greet friends, to moan at someone, to stare at the toubab (white person), or just to enter the café On the road, horses, carts and freezer–vans dripping with melting fish–ice and skip–loads of small rotting fish, trundled away on lorries called "city boy", to be made into fish paste. Some trucks were dismantled on the sand roads. One day an extracted lorry axle with differential gear appeared. Sand paths between shanty dwellings led past boutiques, small grocery stores and children playing football. Chickens stared into grey puddles of waste water. Goats wandered in search of mountains. Flies swarmed in forgetful loops.

Further from the beach were hairdressers, tele–centers, wood carvers and a freezer repair shop. Each day the wood carver said he had no money and asked me to give him an advance on a carving. I greatly admired the convoluted, abstract, hardwood sculptures, particularly a stool of shining hard wood in the shape of a flopping whales tail. However I dared not enter any type of negotiation because I would surely end up with the piece aboard Storm Petrel, but it was too big. Stalls offering sacks of dried beans, herbs in tiny plastic wraps and vegetables, were crowded in lines, or haphazardly arranged where people walked, which was anywhere. Market stalls were shacks and dens, ranging from cement closets with corrugate roofs, down to three tomatoes, an onion and an aubergine laid on a piece of cloth, unshaded on the ground. Lemons, green peppers, chillies and bananas wrinkled in the sun and were gripped by flies and still more flies formed holding patterns above them. Raw, unchilled meat was chopped and laid out for sale on a bare wooden counter. Hardly any flies landed on the meat. Wheelbarrows of oranges scented these shack alleys with piles pre–peeled in perfect spirals, stacked in pyramids and the scent of cut lemons pierced the stench of putrefying fish guts. Other smells, like burning shoe factories and smouldering waste tips, blew on the wind from a nearby petroleum refinery. Children offered handshakes, saying, "toubab," white person – others said, "Bonjour," good day. Some grown–ups asked for money, but children were radiantly pleased to exchange greetings with the toubab.

Capa village continued up from the fish market. People sat, lazed, stood and walked everywhere. Next to the road was a table football game, in continuous use, crowded round and twisted–at aggressively by grubby boys. They rarely glanced up as this "toubab" passed by. The little moulded footballers had been freshly painted with black hair and deep pink faces. Flies landed on everything and then settled at the edge of my mouth for a quick drink. Men lay sleeping in the midday sun, in empty sand filled lots and on unused stalls, anywhere. Men slept everywhere, an anorak over the head out in the midday sun. A hairdresser worked with a wooden framed mirror hung on a tree and a wooden chair for the client. Men and boys invariably had a head shave.

Baobab trees had bulbous trunks and wriggly, strange branches making them cartoonish. Ancient baobabs gain a spirit which could be consulted for help. A baobab lived next to the internet café in Capa, called "Capanet", a signboard attached high up the massive baobab tree trunk offered, "cle minute", one minute key cutting.

The CVD had been open for seventy years. Senegal had had independence from France for forty three years. France continued to reduce financial support for Senegal. Throngs of humanity lived in and around the crumbling French colonial city of Dakar. It seemed everywhere things were offered for sale – an old office telephone, a couple of fish on ice in a black carrier bag, shoe shine, toothpaste, sunglasses, peanuts, dried hibiscus flowers from which a tea was made, cassette tapes. These items were continuously waved past the windows of traffic jammed cars. At least it was easy to say no, with the sellers so beset by dust and exhaust fumes they floated wearily onwards to another vehicle.

La Place de l'indépendance was a large square at the centre of Dakar where dusty children thrust their hands out for money and the streets were busy with hawkers and hustlers. A man walking on all fours, with arm–like legs, winked charmingly, flirtatiously. He was good looking and I gave him some coins because his need was immediate and great. People talked, greeted, engaged and followed me, the white tourist.

## Mr Gambishirt

I was sold a mauve tunic I had no intention of buying. A "boubous" or "gambishirt" was a gaily coloured batik dyed, long sleeved garment. Tourists loved to bargain for a gambishirt as a souvenir of Gambia. I met a Gambian – many Gambians lived in Senegal – he looked wholesome enough, with a big smile and sparkling eyes and he disarmed me when he said he knew me from the CVD. He wore a long white boubous with embroidery down the front and a large watch garishly decorated with fake blue jewels. I should have judged him by his watch rather than by his face. I needed to break down a 10,000 and two 5,000 CFA notes – a total of about £19.00. In the stores and restaurants around the CVD it was only useful to have smaller 1000 CFA notes. Mr Gambishirt said he could help and introduced me to a street money changer, but he could not break down the notes so Mr Gambishirt led me, eventually, to the shop of a friend. In a spirit of openness to new experience, I followed the man into the store. I was led through two dim rooms stacked with shelf loads of clothing and then upstairs. Looking back I just do not know how I could have been so naive. At some point between admitting they were nice bright colours and nonchalantly asking what kind of prices they sold for – you know, when the type of people who bought these sorts of things actually bought them? Unfortunately this question seemed to mean – I am going to buy this boubous and now we can agree a price between us. The asking price was 39,000 CFA, about £39.00 and a huge amount for a boubous. I countered with 1,500, which was what a local would actually pay, around one pound fifty pence. An intake of breath from the seller told me my offer was unrealistic and downright rude. He said, "that is only two euros, the price of a cup of coffee! Come on." Mr Gambishirt smiled kindly and chuckled at my super low offer, which at least had told him I had been in Senegal for more than an hour. Many tourists would knock a third off the asking price and be happy to bargain upwards from there. However, I had been feeling "Dakar struck" when he first approached me and Mr Gambishirt would have recognized the overwhelmed tourist in me. Despite my initial hard nosed offer he knew he could make more out of me. My low offer nonetheless, had given me composure and some courage to resist what then quickly became a tedious and persuasive sales pitch. I was committed, but then I noted to myself that every garment in the store was short sleeved. I very nearly escaped after declaring I definitely did not wish to buy any type of short sleeved garment. I explained how mosquitoes would bite uncovered arms. Clutching this new tactic perhaps a little triumphantly, I moved towards the front of the store and the exit. Within fifteen seconds armfuls of different garments were arriving in the room – long sleeve garments – and somewhere deep inside I knew I was going to have to buy one. This would not have been the case after a couple of weeks, when I learned to be more direct in the face of sellers and hustlers, to say, "No!"

A bespectacled man in a round hat and sunglasses looked much less trustworthy than Mr Gambishirt. He told me the profits from the store went to aid families of a recent ferry disaster. I remembered hearing about the ferry in the news. It had been over crowded and hundreds of lives were lost in the sea between Senegal and Gambia, but this was not charity it was intimidation. Mr Gambishirt had more than his blue bejewelled watch up his sleeve as he told me he had a new baby, as he pressed a fetish and a gold trinket into my palm and said I would bring good luck for his baby if I simply accepted the tokens and sent a postcard from England when I returned, insisting, "No, no, no, I don't want any money for these. They are a gift to bring good luck to my baby. That's right put them in your pocket." Alarm bells were ringing in my head. I'd read somewhere of a scam involving tokens, babies and eventual demands for money. A lizard ran into the room, bobbed its head and disappeared behind a new pile of long sleeved boubous. Next I had one on. It was a fetching mauve, my favourite colour because it picked out my blue eyes and blond hair. Mr Gambishirt complemented me on my choice of mauve, saying how attractive I was in it as his watch and eyes twinkled. The other seller was still smarting from my first, depressive offer and stayed voyeuristically silent. If he spoke he only spoke prices. Other workers glumly moved around carrying arm loads of folded boubous, which one day would be foisted on other unwilling, frightened tourists. I went to remove the boubou and several voices said, "No, no, it looks so good, you must keep it, keep it on." I dragged it off over my head and then delved into my bag to find my purse which momentarily captivated the peering faces now wanting to see what it contained. I may have been from a ship picking up petty cash and in possession of several hundred thousand CFA.

The bargaining process ended as I wriggled my way out of the bowels of the clothes shop, clutching a fetish, 25 grams of gold coloured trinket, a mauve boubous and barely my patience. I had paid 10 times a days wages for a Senegalese unskilled labourer. Also, I was tricked out of two days pay for the same unskilled labourer by the switching of a five thousand CFA note for a one thousand CFA note, by the ugly one in the hat and sunglasses. When I scoffed at the switch, an even bigger scoff went up in the now gloating group of workers who had assembled to watch the toubab spend like a toubab. The fetish and gold trinket trick came next. It was now only hard cash, there and then, which could bestow any benefit on Mr Gambishirt's new baby. I refused outright and there was a moment when Monsieur Gambishirt tried to take money from my jeans pocket. This made me cross, which gave me the presence of mind and an opportunity to walk defiantly away. Gambia–man's fingers beckoned for the return of the fetish and trinket and I angrily said, "But you gave me this as a gift", he looked surprised, even guilty and I shoved the objects into his hand and stomped resolutely away toward La Place de l'indépendance. The gambishirt was a lovely shade of mauve. I would probably never wear it, but I would keep it as a souvenir of week one in West Africa.

Supermarkets had names such as, "Fili Fili", a much richer use of language than the UK's "KwikSave". The trouble was supermarkets lacked the seduction of European ones with shopping consisting of swapping value, rather than the more exciting search for solutions to ones own unique needs and aspirations. In Europe, shopping was largely a ritual of self–actualisation and discovery. In Dakar, self–fulfilment came through the direct exchange of goods and money.

## Chez Taty

Close to the CVD was a tiny restaurant called Chez Taty where I took breakfast and lunch. Breakfast was a baguette, spread with butter and wrapped in newspaper. This was taken with an extremely sweet milky coffee made with Nescafé instant. Lunch was the national dish – riz au poisson stewed fish stuffed with pepper, tomato and onion, with boiled yam, aubergine, cabbage and a yellow, tomato shaped vegetable which tasted deliciously firm and bitter. The rice was cooked in the juices of the stewed fish. The price of lunch was 30p. Marie was one of five women who worked in Chez Taty. She loved the tiny, bright, screen images of her and the others in the café on my digital camera which was swept away from my grasp as Marie rushed off to show the others the images. Marie asked how much the camera cost and it seemed meaningless as I told her it cost me 250,000 CFA. That amount would pay for eight thousand, three hundred and thirty three scrumptious plates of riz au poisson. Did my camera cost so much? Or, was riz au poisson so cheap? I wanted to tell Marie that my digital camera was priceless and that the fleeting moments it bagged were precious as jewels – the split seconds it captured were chiselled silver and that the treasure it landed me made me richer than I ever imagined I could be. Nonetheless Marie gave me delicious food at delicious prices.

I had been getting along really well with the local people of Hann, with my survival instinct of firstly befriending everyone and then gradually retracting from people who were ill mannered. The people I met were friendly and open. Older children sometimes stared rudely but they could usually be disarmed by a greeting in French, "Bonjour, ca va!", when purchasing items in small stores or markets, children often rudely moved in close to stare until the sellers sharply told them to go away. Amusing for the local people was when I talked Wolof, "Nangadef" – hello. "Mangifi" – it goes well. It was not for everyone to say, "Ca va bien" – It goes well – and often the response was "Ca va, un peu" – It goes, a bit.

Most evenings a woman came to the CVD to sell peanut brittle, cheese, or a plate of deep fried fish snacks, called "pastels". Pastels came with a hot pepper sauce. One evening the trader, the bar woman – Nday – and I, sat at the bar. She was waiting for more people to arrive in the hope of selling something. When she did not order a drink, I offered to buy her one. She thanked me and said something I did not understand. After a few moments, Nday explained the seller would like to have the money for a drink rather than taking the drink itself. This made me suddenly aware of the sharp contrast between my world and that of the seller. I gave her 500 CFA (fifty pence), the price of a coke and she gratefully accepted it. I also gave her another 500 CFA for a delivery of peanut brittle the next day. She was a small, married woman, with a broad smile and bright eyes. She wore an anorak and a headscarf and a long skirt. She carried her wares in a large plastic tub. The following day when the evening came around and the seller turned up again, I greeted her, "Bonsoir. Ca va?". She beamed at me and said, cheerfully, "Bonsoir, ca va bien". She had extra wares, a couple of bottles of perfume and several eye shadow kits, in the shape of mobile phones.

Each morning at the ambrosial hour a din of train horns carried over Hann Plage from the junction in Capa where the railway from Dakar passed out through the suburbs. Goats, hawkers, labourers, buses, cars and taxis lingered over the junction of railway and road. Shanty huts lined the scar of dust and sand. Paths, tracks and roads, wended and criss–crossed the tortuously parallel railway lines, only briefly occupied as the trains passed, the press of humanity flowing back over the railway in front of and behind each horn blasting train.

Many fishermen worked all night, offshore in pirogues and the dusty figures asleep in the sand or between stalls were not idle, or unemployed. Fleets of unlit pirogues between Dakar and Gambia were considered so much of a risk to sailors it was dangerous to try to sail by night. I heard a story of a French yacht being boarded by fishermen from a pair of pirogues after it had unknowingly passed between the unlit boats at night and fouled a large net, damaging it. A demand for the cost of repair was made, the equivalent to two hundred UK pounds.

Fishing boats have the right of way in general but surely not when they work with no lights at all?

Telephones were expensive for international calls. I paid 5000 CFA for a seven minute call to my parents in the UK. The internet café was much more affordable, costing 350 CFA per hour. This was five UK pounds for a seven minute phone call or 35p for an hour in an internet café. The walk to Capa was less than a mile. Sometimes I took the high street which was groaning with trucks, whistling taxi drivers, horses pulling carts, as well as cars and Land Rover Discovery type vehicles.

Alternatively I walked along Hann Plage to enjoy the view out over the bay. The bay was under Presqu'ile, a peninsular with the major headland of Cap Vert, the most western point of Africa. The city of Dakar was also contained on this lobe of land. Dakar was the capital of Senegal and the most cosmopolitan city in West Africa. The beach led away to the east and then the south in a great curve disappearing into the dry season haze within 5–6 km. Beyond the limit of visibility was the river country, Gambia, 152 km to the south. Reports came of a military confrontation in southern Senegal, the area of the Casamance river, between southern Senegalese separatists and the army of Guinea Bissau. Despite this ongoing situation the Casamance river continued to be visited by a number of French yachts. The people who went to the Casamance said there was no trouble in the navigable section of the river. The news in early March reported armed bandits emerging from Guinea Bissau to raid villages, stealing cattle and robbing banks in the eastern Casamance.

My main navigation chart reached right from Lisbon in Portugal, to Freetown in Sierra Leone, a distance of over 2000 km but for several weeks my visible horizon became reduced to the CVD compound. A daily stroll to Capanet, the internet café was as far as I went away from the boat and CVD. Having found central Dakar too much hassle and not yet having planned any exploration of the hinterlands. Until the mechanic, Aruna, mended my engine I had to stay in Dakar as a motor would be essential to travel up the River Gambia. I learned to go around alone, although not at night for initially in Senegal I felt everyone was calling, laughing, asking my name, trying to trick me and wanting to get to know me. I felt intimidated during the day and drained by evening.

During my second week in West Africa, I was happy to move about freely, with composure and resistance. Teeth sucking noises from solicitous taxi drivers continued, as did all the other attention grabbing attempts, "Ello!", and "Bonjour Madam," but I stopped jerking around to them and the hassle rolled off me to be reabsorbed into the heat and dust – eaten up by the famished road.

*Dakar yacht club moorings*

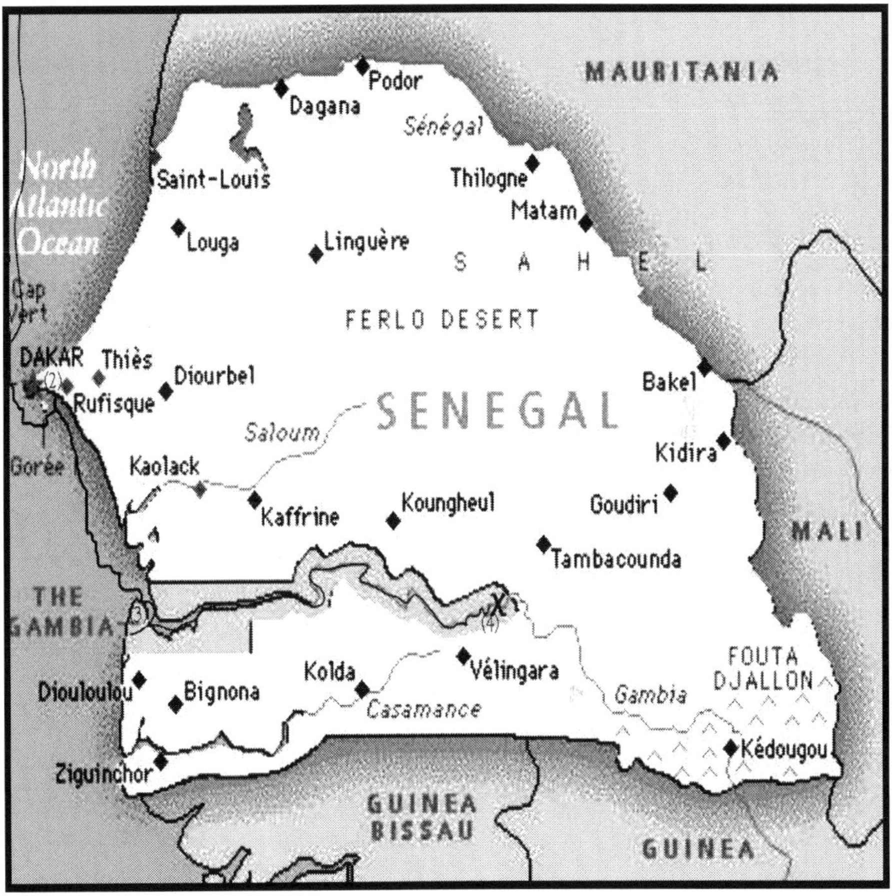
MAURITANIA
Podor
Dagana
Sénégal
North Atlantic Ocean
Saint-Louis
Thilogne
Matam
Louga
Linguère
S A H E L
Cap Vert
FERLO DESERT
DAKAR
Thiès
Diourbel
Bakel
(2)
Rufisque
SENEGAL
Saloum
Kidira
Gorée
Kaolack
Goudiri
Kaffrine
Koungheul
MALI
Tambacounda
THE GAMBIA
(3)
(4)
FOUTA DJALLON
Vélingara
Kolda
Dioulouiou
Bignona
Gambia
Casamance
Kédougou
Ziguinchor
GUINEA BISSAU
GUINEA

## The Fish are in the Trees

I lay down in a hammock in the yacht club garden. I was calming down after my Psion 5 spontaneously reset itself and I lost a weeks writing. Through overhead branches I watched black kites wheeling against the sky, until I noticed a fish hanging there, probably dropped by one of the kites that landed in the tops of the trees. A sentence formed in my thoughts, "Le poisson c'est dans l'arbre". I laughed out loud and it was pleasant to find life funny again after the frustrating loss of text.

I was sad to see lions in a zoo, the Parc Zoologique du Hann. Monkeys and other primates were utterly captivating. A big male clung to the front of the cage, fielding nuts and exhibiting an erect, red penis and a tumid and hairless anus, like a pink cushion tied to his rear. Occasionally he would throw things hard and accurately through the bars. Something wet clipped the back of my hand. He wore an original 1970s mullet hairstyle. The female screamed and bobbed behind and to the side of him, lips drawn back, bearing her violent teeth and flicking her eyebrows, advancing and retreating again and again. She monitored every snigger, caught each grin, glowered at glances and rushed at foot falls of the four human animals standing before the cage. They were fascinating and another primate in the next cage along bounced up and down, hair plunging and flopping around a face like a rock musician. Theirs was an absolute body language and their behaviour and expressions were unsettling – so similar to our own human ones.

A camel stood, head and neck projecting over an enclosure fence. I walked toward the huge, chestnut brown creature when a rumbling, growling groan began, low in the base of its neck, working upwards towards those camel lips. I thought it was going to spit at me, so I hid behind a tree. Instead, a purple tongue lolled out of the side of its mouth. Next it swallowed everything, noise and grotesque tongue, down into place again. The camel looked at me peeping from behind the tree as if I was foolish, but I had no reference for camel moods and its expression was as much that of a hellish spitter, as a friendly cow. I wished the camel well with a spell of positive visualisation – imagining it bathed in sparkling blue light – an intuitive outlet of compassion driven by my feeling helpless in the poorly furnished zoo filled with ailing creatures in cramped cages.

There was even a herring gull pacing around with no space to fly inside a bare cage, an end section, next to a pair of huge fish eagles. Alternatively, I may have been struggling to impose a mental image of a perfect creature in place of the unhappy one in front of me. Just before the rumbling, growling throat noises began again, two heavily lidded camel eyes met my gaze and I wondered whether maybe the camel felt sorry for ME. The camel said, "Bonjour Madam, avez vous du pain?" Then a spirit, shaped like a vulture, flapped onto a tall tree stump, drawn by the camel talk. I kicked the tree and it flew away. For a brief, irrational moment I was a spirit child, the camel was talking and the vulture was also a spirit. The camel began rumbling and gurgling deep in its neck as I strolled off towards a pair of horses tethered further along the path which I tried to console by telling them they would become unicorns, one day when this horrible, cruel zoo was closed.

I enjoyed those peaceful, sad, funny, enchanted moments out of the realm of people. I was more disturbed by the captivity of zoo animals than by the toil of working beasts – mules pulling carts and goats foraging along the great Rue de Rufisque, the main road running through Capa into Dakar, which at least were able to negotiate with a flow of life, even if it was harsh and laborious, even cruel. The state of zoo animals locked in concrete and steel was a terrible, frozen captivity that denied almost all natural expressions of vitality. Creatures unable to fight, or flee were driven into bad tempers and dangerous moods for human spectators to gloat at, the violent, savage creatures thus produced, and to say, "Look at the animals, how savage and brutish they are." A beautiful, weird faced hyena was lame and incontinent. The ears of a fox had red bubbly growths pestered and inflamed by flies. A panther paced around in a repetitive pattern; into the box; out of the box; nose the wire mesh and bars of an opening;

two paces down to the rear bars; about turn and back into the box. It was unsettling to watch. With no mud to roll in, no plants to munch and cure, and no running water, zoo animals such as these had no resources to keep healthy.

They were fed with heaps of baguettes, regardless of the type of animal. I watched a huge brown bear pawing through a fall of baguettes. The bear glanced skyward at a soaring vulture, instinctively reacting to the form of another hunter, or food, moving within its range, but seemed oblivious of me as I approached the cage, as if deadened to the presence of its human captors and tormentors. My friend Alu reappeared after going off to find a cigarette. He was not completely at ease accompanying me and frequently took opportunities to be separate. This became tiresome as Alu walked well ahead of me along the road, even crossing the road and I thought, "Hmmpph, I'm paying you to repel ill suitors and you're letting me walk alone and undefended." The next time I visited the park I went alone and found it less tedious to fend off a few suitors and people simply asking for money, alone, than it was to be accompanied by an unwilling protector. Alu wanted to leave, he'd seen enough of the park. He wanted to take a taxi – walking along the road was a waste of time – I told him I liked walking because it gave me exercise after being cooped up in the boat. Alu said he wanted to leave and try to find work back down at the CVD. I reminded him he had accepted a days pay, to be my guide to the park and that now it was only noon and I had thought of discovering the rest of the park. He fudged an excuse and I could tell he was not comfortable so I thanked him for walking me this far and bade him adieu.

I was alone. A lizard ran up a tree, spiralling around the trunk and out of sight as I moved closer and then peering round to see if I was chasing it. I was happy. I liked the lizards best in the whole zoo because they were free. Another lizard ran through the hyena cage. The hyena had weak back legs. The lizard was strong, flexible, bright-eyed, alive. It moved in sporadic bursts of fright interspersed with audacious occupation of space. Exposed when stopped, but the lizard could run in any direction, climb anything, go under, between, behind. It stopped in front of the hyena, looked at me, bobbed its head, then ran out between the bars of the cage and climbed a tree. A moment of joy in this sad zoo. On the way home alone, I exercised my simple right to walk unhindered and pay no attention to the hisses and other comments by men. Quickly I realized it was only a few individuals who had to be brushed off. The majority of people were either pleasantly mannered or unconcerned by my passing.

Over two weeks Hann Plage had changed. The local council had decided to clear a mass of huts, water butts, benches, tables, storage containers and corrugate lean–to's which were becoming established between the CVD Jetty and the main fish market. Initially personal items were taken away on donkey carts. Then the structures were dismantled. Within three days there was half beach and half settlement, until on the fourth day, a mechanical digger unearthed the remaining foundations and buried water butts. Then a horde of workers strolled towards the cleared section.

Twelve men pushing green wheelbarrows with twelve squeaking wheels along the sand and thirteen women, each carrying a metal rake behind the men. Five black herons and seven white egrets stood at the wave–edges. Sixty black kites dwindled upwards in a thousand foot spiral. A vulture strode among seaweed, plastic bottles and dozens of dead porcupine fish laying inflated in death. The wind drifted wood smoke over the squint forcing sand and muscle toned men did backwards jumps up the beach, sit ups, stand ups and jogging. The wheelbarrow men lay down in the wheelbarrows like reclining bathers. The rake women leaned and flirted beneath the shade of beached yachts. In the calm of the CVD compound I wrote under liquid bird calls and dappled shade. The small amount of money I had went a long way, up to ten times further than in Portugal – so this was what it was like to be rich.

In Chez Taty's I ate rice, vegetables and fish, along with six or seven other customers. My favourite time in Chez Taty was mid morning, when it is almost empty apart from five women moving around, pounding spices, cleaning grit from huge bowls of rice and bringing in plastic tubs of water on their heads. Chez Taty had a corrugated roof with breeze block and concrete walls. Benches were roughly nailed together planks which worked best leaning against the wall, because they were on the verge of collapse. A gloomy, masculine picture of a maraboo – part Muslim and part African spiritualist, was stuck to a grimy cement wall. The words "Chez Taty" were hand painted in grey/silver paint. In front of the name hung a brilliant red spiral wind catcher. Directly beneath the ornament was a wooden stool and when someone sat on the stool it looked as if their thoughts were turning in a deep red coil above their head. Flies gathered on every surface in groups of twenty. Balls of crumpled newspaper and magazine pages littered the floor and would be swept up before lunch. At the rear a tiny cubicle held one woman who pounded, fried and chopped food. An aperture showed her scarf covered head bobbing as she laboured. She occasionally looked out to check the customers and grinned at me. A single wooden shelf held folded scarves and personal belongings over a rusty, inoperative fridge. High up in the rear wall seven vertical slots let in flies and light. I hoped to see geckos running around the walls but there were none. An electric fan hung haphazardly in the centre of the ceiling. An infants shoe was nailed to the top left hand side of the entrance lintel. One day, a man arrived, attached another small object at the opposite side of the door lintel to the shoe and left. A guide book claimed that animism made up about three percent of the Senegalese religions but it seemed far more ingrained than that so, perhaps three per cent was not seeing the wood for the trees. Plastic jugs of water were placed on the tables and plastic beakers were communal. Before a drink of water was taken the contents of the beaker were ejected through the doorway past hanging strings of wooden beads onto the tiny front patio, where one small table and two wobbly benches with nailed on legs held three or four customers.

    One of Chez Taty's women had cat like eyes, pouting lips and wore her hair lifted up in a knot. Her crown and hips were decorated with lace. One day when I stood up to pay she gave me a wicked look which caught my eye, wiggling her tongue and lowering her eyelids in a fantastically suggestive motion. We burst out laughing. The day before she had asked me directly if I wanted to be together with her and I had claimed not too understand, even as she held her hand out with two fingers spread as an upside down V. She pointed alternatively at me and her hand, in a drastically suggestive way, while I continued to pretend not to understand. I blamed the coiling, libidinous, red mobile and fled.

Outside on the tiny front patio on the plank bench sat a tea seller swathed in bright coloured wraps. Two small teapots shared the top of a cardboard box with several tiny glasses. She asked me if I would like some tea and after stewed fish, rice and vegetables I did, so I sat down again. The tea was poured from one pot to another and then into a tiny glass as a sticky sweet, dark liquid with toffee coloured bubbles on the surface and greenish leaves at the bottom. A Chinese portable world radio screeched out Senegalese music and a blue wire aerial led from the radio up to a broken, dirty cane screen between this and another restaurant next door. The tea cost 50 CFA, about 7p.

Various yachts arrived, mostly French. One Danish and several South Africans arrived on a delivery of two yachts from Croatia to South Africa. Some people had been around for years. One elderly French sailor died in his boat after refusing to take medication for malaria. A number of young Senegalese men got work on the yachts after they were hauled onto the beach. I overheard a European man talking to a young Senegalese employee, "Take off your bobble hat, you are much better looking without your bobble hat." The Senegalese man's voice was usually sonorous, but he only mumbled the reason for wearing a hat. His face was young, amiable and he had much to gain in maintaining a positive friendship with his employer. Use of the word "boy" to describe a young black employee turned up a few times. "Boy" was said by the same European man, as a joke to Dominique, the barman of the CVD and Dominique made it clear it was not appropriate. The man claimed he was only joking, ha ha ha.

Another use of the term "boy" was by some Danish cruisers who had written an account of their visit to Senegal on the internet. They recommended other cruisers take a "boy" up the river, who would act as pilot, negotiator with fishermen and other sellers and know where to pick up water etc. The article was most positive in all respects apart from this use of the word "boy" to denote an employee or guide and so full of negative implication. To me it was no more than a condescending colonialism and smacked of racism.

Saturday 21 February 2004. I was troubled by mosquitoes in the night. The air was absolutely still and the dust of daytime soaked up heavy dew, making dirty smears. After several blasts of aerosol insect killer I lit a mosquito coil for the first time. It made a pleasing, woody, smoke in the cabin and no more mosquitoes bothered me and I had passed into dreamland. Through the night a waxing moon shone and the boat lay peacefully tethered to its anchor while wavelets plipped and splocked next to my ear and fish made little cutting noises with their teeth as they ate the weed growth on the underwater part of the hull. From the shore came the noise of drumming, calling and singing. A black strand of water, lit by the screeches of herons was like a protective moat and let me fall soundly asleep, knowing only noises would arrive out of the wild, moony night.

I awoke after a most satisfying dream, although the memory of what the dream was about faded quickly. I remembered waking up with a start, thinking the boat was filling with water until a check in the bilge with a torch put my mind at rest. Sinking anxiety is no bad thing on a boat. After this initial fear–jerk my dreams came radiant with symbols. In the morning the rich, but forgotten dream had distilled into the words, "Consciousness is a narrative".

## The Sails are in the Trees

Sunday 22 February 2004. In the delicious shade of a rear courtyard of the CVD compound I sat writing on my little Psion computer. Between the "T", "Y", "G" and "H" keys, a tiny shit dropped. Above me was a bird the size of a firecrest, with almost no tail, an orange–red belly and breast, sage green wings and back, with a white and black eye stripe. The bird flitted in the dappled leaves, feeding on minute food. Tiny, ruby red finches, with a white circle around the eye fed on the ground, hopping about in threes and fours and coming fearlessly close, as if no one had ever tried to catch them. Perhaps they lived at such a quick metabolic rate that the human forms around them appeared like slowly moving giants. A hummingbird landed in the foliage above me, squeaking out a shrill, high frequency song. It was delicately toned with a white eye stripe and the thin, long curving beak of a flower feeder. It flew off to hover at some large red flowers. There were several unseen voices up in the trees. An iridescent black–blue bird landed, the same slim shape as the humming bird. Another day I saw two green parakeets land in the tree tops, green tapering, fluted diamond tails and plumage. On the beach charcoal grey–black herons, with black legs and yellow feet, mixed with white herons. Each evening flocks of white birds flew along the seashore through the anchorage, to alight perhaps upon some enchanted table where spellbound knights sat in limbo.

Often when I came ashore in the morning, one of the two dogs who lived in the CVD compound was asleep on top of one of two stone tables. My strongest impression of West Africa so far was the way so much seemed to resonate with and emanate from the heart. The white birds returning along the shore each evening and the dog on a stone table – came to me as pertinent symbols of the voyage I was on – a Narnia voyage after The Voyage of the Dawntreader. Even the Mauritanians to the north were known as Nars. I was enchanted by my journey and how it resonated with stories I'd read.

Perhaps I was lost in my own dreams, but I was sensing around me that Africans seemed to understand each other instantly through their emotions. The experience was one of relentless exchange and interweaving of fortunes in millions of tiny interactions. On the beach in the evening singers sang in a question answer pattern, a male voice leading and a female chorus answering. Flocks of cormorants harassed the fish, surfacing in thirty or forty necks, upward angled beaks twisting this way and that as they looked around. The stench of rotting seaweed and the open sewer inhabited the cabin. And I absolutely loved it all.

The following morning in the CVD two large mainsails had been washed and were stretched between tree trunks to dry. They were skilfully constructed to take up aerofoil forms when tensioned on a yachts mast, between the head, tack and clew – the three corners of a tall triangle. Leaf shadows danced on the curving surfaces. I talked to sailors around a white painted table and a Spaniard spoke the scene lyrically, "Le voiles est dans les arbres" – The sails are in the trees.

It was interesting how much of travel was an exploration and discovery of ones own internal topography. Living away from the constraints and influences of both peers and culture allows one to try many new ways of being and communicating and this was made easier by the fact that most people encountered in far away countries would never be met again. Given this freedom from accountability, rather than going wild, if anything I adhered more to social convention. Often I found formality had clear effects which were useful and the result was a sort of universal friendliness with minimal confrontation. The friendliness of foreigners, the more so the further from the UK I travelled, was one of the most pleasant discoveries of the voyage. I sometimes felt lonely too, just for the odd fifteen minutes and once in a while I was fearful of the long journey home – as if I had so far only scraped by with a haphazard mixture of luck and chance success. My fear was of being shown to be incompetent and flimsy in everything I did after all. I was far away from home although there was no longer such a place as home and all courses led further into life – there was no returning, only going onwards. I had travelled beyond my own limits of caution and become comfortable at the edge of my world.

The UK shores were a far off land, even quite exotic.

Way back in Bristol Marina I had been deeply prepared to go somewhere remarkable, like C.S. Lewis's "The Voyage of the Dawn Treader". "Narnia" – a place of the imagination, had been my way to name the setting out, without imposing limits. That had been a long while before I became captivated by the idea of sailing to Africa.

## Dakar and the Senegalese. Banjul and the Gambians

Wednesday 10 March 2004. Two Fula musicians stopped in front of me as I walked through the fish market. They were young. One had a pair of shakers – a branching, curved stick, stripped of bark with palm wood discs loosely threaded on the branches. Asymmetric wrist movements of the "Bonco" made a double para–diddle shifting in and out of phase. The second musician played a kind of violin with six strings, called a Susa. A gourd sound box connected to a neck of round stick, strung with gut, or perhaps bailing twine, was held at chest height and bowed with twine stretched between the ends of a curved twig. They bobbed and grinned in front of me, dancing from one foot to the other. With my back to a fish lorry I soaked up the music and watched the instruments being played. The song went on, the string player opening and shutting his fingers over the neck in several patterns to make a tune evoking mud hut villages, cooking pots over smoky wood fires and a ring of clapping dancers. Then the music shifted into a sort of Irish jig. The street scene came back into the music; a horse and cart carrying a load of truck tyres; a young woman cutting up smoked fish; an empty fish–lorry, full of dents, with painted eyes and women carrying plastic tubs on their heads daring to glance sideways. After five minutes they walked onwards and took the tune with them.

Three men who had also enjoyed the music spoke to me. They sat in a line across the cab of a fish lorry. Over the windscreen a banner, *City Boy*. Painted eyes with strong eyelashes gleamed above each sidelight. They told me it was Senegalese folk music and I told them I found it beautiful. I continued back towards the boat, past the wood carvers and again as I admired the carvings was asked for a deposit on a purchase. The stool in the shape of a flopping whales tail was still there and almost mine, but I was reluctant to discuss any price, for I knew the power of those words would inevitably lead me into a purchase. I also knew a hardwood stool would be too heavy and bulky aboard Storm Petrel.

Sorting through clothes I'd not worn for ages I found them smelling musty so I washed several tops and skirts which hardly got worn because I preferred to cover my arms, shoulders and legs. A slinky pencil skirt in shimmering mauve velvet was perfect for Marie, my friend in Chez Taty. One morning she had her hair in plaits and looked radiantly pleased and a little self–conscious at her augmented good looks. She told me it was her twenty–fifth birthday. When we first met Marie had said she was twenty three years old. A perfect coincidence. I handed her the skirt, wrapped in a glossy carrier bag to make it gifty in slippery, luxurious plastic from "El Corte Ingles", a swish department store in Las Palmas. Marie looked really chuffed as I handed her what had suddenly become a birthday present. The following day Marie wore the skirt which suited her absolutely with her plaited, aubergine–black hair and she looked beautiful. A few days later Marie handed me a folded letter – an invitation to her house the next Sunday – it began, "Chere Clarissa,"– Dear Clarissa – but it was from Marie's older brother and in giving his height, weight and skin colour he sounded very keen. A request for a reply, "by Thursday" made me feel cornered and compounded my resistance. He wrote of Marie as his "little sister", but to me she was a 25 year old woman. I decided the best reply would be none and I spoke to Marie, telling her I enjoyed talking with her in the restaurant but I did not wish to agree to become the friend of a man I had never met. Marie was happy with this. I wanted her to know she could form friendships of her own choice, without the mediation of her "big brother".

On a crate outside the CVD sat an artist with a selection of paintings stacked in a large carrier bag. Landscapes on rectangles cut out of cardboard boxes depicted mud hut villages with splodgy, or stick–like figures carrying items on their heads, sitting under the shade of trees or thatched roofs. Huts were made of brushwood glued to the picture. I choose a river scene including several canoes. Another artist was staying at the CVD and I showed him my new acquisition but he laughed at the brushwood huts and scoffed at the crude, brown edging suggesting a wooden frame; discriminated against the bare cardboard rear side; became impatient at the cotton hanging loop sellotaped to the back. At the bottom right hand corner in damn–this–pen–it–doesn't write blue biro was – J.P. Ndong – the artist's signature. The picture was not a representation of West Africa it was a part of it. The makeshift use of scrap materials and carefree technique was a slab of African village. The derisive laughter of the French abstract expressionist painter drove me and the picture away. When I saw the French man's work, full of sophisticated colour contrasts and harmonies, he explained the symbolic elements and impossible perspectives in relentless French. I saw gawky, hideous monsters formed out of splashes and runs and human figures with root–like arms and legs, reclining in pools of dry, flat water colours – "This one sold and went to England," he told me and sunk back into French philosophical art theory which made a richly soothing texture way above the pictures.

The explanations of J.P. Ndong were in total contrast, "That is a canoe; those are people standing in the village; this person is sitting against the hut." Beams of simplicity. He pointed at two black arms and a black head in the sky blue water, "He is swimming." In the blue air, bird Ms flapped to become Ws. In plant green bushes were red and yellow flowers over a wall of over size, painted bricks. I gave him 2,000 CFA, the asking price, which would buy a week of rice, vegetables and fish dinners at Chez Taty. His work, like the egotistic French abstract artist, would also be taken to England, but J.P. Ndong would probably never feel the need to mention this fact to his customers.

Thursday 11 March 2004. Seven taxi drivers sat or lay on mats, wearing robes, in a shaded sand lot. I bargained for a low price but managed only a bilateral price – If there was heavy traffic it would be his asking price – if the roads were not blocked it would be my price. The taxi driver knew well the road to Dakar was always chock–a–block.

Along the tired road to Dakar were sellers carrying tools, dangling telephones, lugging sunglasses, angling racks of music cassette tapes, wheeling cartloads of fruit, sitting behind stacks of peanuts and brandishing shoe polish. Further towards the city, in a traffic jam, the driver hurled a one hundred CFA coin onto the roadside, telling me it was for those who could not find work, so the higher taxi fare was a good thing. The driver haggled with a pedaller walking along the traffic jam. He was interested in buying a portable radio. Finally, as the traffic began to grind ahead again he decided, at seven thousand CFA, the radio was too expensive.

Later, back at Hann Plage I met Ibrahim, a fish seller, who said he would like to join me in a trip to Gambia. He became sexually suggestive, grinning and flicking a big pink tongue around like a snake, eyes twinkling. It was always awkward to have to thwart the hopes of strangers who saw me as rich and free to choose to take them on as fellow adventurers. The next time I met Ibrahim I immediately discouraged him by greeting him, "Bonjour, Ibrahim qui grimace." I meant to say, "Ibrahim qui rit", like that French cheese called "La Vache Qui Rit" – The Laughing Cow, because Ibrahim had such a cheesy grin. What I had come out with, the word "grimace" meant literally grimace – an ugly face. At least my wrong word clouted that improper tongue back into place.

Each day around 2.30pm a mauve robed man with a violet scarf wrapped around his head and deep black skin arrived on a scooter loaded with a pile of newspapers and magazines. They were all in French and after he realized I was English, he included the Herald Tribune newspaper, Time magazine and Newsweek. I did buy a Herald Tribune one day, but found it less interesting than listening to the BBC World Service. Time magazine was too glossy and Newsweek too narrow, so I gave them to the seller and told him to feel free to sell them again to someone else and he was really grateful.

After two broken engine mounts were replaced I had the hull scraped by a local fisherman. The anti–fouling I applied in Portugal was struggling to shed off the growth in the warmer water. The engine had been idle since arrival in Africa, seven weeks before, which made it awkward to start and Arona the mechanic squirted Easy Start at the air intake, until the motor jostled into life. He told me a diesel should be run weekly to keep it clear of build ups. On the afternoon of Saturday 27 March I pulled up the anchor to take the boat for a test to see how the engine and new clean hull were, but found myself putting to sea and sailing away from Dakar. The Gambia was 130 km to the south. I ran the engine hard for twenty hours which really set it into a healthy condition as after that it started willingly and would run with very few problems for 1200 km of river travel.

The journey to The Gambia went uneventfully and I saw only a few pirogues out fishing in the early morning light. I headed into the River Gambia through a channel called Schooner Gap past a sand bank called "Stop In Time" and Banjul appeared around Sunday lunchtime. I eventually swept into the river proper on an ingoing tide, past Banjul to anchor off Half Die, named after a cholera epidemic. Several men hanging around a tug in the docks beckoned me in and I started heading towards them, thinking I could anchor near to the tug and work out what to do next, but suddenly I thought better and veered away to choose my own spot. They passed by later in a tender and introduced themselves with big toothy grins, "Welcome to the Smiling Coast!" I humoured them and mentioned my husband was sleeping down below so not to wake him because he would be grumpy. They went and left me in peace.

Monday 29 March 2004. I cleared in to The Gambia with the Banjul Port Authority charging twenty two euros – 817 dallasi, for entry of a private yacht. They showed me the official regulations with this amount plainly correct. Twenty two euros was a large amount of money to pay, but at least I knew I was not paying a corrupt official. There was a delay while the accounts department confirmed the charge to the cash office, via the marine department. Customs stamped my passport with a twenty eight day visa which cost nothing and both harbour officials were very polite.

I walked around Banjul's Albert Market and bumped into Asmat, an English sailor I knew from Portugal, Canaries and Senegal. Despite the success I found being independent and alone it was so nice to meet a friendly face and share a coffee together. He told me Bendt, my

Danish sailor friend was also in The Gambia, anchored at a place called Oyster Creek and that I must go there to pull Bendt out of a habit of a bottle of brandy every day.

## Bendt

In the morning Bendt turned up at Storm Petrel on a local fishing boat, offering to pilot me through the Chittabong Bolon to Oyster Creek. Chittabong Bolon was a tortuous creek winding 5 km through mangrove swamp. It led to Denton Bridge where most cruising boats gathered.

Banjul was built on sandbanks at the mouth of the River Gambia. A ferry ran across the wide estuary to the north but the south of Banjul was served by a single highway which crossed Oyster Creek at Denton Bridge. Beyond Denton Bridge a white line of breaking waves was the Atlantic Ocean. On the landward side of the bridge a fleet of moored sports fishing boats, passenger carrying pirogues and foreign cruising yachts lay.

At one end of Denton Bridge a police station served a permanent check point for vehicles. Behind the police station was a quarter of an acre of waste ground, or what was once waste ground for now there were neatly hoed rows of beans, peas, carrots and banana trees. The garden was a place of value, calm and philosophical reflection for the gardener, police sergeant Osman. At one end of the vegetable patch a water stand pipe was the one source of the gardens success as well as filling the water cans of cruising sailors. Osman would always appear smiling out of the foliage to talk with trespassers arriving in his garden to seek water. Osman spoke in quirky, godly, sayings, pontifications and observations on the state of man were served as free gifts with the water.

I took the bus to Westfield Junction with no breakfast one morning and spent an hour in the internet café, then stopped off in a Lebanese restaurant for brunch. The toilet was without water so I asked to wash my hands before eating and I was led into the kitchen where the woman held up a green plastic dustbin with a pint of water remaining in the bottom. I gratefully washed my hands which felt really grubby after pawing the keyboard and using the waterless, stinking toilet.

Westfield Junction was a crossroads, busy with traffic and shops. One day I sat down to eat under a large tree, at a restaurant consisting of a couple of cardboard boxes covered with plastic as a table with wooden benches surrounding it. A meal of rice and fish cost ten Dalasi. A woman sitting next to me asked if I was a Gambian and I laughed, "No, do I look like a Gambian?" She just smiled and told me her name was Mariama. Being told you look like a Gambian was a way to complement toubabs into thinking they really were blending in. When a very poor, elderly man asked me for ten Dalasi my initial response was to say I had no change but when he said he had not eaten since the day before and muttered about the price of a plate of rice while calling on the mercy of god I gave him ten Dalassi.

Back at Denton Bridge a Senegalese woman called Rosemarie made daily attempts at selling me something. I purchased a sky blue cotton top with embroidered neck, a mauve cotton top and a beautiful green and fire coloured wrap with matching headscarf. Rosemarie's marketing plan moved on to a djembe African drum and a bed sheet, both items I had expressed mild interest in. I told her I only ever used a quilt cover, not bed sheets, so she immediately said she would sow it into a quilt cover as she thrust the djembe at me. The only way to handle this constant selling was, "NO, THANKYOU".

Any interest whatsoever was seen as a willingness to buy. One trick was to say they had the item you ordered, "But I didn't order anything". I tried to walk away towards the bar and a hand on my elbow spun me around. "Yes, you want it, look, you say get this and I get it for you". The drum, or blouse, or cover or all those hung inside a half size shipping container. "Well I will look at it, but I really didn't want to buy one just now". Rosemarie would not have her bus fare home unless I bought something. "It is very nice, look at that". I realized the cost was almost irrelevant to me and a days earnings for her. "Oh yes it is very nice, but I do not wish to buy anything today". A tearful Rosemarie told me she would not have the bus fare to get home let alone anything to eat and begged me for a down payment. "No, I can't give you an advance payment on this or any other thing I might want in the future."

Next a story emerged which was so believable I felt rotten. "I realise you gave 900 dallasi to your neighbour to pay your electricity bill and then he spent it without paying the bill and you have now been disconnected from the electricity. But I do not wish to buy a drum, thank you". A loan, a gift, please, anything she begged again. "No I do not want to lend you 500 dallasi", because I would never see it again. "I don't want to buy anything thank you. Goodbye". A sobbing Rosemarie sat defeated in her container and I felt rotten but also like Arrrgghhh, just leave me alone!

Saturday was "Operation Clean The Nation", a day when all vehicles were banned from the roads, except police, fire, ambulance and tourist businesses. People were told, by President Yaya Jameh to stay at home and clean their compounds and neighbourhoods. In fact it was "Operation Stop the Nation" because it hindered everything and caused a huge congestion in the late afternoon when things were permitted to move again. Much cleaning was done, mostly the burning of piles of rubbish which lay alongside the highways causing stinking plumes of smoke and numerous small brush fires.

Some UK friends ran a sports fishing business from Denton Bridge. They gave me a lift to Bakau 6 km to the south west and on the way a short detour took us to see a giant baobab tree. Children kicked around the dust bowl square under its shade and the boys came up to us and explained they were a football team, but they had no ball and no boots. I told them that a ball would arrive soon out of the baobab tree as my friends told me all boys asked tourists for footballs. Girls asked for pens because Gambian girls received free schooling, but not the boys. The baobab tree must have been many hundreds of years old and buttress roots stood out in great folded ridges with a smooth grey trunk as thick as a tube train. The baobab produces a gourd like fruit, filled with fibrous pulp surrounding hard round seeds. The white pulp is called monkey bread "Sito" in Mandinka and was good for the digestive system. It tasted slightly bitter with the texture of wall insulation foam. Serekunda market served a sprawling urban area and only the hardened tourist attempted it on foot, most toubabs passed through in a taxi gazing out like ghosts.

Albert Market was so convoluted as to need a G.P.S. to navigate in and back out again. One day, after trying every polite and direct turn of speech to shake off a bumster in Albert Market, I needed to use the "Acha!" command. He joined our group of three, uninvited, introducing himself as the "King of the Market", then jumped in front of us at every turn suggesting we choose the way we had just chosen. "Yes, you can go this way". He would decree. My friends asked, "Who is this fellow?"and King of the Market glanced at this ripple of unrest in his people. "Where did we pick him up?" King of the Market grinned at me like a friend. "Why does he keep telling us where we want to go?"

I said I would deal with the King of the Market, so thanking him for his suggestions and comments, then telling him we did not wish to be given a running commentary on the stalls or led around like tourists, I said we wanted to walk alone and so to leave us and goodbye. He sponged up the attention, seeing my talk as a strengthening of our relationship. I got angry, "Excuse me, leave us alone, now!" He glanced down a side aisle and stayed right next to us. "OK. Now go". He was still attached to us, so I said, "Acha!" It worked. Acha! meant "F**k Off!". and he did.

A choice of three main markets lay within a ten minute bus ride of Denton Bridge. Bakau market was laid back and even quaint, being on the edge of the richer tourist strip along the coast. Serekunda was a sprawling urban market in a kind of suburb of Banjul and Albert Market was central Banjul. Asmat and I went to Bakau after seeing some beautiful batik paintings when my friends had driven me past. I wanted to buy two for my sister's birthday. We were approached by a man who convinced Asmat he had just got married and would love him to meet the new wife. I knew it was all false and so I let Asmat go alone into the alleys behind the market street with the fellow. I went to drink a coffee alone in a nearby restaurant which I liked for the fantasy posters of unicorns on the walls. When I found Asmat again he told me the inevitable story of extortion.

He had been led into a small orphanage run by a treacherous looking man. He was shown a guest book with various celebrity English names written in with a large sum of money recorded by each as a donation, mostly around seven hundred to a thousand Dalasi, £15 to £20. The names were all written in the same scrawling biro pen and had obviously been made up. Asmat gave fifty Dalasi and left under a hail of insults from the treacherous looking man and his many wives who were laying around on mats. I was pleased to have avoided it and up till then it had been Asmat who had taught me the resistance and directness needed to keep out of difficulties. When I met the newly wed bumster again in another area on another day, he greeted me like a friend and called me by name a good memory – trying the ploy again. He said he had a new born baby and gesticulated across the road at a young woman carrying an infant in a scarf wrapped around her chest. I immediately severed the conversation, "No, I do not want to see your new born baby," and, "I'm going to walk along the road alone now, goodbye". And, "Excuse me I do not want to speak to you, please go away," and then, "Acha!" and he was gone. "Acha!" was a good Mandinka word which could shoo dogs away, disconnect with annoying children and harass the hustlers. Later, during two voyages far inland up the River Gambia, I only used the "Acha!" word once – to shoo away a very friendly dog who lay at my feet and was just about to be bumped by a table.

## Yes, We'll Gather at the River

Tuesday 20 April 2004. After a week in Denton Bridge I was considered a local and in reaction to this pernicious familiarity I began to plan a voyage up the River Gambia. I wanted to go all the way to the fresh water section, which began some 200 km up river from the sea. So three weeks later I set off to explore up river. The anchor chain was wrapped around a large anchor which had probably been laying under 9m of water for years. I managed to winch the weight to the surface and get a rope around it.

Asmat and Bendt arrived to help. After half an hour of huffing and puffing we had the stock removed and the chain unwrapped from the shaft of the derelict anchor. Finally I extricated myself and boat from Oyster Creek and found myself wending through Chittabong Bolon amid dense mangroves. I anchored at Half Die from where I would depart up river the next morning. It had not been difficult although I ran over a mud bank in the bolon and hit a wreck near Half Die. I anchored in the same place as when I had first arrived in The Gambia. Here, a gentle and friendly security man called Dodou helped me again to collect water in cans. I tipped him ten dallasi which he refused, but I insisted until he took it. The plan for the morning was to leave at first light, 7am and make for Kemoto, 52 km up river. Bendt had been to Kemoto and described a friendly village with an easily accessible anchorage.

I travelled the hot, wide open river estuary all day and stopped at Kemoto. A pirogue with three fishermen aboard bumped alongside as I tidied the boat after anchoring. I thought, "Here we go, what do they want, oh well, just be friendly and let them know I do not want anything". One of the fishermen was called Buba and he sprang aboard to help me lift my dinghy off the fore deck into the water. I rowed ashore and Buba, who had moored the pirogue, met me and offered to introduce me to his family and friends.

I quickly realised how difficult it would be to arrive in these small villages alone. The complex web of extended families living in interlocking compounds was no place for a stranger to go wandering alone in and as insensitive as an African strolling about the gardens of a UK village.

After spending the afternoon with Buba's family in Kemoto and walking the little paths between interwoven households I began to realise Gambia would best be done with a Gambian, for to walk into such complex social arrangements uninvited and then wander around unaccompanied would be insensitive. While in Kemoto, Buba's brother Lamin showed me around a closed hotel, or tourist camp as they were known. Foxy looking fruit bats hung from the deserted bar roof, grinning and flying in our faces, as big as rabbits. I rowed back to Storm Petrel with Buba just to show him inside the cabin, but I soon realised he thought he was invited for the trip up–river, so I told him I always sailed alone. Then I wondered whether it might be enjoyable to share the journey. I liked Buba, so I changed my mind and when I invited him after all, Buba shrugged, as if to say well, naturally it would be better if he showed me the river, the monkeys, the crocodiles.

I upped anchor at 9am after Buba had rowed ashore to collect mangoes and buy cigarettes. While scoffing smoked cat fish and mangoes a large crocodile appeared laying dead on its back with legs and claws sticking up, nearly 3m long. Buba told me the bush was not dangerous and he sometimes walked 10 km to another village in the cool of night. He said when there was a football match many people would walk in a large group, women and girls carrying dishes of food and water, the men and boys talking and running about. Buba said he often saw monkeys, baboons and bush pigs and that hyenas called to one another at night. The day became searing hot and we drank a mug of water every half hour. Buba liked my cups of tea. The river narrowed from 2.5 km wide to 1 km.

More endless wide waterway with nothing but high mangrove either side. The river curved and numerous bolons led away through the mangrove, as tall as large trees. The shipwrecked Lady Chilel showed as two steel plate masts occupied by pelicans with rippling throats. Buba explained the Lady Chilel ran weekly between Banjul and

Georgetown with supplies and passengers and one day the drunken captain ran onto a mud bank between Krule Point and Devils Point. With the force of the tide pushing against the immovable hull, the ship turned over and many lives were lost. A small building and jetty made a place called Balangar, pronounced by Buba as, "Balem". A few figures sat in shade watching Storm Petrel of Narnia pass as an anomaly. Elephant Island and then Sea Horse Island, stretching 8 km, saw the late afternoon into evening. Dense, high mangroves still dominated the view but occasional glimpses of red crumbling lands showed above and behind the foliage. Nipa Palms rose over the tree line. Mangroves wended off into the bush following each bolon for a kilometre or more and Buba told me these creeks were busy with crocodiles. Parrots screeched, whistled and squeaked in flocks at dusk, flying in flocks, like swifts with long straight tails. We tried to reach Kauur but darkness filled the river and I wanted to stop because I was the captain and could no longer see, but Buba laughed and said he could see fine. We laughed as I bumbled about with a torch and made increasingly anxious remarks about stopping for the night. Eventually we anchored next to a large tree and the mouth of a tiny bolon. A cooling night breeze and a new moon treated us for a couple of hours and we ate fried pork luncheon meat with baked beans Buba liked that.

 Buba was on deck at 5am quietly watching the river and listening to the radio. I got up at 6am. And we pulled up the anchor with a fair tide beginning. The character of the river banks changed from impenetrable ranks of mangrove to reeds, flood meadows, rice paddy with banana trees and nipa palms. When the water became sweet rather than salt I was so excited and after tasting it to make sure I washed my hair with cooling bucket loads. The fresh water made me feel nostalgic in a river scene reminiscent of an English river, such as the River Nene or the river Avon, winding through thick green woods and flood meadows, lined with hissing clumps of reeds. This impression was countered by the searing, heat rippling bush, rising up beyond the flat river plain. Strange baobab trees and a crumbling, dry red–tinted surface looked like a volcanic field ready to burst with heat energy. At Kudang Tenda small round mud brick houses thatched with reeds came right to the low waters edge where dug out canoes rested and figures wandered about busily under conical reed hats and long loose robes. As Storm Petrel passed a ground nut wharf, dozens of dug out canoes, each holding two or three children paddled madly towards us. Buba suggested we stop for cigarettes and the fleet of children in dug out canoes frantically raced beside and behind us. Buba spoke in considerate, but authoritative words and hollered at them to not go across our bows. We slowed to a halt and Buba gave one boy five dallasi to go and buy the cigarettes for him. Ten dug outs and twenty five children swarmed around and sat on the back deck grinning and peering.

Buba's authority held them at bay and we shook their hands and greeted them warmly. They were between six and ten years old. As a parting gift we gave out bits of maize pancakes that had been eyed up constantly on a plate in the cockpit. One dug out canoe became glued alongside by the flowing water between the two hulls. Another capsized as two boy racers collided. The dug out canoes were so low in the water it took no more than a splash to flood them. They were made from a single hollowed out log and very heavy, even so the fleet of ten or so raced us at three knots. We stopped to release the trapped canoe and the rest of the fleet caught up so the race began again. One was called Momadou, a round faced boy of ten or so, with his ship mate, Mama had a quiet, serious expression and a pink hair scrunchy around his wrist. I felt an aura of affection between strangers. Perhaps Momadou saw something in Buba and me which resonated with his dreams – freedom, travel, liberty to be who you wish and to move at will in the world – things many Africans do not possess.

The children told us there were hippopotami living around Deer Island, opposite Kudang Tenda. We passed a mass of nets strung across the river, but Buba understood the way these nets were either freely floating, as a drift net, or anchored and he steered us expertly through in a series of zigzags. We got talking about my river, the River Avon at Bristol and I drew a picture of the Avon Gorge with the

Brunel's suspension bridge spanning it and a tiny Storm Petrel passing beneath to give the scale. I told Buba that each year many people jumped to their deaths from that bridge and he asked why people jump and kill themselves – all I could say was *because they were crazy*. He asked if they were mostly black people and I said no, because black people were too busy dealing with problems to think about killing themselves.

*That is definitely a crocodile!*

*Three fingers of whisky each and a jam with Buba on The River Gambia*

*Buba sheltering from the sun*

*The tiny black humps are hippopotami*

*Kemoto village. Everything carried on the head, even an axe.*

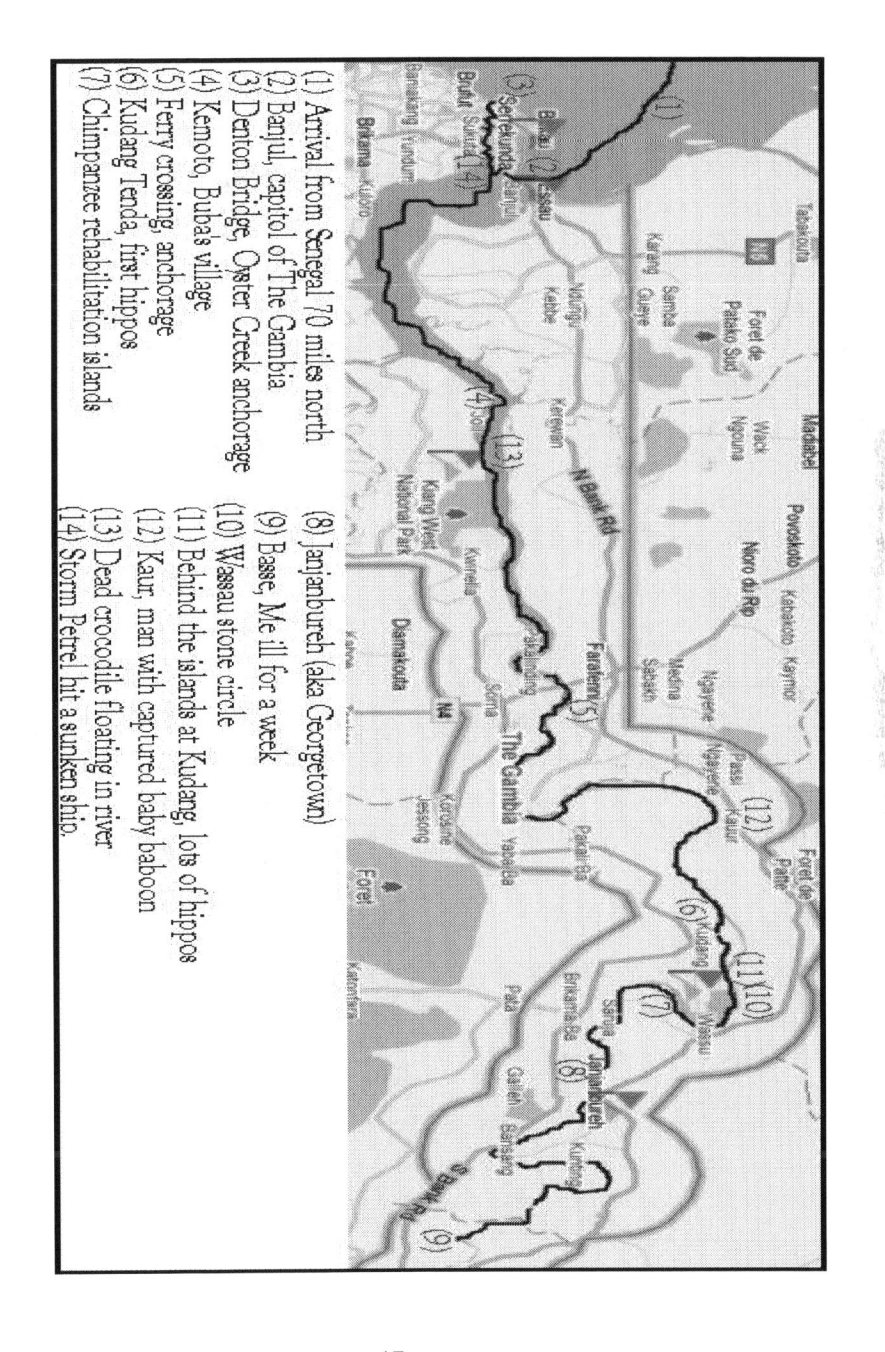

(1) Arrival from Senegal 70 miles north
(2) Banjul, capitol of The Gambia
(3) Denton Bridge, Oyster Creek anchorage
(4) Kemoto, Buba's village
(5) Ferry crossing, anchorage
(6) Kudang Tenda, first hippos
(7) Chimpanzee rehabilitation islands
(8) Janjanbureh (aka Georgetown)
(9) Basse, Me ill for a week
(10) Wassau stone circle
(11) Behind the islands at Kudang, lots of hippos
(12) Kaur, man with captured baby baboon
(13) Dead crocodile floating in river
(14) Storm Petrel hit a sunken ship

Just downstream of some remote islands, the larger of which was Bird Island, we saw four big heads, like horses, but as black and fat as whales, rising to look straight at us, or sideways, then plunging beneath a ring of seething water – Hippopotami. Buba steered nearer, between the two islands and I missed them repeatedly rising to breath, always pointing my camera somewhere else. As we arrived at the place they had been, the hippos had out manoeuvred us by being where we had been. They were now between us and the main river and we moved closer to them again. They each rose to breath, with an expulsion of breath every minute or so. As we again passed near to them they once again moved under and around our position. A big male let out a series of angry grunting snorts so we left them alone. The head of a hippopotamus was of great size with small bent ears and eyes and a long nose ending in prominent and distinctly horse–like nostrils.

I spotted a dark red monkey sitting deep in a shady tree, looking back at me. We saw more and more as the river grew narrower and we passed through channels around islands. Lush and sweaty vegetation, full of parrots and the sounds of Africa, yelling indigo starlings, bubbling purple doves, buzzing, unseen insects, bell–like plaintive parrots. Monkeys could be seen from 500m away because they caused great disturbance in the trees as they jumped about. More "towns" not really towns at all collections of mud houses with thatched roofs, always with women washing clothes at the waters edge and children standing naked – more involved with daily concerns rather than a sailing yacht passing. The men were mostly out fishing in small dug out canoes, sitting so low in the water the aft end, where the man sat paddling, was semi immersed and his legs dangled in the crocodile and hippo infested water.

The temperature had risen to very hot and it was extremely pleasant to soak self, clothes and hair with buckets of river water. The sun cooling me further as it evaporated the wet. Many times people called out, "Hey! Come!", but we sailed past with a smile and a wave. Buba often recognized fishermen in pirogues and he talked over the water, some 150m, in Mandinka. Despite the diesel engine roar they managed to make each other laugh across the water gap. Much of the Mandinka language seemed to consist in short, chesty, guttural phrases which carried well.

Later in the afternoon we came to Baboon Island, which was occupied by a rehabilitation reserve for rescued chimpanzees. A Cheltenham, UK, based charity funded the project and the Gambian government aided its development and continuation. A metal dory came alongside with two, dark green safari suited men. After a long description of the chimpanzee rescue project they asked me to pay one hundred dallasi before we passed the island. I felt indignant at being asked to pay to navigate the river and stated my right to unimpeded navigation, supported by written permission by the Gambia Ports Authority. I had not intended to visit the chimpanzees – poor animals, now rehoused and peaceful after being used as entertainment in circuses, restaurants and zoos because I was content to know they had a natural place to live together and I only wished to peacefully pass the island. One chimpanzee had been taught to drink brandy and smoke cigarettes in a restaurant to amuse diners.

The chimpanzee was not indigenous to Gambia. The rangers agreed to let us pass unimpeded as I had argued, so I conceded by giving a donation of fifty dallasi to the Chimpanzee Rehabilitation Trust (UK registered charity No. 1081151). The rangers were very pleased by this and roared off at high speed to collect mangoes for the chimps. I pondered the horror of chimpanzees being used in scientific laboratories to test cosmetics, cigarettes or even medicines. Part of the rangers spiel was to say scientists had found the social and emotional intelligence of chimpanzees to be similar to that of human beings. We were given a full colour leaflet with twenty or so portraits of individual chimpanzees with their names and a series of extremely endearing, short biographies of Beng, Frankie, Diao, Hexel, Stella, Nellie and Nelson, who could all be adopted. At eighteen months old Pooh was rescued and he had reached the age of thirty two.

We were left to transit the eight kilometre long Baboon Island in solitude, with fish eagles, palm vultures, green parakeets, a spur winged plover, white egrets, herons, pied kingfisher, terns, swallows, palm swifts and weaver birds building hundreds of pendulous nests in the over–hanging foliage. Many small colourful birds were too elusive to identify.

Near to the far end of Baboon Island another dory came hurtling around a long bend and a sole, white woman sat mesmerized at the bows. The boat was driven by a local man with dread locked hair and she was obviously doing a "see the chimps" trip out of the Bird Safari Camp, 12 km up river. The dory was brought to a swishing halt under a large overhanging bough on Baboon Island and immediately a screeching and screaming noise began as a group of black chimpanzees climbed out over the river on the tree trunk. I felt happy to know the sixty five odd chimpanzees on the tree filled island with delicious sweet water flowing around were protected by the charity and backed by the Gambian government. In the dry season, December through to March, large tourist pirogues arrived to see the chimps, with forty to sixty people aboard, each paying the one hundred dallasi ticket, as many as five pirogues a day.

Despite the goodwill and cheer of seeing and hearing happy chimpanzees I nevertheless felt my own River Gambia the one I'd woven gradually into being by travel, patience, effort and idealism was interrupted by the request for money to pass the island. I felt to be in someone's area of control, whereas the River Gambia was so wild and remote with it's small villages and fishing fleets of no more than three or four dug out canoes. The only other boats using the entire river were occasional movements of the municipal ferry from one crossing to another, tourist pirogues in the high season, one or two cruising yachts per month and the groundnut barges. Ground nut barges were three large steel barges tied abreast with the centre vessel powering the outer two and at the bow a huddle of watch men under a matting canopy, brewing tea on a little charcoal stove.

We passed a shipwreck with only masts exposed after many years, the Lady Denham. A large ferry crossed at Eltenda, on the main highway linking north and south Senegal. This one carried five or six heavy goods vehicles at a time. Barrajalli had a ferry and was also the birthplace of the former Gambian president, Jawara who had retired to live in the UK with his family, the ubiquitous Gambian dream come true, for one family. A third ferry linked Georgetown on McCarthy Island with the mainland. This was about 15m in length with a tall wheelhouse at one end, enabling the helmsman to see over high vehicles. In 250 km there were just three ferries carrying vehicles. Buba told me he would sometimes walk 47 km from his village to reach the main road where a bus to Banjul passed by.

That evening we anchored, near the Eltenda ferry crossing, in the dark. A man's voice called repeatedly, asking for a ferry service. He hissed, howled, appealed, demanded, and re–appealed. Me and Buba could not help laughing at the sound of him howling across the darkness of the empty river. He probably thought Storm Petrel was the ferry moored up for the night. Buba said, "If he keeps howling like that, a hyena will come and get him". Buba recognized the accent as Malian. Several other people had arrived – a motorcycle and a flock of sheep but I could not do a favour with Storm Petrel's deep keel making it impossible to approach close enough to the shore and I was not prepared to carry a motorcycle and sheep. On the opposite bank was another huddle of late comers washing their white Mercedes car while they waited for a ferry which had departed up to Georgetown for the night. Eventually a small outboard powered dory turned up, a local opportunist, who putted across towards the Malian and the bleating, chatting rest. We listened to the price negotiations, the voices carrying clear over the night water. The boat man refused to go near the shore until a price had been agreed and the Malian scooter rider grew exasperated at being stranded but remained full of humour. They settled on twenty five dallasi and fifteen minutes later we heard the moped drive off the dory and head up the track in the direction of Kuntaur, probably still laughing under his helmet. Malians have a social bond called a "laughing cousin" – People from different tribes and families are denoted laughing cousins. Disagreements between various groups or individuals are sorted out by selecting the laughing cousins from the offended or arguing parties who then mock, parody, ridicule, taunt, belittle, deride and jeer each other to a point where they fall about laughing and the hurt is mended.

Again we had the river to ourselves with a thin, new moon setting into the bolon (creek) and the high ringing note of insects filling a sweating darkness. We sat without saying much and drank several mugs of strong tea, watching shooting stars, or meteorites fall in long slow, vivid violet streaks. Strangely, in this remote place, the sound of a discotheque came and went within a gently folding breeze. Later a cooler breeze came and blew away the mosquitoes. The diesel engine cooled enough to enter the cabin and we moved to our bunks. A hippopotamus snorted nearby, the fifth hippo of the day.

# Chapter 2

# Mind out your tea's getting hot!

On Sunday 25 April we anchored at Georgetown. The African name was Jan Jang Bureh, after two brothers who founded it. A family of repatriated, freed slaves were housed in a wooden house which still stood. I was expecting traffic fumes, internet cafés and hardware stores. There were none of those and after two days in Georgetown we'd seen one vehicle. Shops consisted of neat little piles of wrinkled fruit and vegetables set in lots on a scarf spread on the ground. They looked poor. Small fish smoked and charred were for sale at five dallasi for two. A grocery store was well stocked with tins and packets, even corn flakes, but no butter anywhere and margarine absent. Dried milk powder, tins of condensed sweetened milk, eggs, cooking oil and locally grown rice were plentiful. Ten cups of rice, about one and a half kilos, cost twenty five dallasi, about 50p.

The fresh water was pure delight with buckets of river water giving instant transformational cooling in the 38C heat. We washed clothes and scrubbed the Sahellian dusts from Storm Petrel, choosing chores which meant getting soaked. The heat became overwhelming when no breeze blew, so we jumped from the boat into the sweet, brown river.

It was at Georgetown we found palm wine to buy after being shown to the palm wine collector by a crowd of five boys. We passed along the high street, past the wooden ex–slaves house, past the police station and the policemen laying around on mats and brewing attaya. Buba said police cars were known as "bad cars". Next we passed the Peace Garden built and planted to commemorate the reform of slavery. Further into the back of the town we passed a tall radio mast with wire stays interrupting the roadway. The GamTel international telephone centre was near a small concrete house with a hand painted sign, "GAMBIA METEOROLOGICAL OFFICE". Three men in the porch around a tiny charcoal stove brewed attaya in the ubiquitous weeny enamel teapot. Two miniature glass tumblers stood on a wet enamel plate as the gunpowder green China tea boiled and bubbled. Weather observations were telephoned through to Banjul several times a day. Peering inside the weather station I saw an almost bare room, just several wooden chairs and a table with sheets of paper on it. No other equipment existed, I did not even see a barometer although I had noticed barometric pressure remained fairly constant apart from a diurnal rise and fall with daylight and nightfall. Barometric pressure may as well have been determined by the height at which the cobalt blue and chrome yellow agama lizards clung on the walls outside.

Wind direction, rainfall and cloud cover, in octas were noted hourly on a pro forma. I talked to the meteorologists because weather and sailing were absolutely linked and I was always interested in what the weather was doing. The head meteorologist asked several times how he could reach Storm Petrel for a visit. When I told him it was only possible to swim there, he protested I did not wish him to visit. Storm Petrel was so small and my only haven from the complexities of humanity so I did not often invite strangers aboard – a testimony to the good nature of Buba. I sensed the weather man was anticipating more than just a glimpse of the ship's barometer.

Buba and I rejoined the throng of boys waiting patiently in the road. We turned right at a large cotton tree with five mango sellers sitting beneath and the sand track led past compounds with washing slung over the rush fences and chickens pacing about with one eye on a hole in the fence, the other on a kid goat butting a post. Toddlers with distended belly buttons peered from compounds, calling, "Toubab!", and then, "How are you?" and, "What is you name?"

The five young boys whose sisters would be occupied by tasks such as carrying water from the river in plastic tubs, sweeping, washing clothes and cleaning rice vied for our attention as they led us to the alcohol sellers compound. When we arrived several families sat stooped, or laying on mats under the shade of an overhanging corrugated iron roof and bare breasted women watched as we were shown into a small dark room. Inside a man sat surrounded by empty bottles and unoccupied chairs. His eyes were half closed and squatting near the floor he looked small and old. The next time we came to buy palm wine he turned out as fit and agile as a thirty year old athlete.

Palm wine collectors climbed to the very top of a seventeen metre tree, twice first to hang the collecting bottles and later to carry the five to ten litres down. He sold us two litres of fresh palm wine for ten dallasi per litre, in open topped brandy bottles. Out of the bottle mouths came the froth of early, natural fermentation. We were offered a seat to drink it there and then but we wanted to savour the palm wine on Storm Petrel. Fresh palm wine was about as strong as white wine, but much more an enchantment than an intoxication. As we made to leave the palm wine sellers compound a bare breasted woman, wearing an ankle length wrap, offered to sell us bush meat, wild pig, so we bought a kilo for seven dallasi (about 14p).

The meat was being butchered as we had arrived and so I was not concerned for its freshness. One kilo of lean, boneless meat was too much for two people, but we managed somehow. I felt very happy afloat in the fresh water River Gambia, frolicking in the water around the boat to cool off and there followed several long hot days supping palm wine and adjusting the tarpaulin against the sun. The unshaded decks were too hot to walk on in bare feet and cups of tea or plates of food had to be consumed briskly or they would become too hot.

Opposite to Georgetown was a tourist camp called Dream Bird Camp. I wanted to spend a day sitting quietly in the deep shade of a large tree out of the sun and gain a little distance for reflection. Despite wearing a headscarf, long sleeved t shirts and long cotton slacks I felt constantly on the verge of sunstroke. I was drinking at least two litres of water as well as five or six mugs of tea each day. The Dream Bird Camp offered a respite from raw Africa, being a version of Africa designed to accommodate tourists in a sort of rough, bushy, restful luxury. Ten guests had left the previous day and a few staff ambled about the place, sweeping, washing table cloths and cooking up surplus food. Others sat gazing over the river with a little charcoal stove at their feet, brewing attaya. I soaked up the profound, leafy shade until dinner time when monkeys gathered in the branches above and scampered along the top of the kitchen walls. A man who had been sitting absolutely quietly for several hours and had the thin, grass seed shaped slanted eyes of a Fula tribesman, picked up a cane thin stick from a pile near to his seat and hurled it at a monkey making for the open bar area.

We ate lunch and the monkeys came closer. Suddenly a large green velvet monkey was standing at the table and as it reached across to take bread I shouted, "Hey!" and reaching over I tapped it on the head as one would a rude child. The creature sped off with a piece of bread. I chose omelet and chips, steering clear of spaghetti bolognaise, which would be a left over from yesterdays tourist crowd.

We left Georgetown to visit another tourist camp on McCarthy Island 3 km down river and surrounded by woods. The manager of Bird Safari Camp was a friend of Buba and he had repeatedly asked us to drop by. In a large, thatched building with a bar at one end we enjoyed more peace and solitude out of the glaring sunshine, reading through a pile of old bird watching magazines. A blackboard had written on it, "Todays Birds", followed by a list of exotic sounding species, including a favourite of UK ornithologists – egyptian plover.

I enjoyed seeing and hearing the swifts screeching overhead in large happy groups and touching the water to drink with ripples spreading outwards from the point their beak touched the water, like pleasure spreading in the heart of a calm watcher. The Bird Safari Camp manager, Lamin, said he saw many geckos in the buildings and that their tails were poisonous and so he killed them. I calmly countered this myth, telling him the gecko tail was not at all harmful and adding geckos ate many mosquitoes and flies. I then told him how much tourists enjoyed having a gecko or two in their room so they were definitely to be looked after. Of course if a gecko sheds it's tail and it falls into a water butt – which stand inside houses with wooden lids loosely covering the open top, an ideal resting spot for a gecko – it would rot and contaminate the water, so there is something in the fear. The manager admitted that many snakes were killed needlessly by people who thought they were poisonous or evil. We agreed that snakes were keener on escaping people, rather than attacking them, even the poisonous ones. I took this positive talk about reptiles to mark a turning point in Lamin's gecko policy. He went on to talk about the big Nile monitors, a meter and a half in length and he said he occasionally saw iguanas running through the bar area when things were quiet, holding his arms wide to indicate their size.

I went for a deeply satisfying wander alone, walking a couple of kilometres along the river, past white horned cows wearing bells, baobab trees, ancient and scarred, inviting old spirits in, termite mounds growing like giant fairy tale mushrooms or gnome huts, mango trees hung with lorry loads of green or orange tinted fruit and monkeys crashing about in their foliage, avoiding me as I padded along feintly human paths. My leather sandal broke and I used a piece of string from the waistband of my slacks, cut free with a piece of glass, to repair it. I found the green shard of beer bottle embedded in a termite mound, perhaps hurled out of a passing tourist pirogue. The glass cut the cord. The cord held my sandal together.

After a couple of hours I headed back and met Buba coming towards me on the track. He thought I might have met an angry troupe of baboons and told me when he was younger, he would go chasing baboons far into the bush and then at a certain point the baboons would turn around and chase them back to the village. Baboons would run up behind and swipe the legs from under people. What fun! We left Bird Safari Camp late in the afternoon. Tourist camps were expensive places to spend more than a few hours in with each coffee, tea and bite to eat going on the bill which had to be paid at the end. The most relaxing place was aboard Storm Petrel, although I always felt a need to get off the boat for a portion of each day if possible. I had lived aboard Storm Petrel for three years solid and she was extremely small for my 6' 2" height, even though she was ideal for my purpose. We reached Barrajalli at nightfall and anchored. Mosquitoes hassled us but the cabin was too hot to hide in under the mosquito nets so we sat sweating and slapping ourselves in the dark, singing air. When we fell hot into our bunks we both lay fanning ourselves until sleep stole us away.

We set off at 6am to arrive early at Baboon Island – The Gambia National Park Nature Reserve – this time having decided to pay the ticket price and be shown the chimpanzees. The patrolling wardens appeared in their dory and we took one aboard. His name was Lamin – all first born boys were named Lamin and first born girls were named Fatima. I strongly stated Storm Petrel's depth was 2m, adding 0.6m for a safety margin and Lamin assured me he knew the channels around the islands and would not let us run aground. We failed to see the chimpanzees on the first and smaller island and motored slowly, close to the thick trees. A crocodile wended across the river, a big one, 3m in length and next, as we crossed the river towards the main channel, Storm Petrel's keel cut deep into a mud bank. The tide did its usual thing of heeling the boat over dramatically and I heard the poor ranger mutter, "Oh, sorry." Instantly Buba whipped off his jeans and urged the ranger, "Go down!" Buba jumped over board up to his chest and walked to the bow to push. The guide somewhat reluctantly followed Buba's example by removing his dark green safari suit, but instead of doing as Buba was, he climbed into the dinghy and attempted to push the boat from there. No concept of deep draught boats and none either of equal and opposite reactions. Mine and Buba's equal and opposite reaction was to burst out laughing. The crest–fallen ranger dragged himself down into the water next to Buba muttering about not being able to swim as the two men heaved. Full reverse engine power helped Storm Petrel slide gradually backwards out of the mud, gathering way in deeper water. Buba struggled back aboard and somehow Lamin had leaped back aboard ahead of him. The thought of being crocodiled or hippopotamised was too much for me and I stuck to controlling the engine and leaning out on the shrouds to heel the boat and work her free of the bottom. The chimpanzees must have enjoyed this spectacle, but did not show themselves to us although we saw colubus monkeys and baboons.

    Just peering into the many secret mud beaches leading away into heavy foliage gave me pleasure enough for the sheer herpetological potential this offered my senses. By lunch time we had left Baboon Island behind and dropped off the damp trousered Lamin. Kuntaur came on the starboard side and we anchored to visit this small town with large broad leaf trees at the water's edge offering an all day ten degree temperature drop.

We tried to buy palm wine but found only a drunken group of old men with slit eyed stares, so we sat under the big tees and were joined by loads of boys. Eventually our coolness set the boys back to their frolicking in the river. Chickens pecked and goats climbed and chewed. Sheep lost and found each other. A white cow moved like light through deep tree shadows. Muscovy ducks wide–eyed in wonder, chuckled to one another about water. A voice hollered across the five hundred meter wide river and a figure waved. The boys called back, "Manjago!". Manjago meant "Christian" and was used derogatorily. After fifteen minutes, some lads set off towards the far shore in a dug out canoe and the canoe carrying four boys and a man wearing dirty white robes approached the shore after sweeping past Storm Petrel on a running tide. They came ashore all grinning and panting and a baby baboon clambered out of the boat on a cloth leash. It had been captured by the man. This was illegal throughout Gambia, but monkeys and baboons were prized pets. I remembered seeing an advisory poster issued by the Gambian government, which stated there was a prison sentence of one year for capturing primates. As the Fula saying went, "Taking what you want isn't theft, unless you are caught". The little creature clung to a stone and stared at pebbles as things it knew and trusted. The boys crowded around, jeering at it. I restrained my curiosity and weaved a calmer reassuring thread into the first impressions the baboon was having amongst the human tribes. If provoked too much the baboon lunged into feeble open mouthed attacks. The boys scattered and screamed. This was exactly what the baboon wished to avoid – angering his captors and I could see him thinking over his options, avoiding eye contact, staring at the floor but heart beating with fight or flight reactions. When the baboon tried to lay down and close its eyes under a tree root, Buba made a very acute observation, "He has made a very big run today". Eventually the boys went back to posing and swimming and the baboon slept under the root. One boy made us laugh by scooping up wet sand, piling it on his head like a crown and strutting about in his underpants. Another boy swung a machete around his head, slashing at the sand and water and pointing at ducks, tossing it flipping to the ground and I thought of the horrors of Sierra Leone, to the south and Rwanda far to the east.

We left the baboon to its fate and went off to anchor further down river at Wassau, a small ferry crossing. There was an ancient stone circle at Wassau and this was what we went to find early the next morning. At 6am we rowed ashore and went looking for the stone circles. We walked through rice plantations, then passed through Wassau into open land behind. An enclosure had been built around the ancient site and several round houses accommodated the gate keeper, a museum, public toilets and an exhibition centre. I paid twenty five dallasi entrance fee and Buba was not charged. The stones occupied an area half the size of a football pitch. Stones were set vertically in circles. The largest was around 3m tall plus the root. Others were between 2–0.5m. A dozen or so circles stood in an arc. Laterite is a red rock with a bubbling structure and a dry hollow ring.

Piles of pebbles had been placed on top of each standing stone by visitors. Long shadows projected from the rising sun. Two blue lizards with yellow heads ran down a tree and onto a stone, then chased one another in an ascending spiral. I took a beautiful photograph of our shadows resting on two stones. A stick I'd shaved the bark off, way, way back in Portugal and used many times on walks, I lay across two stones to charge with earth energy and made a photograph. I was playing like a shaman, a spirit child, at the stone circle of Wassau. The stick was to lay on the cabin top pointing forwards like a finger indicating the way, on the voyage back to the Canaries, where I eventually placed it on the harbour wall, watched a man pick it up, admire it, and walk away with it. That's what sticks are for. We walked back through Wassau at the still early hour of 7.30am and called at a household where Buba had deposited the dinghy oars for security. I was worried about leaving a dinghy with oars unattended at a ferry crossing. In the compound were several round huts with the usual swept earth floor. A red colobus monkey was tied to a tree. I crouched down to say hello to it and it masturbated at me. Several men lay on wooden slatted beds under a round thatched roof. The smell of grass being smoked drifted around and we asked if they had palm wine, but there was none, only the drunken palm wine collector.

The journey back to Kemoto and then me alone to Banjul and Denton Bridge went quickly. The lower 200 km of the River Gambia were wide and inhospitable, with endless mangroves and undrinkable water, not a place to linger. About 16 km from Banjul, where the river was 6 km wide I was treated to the company of very large dolphins. I first saw them leaping on the horizon. They were 3m and more in length, huge by normal dolphin standards and they jumped clear of the water, turning in the air and diving straight down into the sea again. When I approached they came alongside and stayed with me for an hour.

The wreck strewn area off Half Die delayed me as I ran aground in soft mud, ploughing around between the sunken hulks, praying there were no wrecks below the surface. After reaching and anchoring at Half Die I was able to plot a decisive route over to the entrance to the Chittabong Bolon and I arrived back at Denton Bridge by dusk. Rosemarie waved at me romantically, doubtlessly happy to see her best customer arrive back as she stood on the rickety rhun palm pier, like a fish–wife welcoming the return of a lover.

*Illus. Maps - Becky Gilbey*

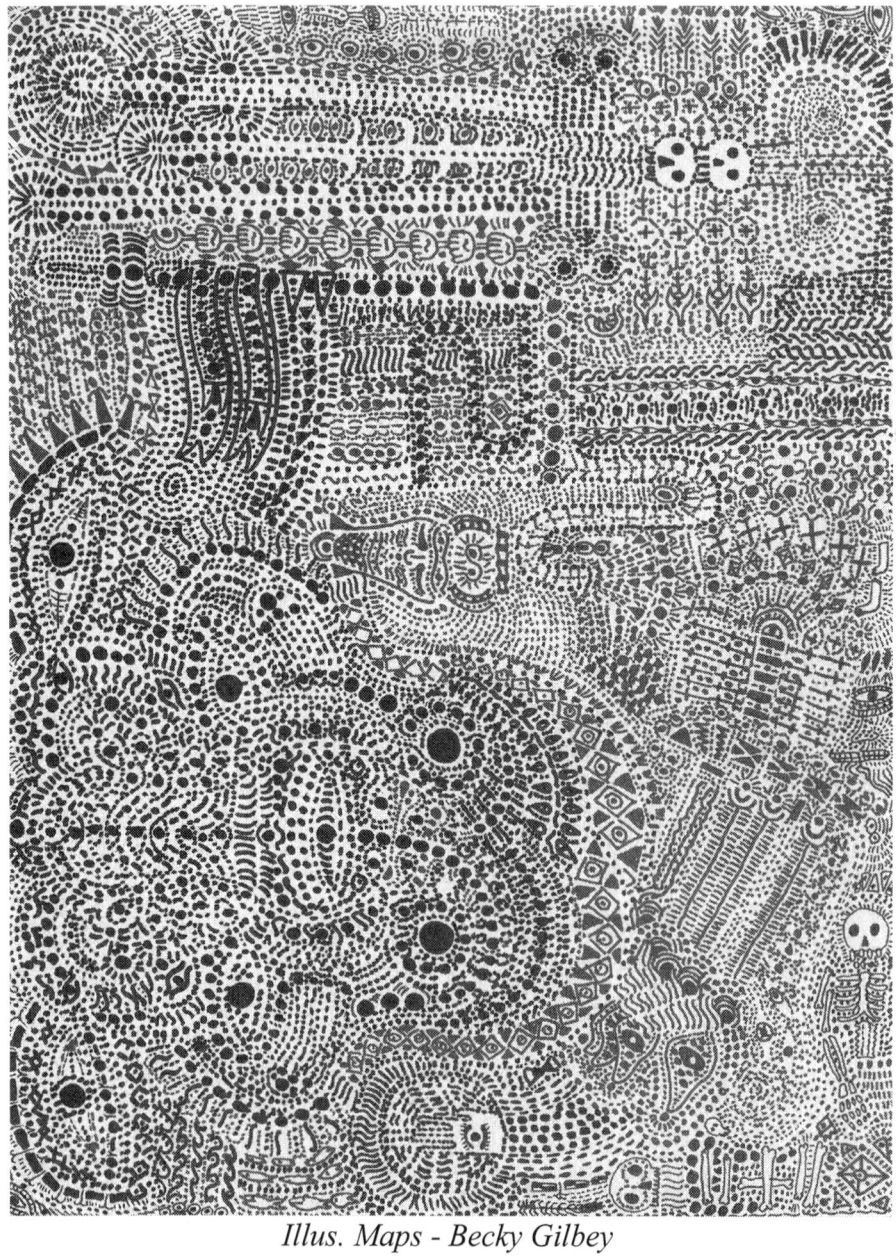

*Kudang Tenda*

*Kudang Tenda welcoming committee*

*Kicking back with palm wine*

*Palm wine drinking at Jan Jang Bureh, named after two brothers who founded it.*

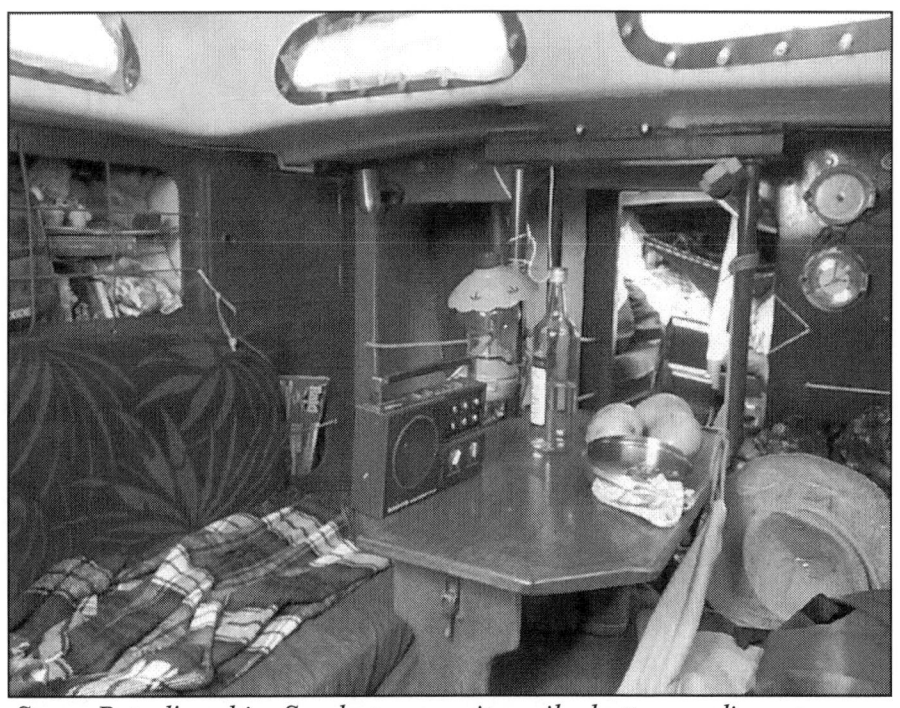

*Storm Petrel's cabin. Sun hat, mosquito coils, battery radio, mangoes, paraffin lamp.*

*By 10am the sun was too hot to do much, apart from shelter and drink palm wine.*

*Captured baby baboon at Kuntaur*

*Kuntaur*

*Muscovy ducks at Kuntaur*

*Drunken musician took a shine to me in Wassau. "Marry me hu?"*

*The lovely girls of Kemoto, Buba's village.*

*Kemoto girls*

## Further in, higher up, The Gambia

Sunday 23 May 2004. I missed Buba during the couple of weeks back at Denton Bridge and when he turned up to say hello I was getting ready for a second trip up the river and so he joined ship straight away. The rainy season was looming closer every day and the sun hotter than ever. We left early on a Sunday morning and ran aground in the winding creek through the mangrove swamp. After half an hour of struggle we were able to continue to Banjul, transiting the wide shallows laden with rusting hulks near Half Die without hitting any. Turning off the engine I was unaware we would not use it again over the following 250 km, all the way to McCarthy Island at Georgetown and further. A fair wind gave us a pleasurable cruise up river and the sails worked their magic on Buba and I. On the fifty six kilometre sail to Kemoto I plugged in the electric bass guitar (powered by solar panel) and Buba picked up the acoustic guitar. A glass each of ships whisky celebrated our second adventure inland. Buba discovered he liked playing the guitar. The great peaceful river allowed us to savour the music and distance equally without any engine noise.

We anchored at Kemoto and rowed ashore to meet Buba's family again. Brothers and other men sat drinking attaya and smoking in Buba's family compound. Wives and daughters were busy with wood chopping and cooking, usually with a baby on the back held in a wrap around the woman's chest. A young wife swished past in an elegant drop–shouldered, long dress in pretty blue satin with ruffles at the shoulders and a matching headscarf. Her femininity was made stronger by the baby boy slung on her back. Seconds later she was bending over chopping hunks of wood with heavy thumps and cracks of a machete. Earlier I had offered to help her carry water in twenty litre plastic drums but she just laughed and lifted a twenty litre drum on her head, as elegant as ever. In the evening we ate fish stew from a large enamel bowl placed on the bare concrete floor of the house, in a room lit by a single candle placed next to the bowl. Some people ate with their hands, but me and a few others used spoons. Fish bones were dropped onto the floor. Select morsels of fish meat were moved over to my section of the bowl. Afterwards in pitch dark Buba and I walked along the main street of Kemoto, where people greeted one another and torch beams flickered on for a few seconds, searching for items or negotiating tree roots and holes. The whole village was unlit apart from dim candle flames or paraffin lamps (invariably with the glass missing) in some homes.

Figures stood around and sat on wooden benches or the ubiquitous yellow plastic water cans outside their compounds, brewing attaya, smoking, joking, chatting in the blackness. Others lay on mats. Everyone shook hands and said, "Salam malikum," and replied, "Malikum salam.". Peace be with you and peace be with you too. Cigarette lighters flickered along the street, revealing other small groups of people. Houses were all without window glass or frames. Buba said that in the monsoon rains people ran about in the darkness, bumping into one another, trying to reach their compounds. Sometimes the thunder clouds were so dark they would wait for lightning to see where to run next. Caught out in the countryside by a thunder storm, people were afraid the wind would take them away and so they lay down on the ground in fear.

The moon was the 'big light'. Sometimes the moon took the path of the sun – when it was seen to rise larger than usual and was orange like the sun. Then all–night rituals were performed to put it back on the moon path. The same thing could occur with the sun taking the moon path, rising weak and silver and causing all night ritual dancing and drumming to correct the situation. Exactly what I saw when sailing past the western Sahara – the sun and moon appearing almost identical by day and by night due to the constant sand dust in the sky and a full moon.

Monday 24 May 2004. In the morning we filled Storm Petrel's tanks with the delicious, coconut–earth flavoured Kemoto water, coming out of a bore hole and pumped to a standpipe in the centre of the village. Water cost twenty five bututs per twenty five litres (One hundred bututs made one dalasi). This charge went towards the upkeep of the pump. We sailed at 9am. I did maintenance work around the boat while Buba steered and trimmed the sails to suit the shifting wind and changes in river direction. We anchored at 6pm near the ferry crossing of Eltenda, a main highway from south to north Senegal across the two halves of Gambia.

We left Eltenda at first light. The boat drifted slowly all day under sail enabling us to enjoy listening to cd's and the melancholy parrots whistling from the mangroves. When the tide turned foul we anchored near a fisherman's shelter, named Japin on the Admiralty chart. There were five fishermen resting and sheltering from the heat. No one had cigarettes for Buba to buy, but a single smoke was given, of course. After the tide turned fair we sailed the 5 km to Bombale. The wind disappeared and so I towed Storm Petrel using the Sportyak dinghy, over the final kilometre. I was swollen with heat energy and revelled in the expulsion of effort, but a little delirious at the same time. We walked into Bombale in the early evening. Children gripped every finger of both my hands. All they could say in English was, "What is your name?"

A woman asked me if we were from the M.R.C. (Medical Research Council) and beckoned us towards her child who needed some attention. I said we could not help. Buba found a single shop for cigarettes. I asked for bread, but Buba noticed it was several days old and we did not buy it. I stood in the dusty road with eighteen children clinging onto my hands. Two women arrived. A boy tapped a tin. I clapped in time. The woman laughed and danced. The children danced. I danced. Everyone laughed at the way I danced. We bought eighteen sweets for the children from the stale bread shop. Buba met a friend and he served us attaya, sitting on a log in the middle of Bombale with a white cow drifting around and sheep pulling at loose ends. On the track back to the river a huge tree gave up green mangoes which we ate like apples as we walked back through rice fields to the boat. I had shaken hands with twenty adults and thirty children and worried about sucking the dripping fruit juice from fingers without first washing my hands. Before I had arrived in Africa, travel advice stated all vegetables and fruit must be soaked in bleach solution or peeled before eating. Unripe mangoes unwashed and unpeeled were delicious – like hard pears, especially when they had been scrumped, with a tingle of the forbidden in the greenness, much nicer than the red, squashy, ripe ones.

Early the following morning we sailed and drifted on the incoming tide, away from Elephant Island and Bombale. Monkeys called out of the dense leaves. The sound they made was very similar to a plastic toy, called a "Giggle Stick", I had been given by my niece Camilla, in Britain. I shook the giggle stick and this made me and Buba laugh as it sounded so much like the monkeys.

On occasions we resorted to paddling the boat away from the banks in very light breezes, but the pleasure of making way only under sail was intense. After a couple of hours paddling and drifting very slowly a firmer breeze arrived and we tacked to and fro across the river with the tide helping progress. Two hours later the river course turned north and Storm Petrel was able to sail straight up–river at 8 km/h. We passed a very long island called Seahorse Island. This marked the point in the river at which things became more interesting. We had now sailed 100 km inland from Banjul and we had fallen into the idea of making the whole 250 km journey under wind and paddle power. The silence and peace were delicious. The only noise came from parrots and monkeys in the thick mangrove banks. One kilometre drifting slowly under sail took as long as 10 km under engine power, but slow, patient sailing was much more rewarding. The day lasted longer and seemed to brim with impressions and feelings which would not arise under the diesel engines roar. Fishermen sitting in dug out canoes stared in awe at Storm Petrel powering past, heeled over at 20 degrees and making a delectable progress. Each river corner and secret bolon passed was like a gift from the river. When we sat quietly drifting for over an hour it was as a discussion between the river and our will to travel along it and then mid afternoon we anchored as the tide began pushing us backwards. We launched the Sportyak and rowed to the mangrove to climb in among the tangled roots and rhizomic stems. 50m in was dense cane, too thick to go into. Buba said the cane was where hyenas slept by day.

Tiny black geckos sped up and away around the thicker mangrove trunks. Strange looking, amphibious fish lived in the mud between descending mangrove roots at the tide line. They measured about 100 mm, had protruding, frog–like eyes and a pair of fins at the rear flank had evolved into small legs, like tadpole legs. They hopped and swam fearlessly on the mud right below us. Buba cut a stick to use as an African toothbrush. We sat in the hot shade, making our dirty teeth even more dirty with the frayed stick ends.

Later, we set sail again on the evening flood tide. Soon it was dark, but we continued sailing towards Kau–Ur. Several fishermen drifted nets across the flood stream. Eventually we left them far behind in the night. Kau–Ur showed up as a shadowy bluff on the north shore with no lights but the flicker of cigarette lighters and Senegalese music blaring out of a small radio from a group of people at the foreshore. Storm Petrel arrived silently with all sail set, glowing dully under a half moon. I switched on the tricolour mast–head navigation light so the people ashore could see we were a boat, rather than a passing spirit. The wiring of the navigation light melted with a strong smell of burning rubber. I quickly switched it off and used the second set of deck level navigation lights instead.

Throughout the night gusts came between calms. We listened to short wave radio coming from Guinea Conakry and reggae coming from Gambian West Coast radio. At 6am we arrived at Deer Island and anchored, tired and mosquito bitten. Kudang Tenda was just 3 km ahead and we knew there would be millions of children invading us if we stopped to rest there. Mosquitoes had bitten my left foot thirty times. The right foot the same. I clawed at them with my fingers and nails. My feet were on fire.

A sound which had deeply impressed me was the call of hyenas. We heard many of these throughout the night, all of them on the north bank. I wondered if perhaps it had been only a couple of hyenas which had been hungrily following our progress.

We slept several hours but were driven out of the cabin by 9.30am by the hot sun. Soon after getting under–way on a fair tide we arrived at Kudang Tenda. We rowed ashore and walked between small round houses built of mud bricks and thatched with reeds. If young girls tried to touch my hands they were jostled away by the boys. We bought bread, heavy baguettes with sticky dough patches inside and black oven marks on the bottom. Kudang Tenda was on the river and 5 km walk inland was Kudang, a larger town with a tarmac road passing through, so we went to have a look.

Kudang. In the shade of a huge cotton tree twenty mango sellers sat. An old colonial market building housed two rows of sellers seated upon the concrete floor. Wearing cotton shawls and head scarves, they sold more or less identical sets of vegetables – tomatoes, sweet potatoes, bitter tomatoes and green chilli peppers, arranged in neat groups of three or four or five items. Each had a set asking price but Buba could invariably buy things at much lower prices than me because I was a toubab and toubabs were rich. I bought sweet potatoes, a bitter tomato and red tomatoes. The last seller in the row drew my attention. She looked slightly different to the other women sellers – with rougher skin around her jaw line and when she spoke her voice sounded quite deep with a gravelly sound as it dropped at the end of sentences. She sat on a tiny wooden stool wearing the usual wrap and headscarf. She was very pleasant and I felt an affinity between us concerning the possible similarities in our gender histories. Her position at the far end of the line of sellers may have just been the result of her later arrival than the others. I detected no animosity or resentment from the other sellers towards this individual. If anything there was a gentle murmur of recognition from the others as the vegetable seller and myself met with our uncommon commonality.

I asked Buba whether he had met any other people like me or the vegetable seller. He told me he had not. I asked about Gambian attitudes towards sex and he told me about a man who performed male circumcisions who had been well known for offering cuddles and 'love' to the young boys on the night before their ritual. I attempted to define homosexuality as sexual attraction to ones own sex, not to children and at this point the topic rapidly became complicated by our differing social norms, varying religious prejudices and widely separated understandings of the words we were using. The fondler was male, he did not circumcise girls, so I could see Buba's label of "homosexual" was correct, if over simplified, to my 'sophisticated' gender concepts.

At 10am Kudang was hot. We sat in the shade of the market building crunching raw, earthy, sweet potato and biting into mangoes. We declined the offer of a donkey cart taxi ride back to the river preferring the four kilometre walk. A group of Fula boys joined us – they often waited under a tree for adults to come past so they could go together through the bush, not so much for safety as for amusement. We were strangers, a Mandinka and an Anglo Saxon, good enough entertainment for the four kilometre walk back to Kudang Tenda. One boy carried a heavy log on his head. Others had various fruits, berries and seeds picked from the bush. A large green bean in a pod very much like a runner bean, tasted slippery and fresh mint – "suck it like a mint," Buba told me, "do not chew the seed". After ten minutes the hard seed was spat out. Some handfuls of leaves tasted of lemon. I recklessly ate these wild plants and happily suffered nil. I felt the health cautions of travel advisory notices in books and on the internet were over done. Maybe in urban areas there were many more risks but a mango knocked from a tree with a stick was as clean and fresh as any fruit anywhere in the world. Minty beans and lemon flavoured leaves were fascinating and refreshing experiences which added life to travel rather than disturbing it. All my fears of small cuts being dreadfully infected slipped behind me. My hands, particularly, were covered in small wounds from rowing the dinghy ashore into thorn bushes or climbing around in mangroves. My feet and ankles were dotted with mosquito bites which I had torn at with my nails, trying desperately to excavate the fiery aggravation. Eventually, everything healed perfectly, helped by regular plunges into the River Gambia. The main thing to watch were the flies landing on scabs and pestering them.

The project of the fly population was to infect every possible wound and thus disable the wounded so they were more easily pestered into a spiral of decay. I killed every fly I could possibly hit – about one in every two hundred and fifty which landed on me.

Saturday 29 May 2004. We went to collect water from the village well but it was locked. Buba asked some children standing nearby and they found a woman who had a key. The village well consisted of a pair of robustly constructed metal hand pumps, enclosed within a circular wall where no shoes were allowed. The usual crowd of boys and a few girls followed us, constantly trying to prize the water cans from our grip – any way to become involved. I gave a few dalasi to the woman who had unlocked the pump and vigorously worked the water out for us. We bought a packet of small biscuits for the children. The only shop in Kudang Tenda sold no butter, nor margarine.

We left Kudang Tenda and by late morning we reached Kuntaur. Ashore we strolled through the houses along the main street. People sat outside shops and homes on mats and wooden slatted bed couches. We were greeted by amused old men and engaged in Mandinka or Fula by women. Beyond the houses rice fields opened up, wet and verdant. A group of young girls joined us. One stood out as a sparkling personality – called Fama. She was about five years old and both Buba and I fell in love with her strong charm. I shared out nearly a whole box of coloured felt tipped pens. A thin girl of around ten years old asked for a second pen and pointed at a baby held in a wrap on her back. Every few seconds another small child squirmed at the entrance to another compound and called out "Toubab".

I had not felt rain any time since I left Gran Canaria, some four months previously. The first African rain fell heavy in the night. Buba had not felt rain for seven months. The monsoon had arrived. Storm Petrel leaked blobs of water onto my bunk, but it was relieving to feel the cooled air sweeping across the water. The morning smelled sweet earthy and distinctly sandalwood. We sailed on past Baboon Islands. This time extremely slowly as the breeze was shielded by the high, thick woods of the chimp sanctuary. A black cobra swam across the river. Hippopotami revealed themselves out on the banks. They had pink around their lips and eyes. Their skin was frog coloured. A crocodile swam lazily across the river. Red colobus monkeys peered and chomped in the thick leafy trees. We cleared Baboon Islands, reaching just beyond the No Anchoring boundary, to anchor next to a rice paddy set in a flood meadow. We rowed ashore for a wander. Mushroom shaped termite mounds grew on the earth banks between the paddocks. We followed thin pathways along the earthen ridges. Some large boggy gaps made us jump and skid in the mud. Half a kilometre further in we were amongst leafy shrubs, thorn bushes, baobab trees, dry grasses and palms. A bush pig tilted away through the woods. In a large tree were several green velvet monkeys. Buba had a reaction to monkeys which was to shout at them and make them jump and dash about. I doubled up laughing when he frightened a monkey which hesitated before a large leap across two trees. Buba gesticulated and pretended to rush forwards. The monkey glanced between the gap and us, finally doing a four metre free fall like a parachutist jumping from a plane. I awoke that night laughing again at this image.

Sunday 30 May 2004. We sailed along to Georgetown, on McCarthy Island having covered 250 engine–less kilometres. We spent a day in the Dream Bird Camp across from Georgetown. Green velvet monkeys became annoyed with us for refusing to give them any food and pissed into our coffee, a direct hit from straight overhead. We amused ourselves in chasing them and they pelted us back with seeds. I loved meeting these intelligent agile creatures.

A few days later we sailed off the Admiralty chart into the rock strewn upper River Gambia. The first rocks reached all the way across the river leaving a ten metre wide gap at the south side. On a partly submerged tree trunk sat a large, smooth green freshwater turtle. The pilot book stated there were manatees living in these parts, but we did not see them. I was perfectly happy to see Nile monitor lizards. The first lounging on a low cliff with his tail dropping a metre to the water and his body half a metre long. The next was maybe his partner and she was silhouetted against the sky, prowling through the bank top undergrowth, tongue flicking in and out. She measured about three quarters of a metre. The third Nile monitor slithered down a steep rocky bank and straight under water. He was a big one.

We came to Bansang a substantial town with a cable ferry and even a moored fibreglass sailing yacht, named "Schedar of Mindello". Her home port was Mindello on the Cabo Verde Islands. Women washed clothes at the waters edge and I nonchalantly pointed my binoculars at a welling movement in the water between Storm Petrel and the shore. Suddenly a frightened hippopotamus erupted up out of the river and surged full body above water away from the boat in the direction of the shore. Some men sat watching, they warned a young girl collecting a tub of water, "Mind the hippo!" She just looked at it, shrugged, balanced the twenty litre water tub atop her head and moved away up the river bank. I realised just how threatening a frightened hippo could be even from the secure cockpit of Storm Petrel. The massive animal had been in deep water but managed to lift and surge forward, like an accelerating power boat. Hippos kill more people in a year than any other mammal throughout Africa. Crocodiles kill many people also, but mosquitoes kill much higher numbers than both.

We anchored, rowed ashore and found a restaurant where we sat in the hot shade to eat rice and fish. We shared one large dish of food and drank water out of a broken plastic pot. The meal cost the usual fifteen dalasi each – about 30p. We filled plastic cans and bottles with thirty litres of water from a tap in a nearby compound, overseen by an unsteady looking, grumpy man who gripped a large glass of brandy. I paid him two dalasi – a token gesture to quieten his grumbling. We rowed back to Storm Petrel with the water and left Bansang into a looming thunder storm. 12 km on was Monkey Court where monkeys were said to hold court. Dense woodland with palms emerged above the tree–line and higher still a red ridge of crumbling rock. Further away a wild fire flared orange on the low thunder cloud base. Lightning and fragments of rain came with strong gusts of wind. Darkness deepened the orange glow of the developing bush fire to the north.

In the woods a tree fell with a crash followed by the frightened barking of baboons. Buba told me how baboons cower in the trees when it rains and could not sleep. The expected heavy rain did not come. We passed under the thunder cell and anchored in the tense darkness off a village called Kerantaba Tenda. Some lights with figures moving in them turned out to be a safari pirogue from Denton Bridge. Two crew and three white women – a nurse, the boat owner and her friend were aboard. No lights showed from the village itself.

Friday 4 June 2004. In the morning we left Kerantaba Tenda without going ashore. The flooding tide took us past a memorial to Mungo Park. The concrete obelisk unceremoniously protruded amongst palm trees. Mungo Park set off from Kerantaba Tenda to explore Africa on two expeditions. The first was successful, the second not so. I could imagine the difficulty of walking through these scorching, thorny, crumbling lands. Two things kept me going on my expedition – first the bucketfuls of cooling river water applied repeatedly over the head, second was the gift of sighting large Nile monitors on the river banks.

Deep in the heated, dreamy river afternoon I smiled to myself as I remembered my childhood term for a good lizard terrain, "suitably lizardy". Buba enjoyed pointing the big monitors out to me, while I scanned the riverside with my binoculars and missed them. The terrain was so suitably lizardy my eyes were too eager to notice the beautiful reptiles lounging at the rivers edge. If deficiencies in my observational skills impinged, I reminded myself I'd sailed all the way to this suitably lizardy land. Sometimes the reality of being in charge of a sailing boat far from England felt humbling too. Our progress slowed as we crept along past sections where the sketch map indicated rocks. We negotiated between dead trees aground in the safe water channels and tell tale swirls in the water where unseen rocks lay. Later, to our great satisfaction we passed some rocks jutting black above the surface for it was a relief to actually see the obstructions in their full boat crunching potential. We followed the sketch map along the lizard infested banks to the next town. Basse showed the backs of mud brick houses with rusting corrugated sheet patches. Women washed clothes into the night time and carried away water on their heads. Men in bobble hats, baseball caps and wide rimmed, bowl shaped reed hats worked on nets and lines or repaired dugout canoes. A partly collapsed groundnut wharf and roofless ex–colonial buildings closed around a bend in the river where a ferry for vehicles crossed. A dozen steel boxes of around 5m in length, with twenty persons aboard, were sculled across using a single paddle in a notch at the stern. A larger steel work boat lay sunken next to a subsided concrete slipway on the far shore. Herds of white cows with wide set horns were swum across tethered to the ferries. Motorcycles perched on the bows and women carried plastic tubs of rice on their heads. One of the steel box ferries was unable to move with twenty people grounding it in the shallows. The ferry man ordered some passengers to shift from one side to the other in an accusatory tone of voice. The government sponsored ferry ran to and fro, repeatedly arriving and grounding at the concrete slipway with a screeching metallic howl. Ashore Basse was a large town and remained filthy and decrepit right to the centre. Diesel smoke trucks and sagging cars shared the roads with wandering, hairless sheep and stick whacked donkeys drawing carts.

On the Saturday I was ill after swigging foul water from a bottle filled in Bansang – I noticed a taste but put it down to Buba having just smoked a cigarette and taken a swig before me but as soon as I began swallowing the water I realized it was bad. I grew rapidly ill and was unable to face eating food, which left me weak and miserable.

The evening of the next day Buba brought fresh bread and said it would make me better because when a black man had diarrhoea he ate plain bread to cure it. It was a great relief to eat something again after forty hours. I was feeling really debilitated and needed to lay down after standing up for just a minute and my head throbbed when I moved about the boat. Buba told me I must eat some food and went off in the dinghy to buy two plates of benachin – fish and vegetable stew with rice. He arrived back in half an hour with a large plateful covered by a tea towel and I ate ravenously although worried it would disturb my stomach more. Afterwards I gained strength and felt more cheerful. Two days later I was still ill, but eating, so felt stronger, but I had not felt well enough to leave the boat for seventy two hours. Eventually we rowed ashore together to walk and found a large cotton tree to sit under. I felt weak.

We found a café where I ate an omelet and drank a cup of sweet milky coffee. The walls, tables, benches and floor were uniformly covered in green and blue decorative plastic. The entrance was a step through a rectangular opening with a high sill and the windows had no glass. There were no pictures on the green and blue walls – the effect was like sitting inside a pile of Christmas presents which had all been wrapped in the same gift wrapping paper. I enjoyed the stimulation of walking around the town and market stalls. One part was filled with people hammering scrap metals into beautiful three legged cooking cauldrons, large enough to serve twenty people from. A racket of cold riveting and metal being beaten into pots came from dozens of workers sitting around under rotting tents, corrugated lean–to's or just by a wrecked car turned on its side. We found a Gamtel International call centre and I tried to leave a message on my sisters answering machine but I called their old number and left the message with complete strangers. Somewhere in deepest Cambridgeshire an answer phone took my message, "Hello, its Clarissa, I'm fine. I'm far up the River Gambia, with Buba again, at a town called Basse. I've had a bad stomach but seem to be getting better now. Love to you all. Bye."

Basse was the limit of navigation for a boat with over 4ft draft. I heard of a French catamaran which had travelled the 32 km further up river to the Senegal border. I was happy with the lizards I'd been seeing and so we left Basse and headed back downstream. After 40 km downstream we were back at Kerantaba Tenda. This time we rowed ashore to see the village. There was hardly a person to be seen apart from a group of young boys who surrounded us. We showed them our carrier bag containing rubbish and they said they would take us to where we could put it. They led us to the gates of a hospital and it became clear they had thought we were delivering medicines. Buba sent two boys off with the rubbish bag and new orders to dispose of it. We saw a donkey cart where a man brewed attaya under the shade of a tree so we joined him. He was waiting for someone he had brought to hospital. He was a Fula tribe man and had the usual two scars at the outer side of each eye, marking these nomadic cattle herders. I could recognize them by their grass seed shaped eyes alone without seeing the scarification, although that enhanced the effect. There were many Fula people along the river. Some villages were dominated by Fulas, such as Kudang Tenda and Kuntaur. Others, such as Kemoto and Balingo were made up of mostly Mandinka. A crowd of children surrounded us and we kept them happy by giving away pens. One small boy wore a t-shirt ripped wide at the chest with a leather ju-ju necklace revealed by the gape. I thought what a strong fashion statement this would make back in Bristol – punky animist chique.

In the night time the rain fell deliciously for about three hours bringing again the pungent smell of wetted Africa – sandalwood, charcoal, earth dust, fresh lizard slough and decaying sunlight. Soon after leaving Kerentaba Tenda the engine lost power. After deduction we realised the propeller was spinning freely on the shaft. I was relieved it was not a problem with the gearbox. We sailed onwards with the ebb tide and after 8 km reached the thick wooded ridge of Monkey Court. The tide was now flooding and we anchored in view of the long, red rock hill covered in palm trees and bushes. The night seethed with insect life and around midnight hundreds of dog faced baboons suddenly began barking from both banks of the river.

Buba awoke at first light and sensing a fair wind pulled up the anchor and set the foresail. I lay lazily in my bunk, still weakened by the illness of the past week. In a few hours Buba had sailed us to Bansang and dropped anchor. We scanned the river banks looking for a slipway or beach on which to dry out the boat and remove the propeller. I was not happy about the steeply shelving bottom and with less than one metre rise and fall in the tide it would hardly give any advantage – the propeller was more than a metre under water. Also, the Bansang waterfront was a continuation of the rubbish tip which existed in every nook and cranny of the town. I decided to do what I could by diving underneath while Storm Petrel was anchored in the relatively rubbish free waters of mid stream. I could at least begin to remove the split pin, the propeller nut, the propeller and the key–way. It took an hour to draw out a heavy stainless steel split pin during forty or more dives. After this I was able to undo the nut retaining the propeller, but the propeller decided to fix itself as I was unable to slide it off the shaft. It was so solid with the shaft I could not revolve it or slide it along, whereas it had been spinning freely, so I simply replaced the retaining nut and fitted a new split pin.

I thought this could not possibly work but it proved effective all the way back to Denton Bridge. A monitor lizard swam past and looked large enough to me that I asked Buba whether it was maybe the top of a hippopotamus. We watched it swim across towards a concrete pier where some boys were playing. It avoided them by climbing into dense undergrowth which was lucky because very often these magnificent lizards were beaten to death. By 4pm we were able to test the propeller. It worked so we motored away from Bansang to arrive at McCarthy Island – Jan Jang Bureh – Georgetown – at 8pm. On the way we passed the rocks almost barring the river passage with swirling water to one side and tree tops swishing past the mast head to the other. Having come twice this far up the River Gambia I now felt I probably would not make a third visit.

We spent some lazy days anchored at Georgetown, swimming and drinking palm wine, while I became thoughtful as to the voyage of Storm Petrel. Where to next? Under a splintering hot sun rendered docile by a couple of litres of palm wine, I found myself saying to Buba, "We could sail together up to the Canary Islands." And that is what we did.

*Company on the road to Kudang Tenda*

*We filled plastic cans and bottles with thirty litres of water from a tap in a nearby compound, overseen by an unsteady looking, grumpy man who gripped a large glass of brandy. I paid him two dalasi – a token gesture to quieten his grumbling. We rowed back to Storm Petrel with the water and left Bansang into a looming thunder storm.*

*Kudang Tenda*

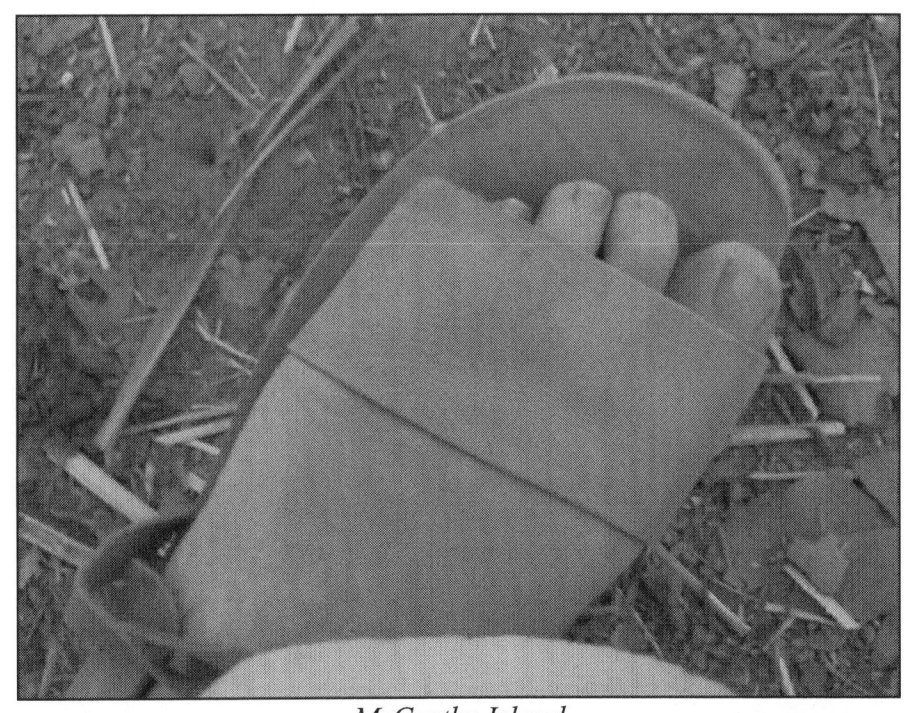

*McCarthy Island*

*Wassau stone circles*

*Wassau stone circles*

*Kuntaur*

*Kuntaur*

*A good omen appeared after we decided to sail together from west Africa up to the Canary Islands*

*Really big dolphins in The River Gambia near the capital Banjul.*

## How we got back from Georgetown to Banjul

The rains circled, advanced, retreated and occasionally fell. Always a barrage of wind was followed by sideways slanting rain. Six months of hot dust was by now entirely dowsed from the mast and shrouds. The Bird Safari Camp on the west end of McCarthy Island, where Buba knew the manager, Idi, and the skipper of a large double decked pirogue moored at the river front, offered shade and quiet. We anchored nearby to visit. The tourist season had ended when the rainy season began so the thatched roof bar and surrounding thatched round houses were unoccupied, apart from the odd spider and geckos, supposedly. After drinking attaya we walked with Idi along a track passing through rice fields, woods, a cemetery and finally arriving at the edge of Georgetown. Idi knew where alcohol could be purchased and we arrived at a palm wine seller whom we had visited before. In the yard there was a still producing fierce liquor from water and sugar. The still was made from two steel barrels, the first with a fire built beneath it and pipes connecting the two. More piping led from the second barrel into a flask. A small measure of the fire water cost ten dalasi, less than a third of one Euro, but Buba warned me the spirit was not at all pleasant. Idi satisfied his craving for the stuff while Buba and I asked for a couple of litres of palm wine. While we waited we were introduced to a palm wine collector, Sam. He introduced us to a second palm wine collector who had recently lost his testicles after slipping down the trunk of a palm tree. The palms get slippery in the rain. We were shown the hospital bill and as a palm wine lover I felt obliged to help him pay the bill, however my resistance was strong as I did not like being pressured to give away money. A hawker arrived with a tray of pastries filled with meat. I bought one each for the curious children gathered with us. After I paid for a dose of fire water for Sam a music session ensued. Sam handed out saucepan lids and sticks and then sang a hilarious refrain, something about Andy Pandy, which Buba translated as, "having many pairs of trousers" and then about 'knowing and folding things'. We all clattered along with our percussion. Sam asked me for a song. I sang, *"It's a long way to*

*Tipperary, Its a long way to go, It's a long way to Tipperary, To the sweetest girl I know, Goodbye Piccadilly, Farewell Leicester Square, It's a long long way to Tipperary, But my heart's right there."*

(Song written by Judge, Williams Feldman).

The old song carried my feelings of being far away from the UK and Sam was pleased to feel the emotion in my voice. A large crowd of children stood around bemused and fascinated, some frowning as they tried to understand what Buba, Sam and I were creating together. Others broke out into little dances or rapped hard on the saucepan lids, until Sam, who was quickly being overcome by the liquor, told them to be quiet and listen to the grown ups. I was also succumbing to the palm wine which we had started swigging freely since it had appeared. Buba and I had intended to save the palm wine until the evening and spread it over several days. The music session was so funny that we finished a litre within the hour. Someone appeared with an acoustic guitar but it was tuned so low – to preserve the strings which were unavailable in Gambia – I could hardly play it.

We were quite drunk by then and needed to walk around so we found Idi and he led us off to meet some more of his friends. Idi had a photographic imagination, often pointing at a scene and saying, "Look at this, it is real Africa, what an amazing photograph this would make, have you got your camera?", even as I repeatedly explained I had left my camera on the boat. We met several families. Idi was quite drunk and I felt his arrival was more tolerated than celebrated. We sat around on oil cans, plastic water containers and discarded engine blocks, polished by years of being sat on, drinking attaya and chatting. I asked Buba how to spell "attaya". He thought for a moment and spelled out, "H, um, I, err, G, and er, G, then I, um, err, T, yes that's it." I spoke the word, "higgit." Buba just said, "attaya, yes, that's how you spell it."

By mid afternoon the heat was overwhelming. I found a strong need to escape for a few minutes into shade each time we came upon it. As I sat down next to a wall or under a tree I would murmur about heat stroke, but Idi was oblivious to my concerns as he wanted to impose us on new sets of friends. I said we had pestered enough people and I wanted to return to the Bird Safari Camp and the boat. We stopped at a small ramshackle store for bottles of water. I bought attaya.

Attaya was usually served between two to four people and each person had two or three cups. Brewing and drinking took about half an hour. The exact method of brewing attaya was explained to me as a precise formula, drawn with a stick in the dust, involving the number of people and servings. The complex part was adjusting the sugar and water in a series of brews. When I eventually learned to brew attaya it was not to a formula, one just aimed for a good strength and not too sweet. What made attaya such a social drink was the tending of the charcoal fire and the repeated pouring of the brew from a weensy pot to the tiny cups and back, while a sticky froth was retained in each cup – the mark of good attaya. Attaya was very sugary and during brewing the tea was almost boiled dry. The taste was a dense, piping hot syrup to be slurped down in a few seconds in a sharp intake of air over the lip of the glass to cool it. The cup was handed back onto the plate to be rinsed, but just around the outside, so the froth in the cup was preserved throughout subsequent brews.

We walked back along the red earth track with Idi pointing out more scenes from the "real Africa" and urging me to photograph his views. I was decidedly sun struck when we stumbled back into the Bird Safari Camp so I sat in the cool shade and drank water, water, water. We left Idi to his world and got back aboard Storm Petrel to regain sobriety and left the following morning. My thoughts were spiralling away from the Gambia now and towards the 1600 km sail back to the Canaries.

For the time being we were still in sweet waters, there were still crocodiles, hippopotami and monkeys, so we bought more palm wine in Kudang Tenda. The local children surrounded us when we rowed ashore in the dinghy, lifting it clear out of the water and up onto the bank as soon as we hopped out. We had been before and given bits of pancake, pens and hair ties so they knew us as good fun. We sat on a jetty while the boys made us laugh by turning their eyelids inside out.

A small girl was terrified of me. She kept glancing round to make sure I was not approaching so I waited for her to forget about me for a minute, then leapt up and ran towards her.

Her face turned towards me in horror and she ran without turning around once, in a dead straight line, the 100m to her home. Some Gambian children feared white people because of stories of slavery. Later she and her mother bathed nearby at the waters edge and I was glad to see she was not traumatized. Physical jokes were a way to be honest, like dancing – a way to acknowledge the commonality between people. Chasing and being chased were universal experiences.

Buba and I paid for a litre of palm wine at a Christian household. Alcohol was forbidden to Muslims so it was always sold by Christians. We wanted two litres, or three, to keep us going all the way back to Banjul. We stopped the next night at Bombale.

After this we stopped at Balingo, anchoring near a European looking catamaran drawn up on the shore. We met the English yachtsman who had sailed there years ago and had now built a house nearby. Jeff introduced us to spirit made from cashew fruits. After walking about the small village we rowed out to Storm Petrel and relaxed in the cockpit, under an ominous sky, drinking palm wine. This bottle seemed very strong, especially combined with the cashew liquor and we crawled into our bunks half drunk, grateful the weather had not broken.

We arrived at Kemoto the following afternoon where Buba told his family and friends about our plans to sail to the Canary Islands. Buba's mother Anja, asked to talk with me. I thought she was going to harangue me for stealing her boy. I was led into her bedroom and sat down with Anja on one side and Buba the other. She told me her feelings in Mandinka. I listened looking her in the eyes, although I did not understand her. After each statement, I turned to Buba and he translated, then I turned back to Anja. Anja said she was very happy her son was able to travel to Europe because they had almost nothing and the village held no opportunity for improving life. There seemed hardly any sadness at the separation of son and mother, at least it was not expressed. Perhaps the opportunity to travel away from Africa was valued so highly it outshone any loss.

The process of getting Buba's documents began with the discovery his birth certificate had been lost when the house roof was blown off one rainy season. To get a passport he needed an identification card and a birth certificate and the first visit was to the Alcarlo – the village mayor. It took three weeks to arrange the three documents. In the Banjul passport office we paid two hundred and fifty dalasi in tips, when the clerk told us Buba's home was not in the lower river division but in the middle river division and therefore we should be applying in the appropriate office. We were given a discount of fifty dalasi because we had to wait an extra couple of days. At the identity card office we were asked for money to get a quick service rather than wait an extra two weeks but we out rightly refused and as we walked away the official came to the railings wanting to shake our hands, saying no harm had been done. The passport office took the only non essential payment I ever paid in West Africa. However I did find out the monthly tourist visa had been costing me fifty dalasi extra – for an application form which was never filled in, but always charged for. I say tips euphemistically, although to call these bribes would be cultural prejudice. I would not view a ten per cent restaurant tip as a bribe, merely a way to say thank you for good service and hopefully good will the next visit.

On the way down river to Banjul Storm Petrel galloped along in a fresh wind, overtaking a fifteen meter pirogue with eight people aboard and a child standing at the helm, robes rippling in the breeze. Storm Petrel shouldered through the seas, leaning in gusts, sometimes rushing ahead through white broken water. Later we got stuck in the mud banks off Banjul. At four in the morning we finally extricated Storm Petrel from the shoal waters and re-anchored in the deeper channel. At dawn we crept tiredly through the mangrove swamps on the Chittabong Bolon to Denton Bridge.

Sunday 25 July 2004. My uncle John had helped build the Denton Bridge about 20 years previously. I remembered the wood sculptures he used to bring back from Africa, so far away – then.

I began preparing Storm Petrel for a hard beat north, away from the tropics. I topped up the engine oil which was well below the lowest level mark. I saw sparking at the dynastart (a dynastart is a combined engine starter and generator) and found wires breaking away, so I replaced the crimped connectors. I tightened the port side forward engine mount hold down bolt which seemed unable to be tightened really hard. I changed the starter motor belt pair and tensioned them.

Storm Petrel was ready to sail the following day. I topped up spare water. I refitted the inner forestay as safety measure in case extended up wind sailing damaged the forestay. I fitted an extra cleat at the mast base, for the topping lift. Buba took an hour to hand drill the bolt holes. Early morning I put Storm Petrel against the Denton Bridge jetty at high tide, for a bottom scrub.

Buba arrived back from a goodbye party at his brothers'. We finished scrubbing, had a final domoda, rice and fish with stewed peanut sauce, at Sina's restaurant, then went into Banjul to clear out with immigration. Both Buba and I got exit stamps in our passports. We got back just before the tide turned to ebb and departed but still in sight of Denton Bridge the engine began smoking heavily into the cabin. After anchoring we found a hole in the exhaust pipe under the cockpit floor. I wrapped it in silver cooking foil and lashed this with twine. It lasted until we arrived at Half Die, off Banjul where we anchored to await the ebb tide the following day. We went into Banjul to look for exhaust repair bandage. A massive rain storm developed. All we found was silver foil backed roofing sealer, but we could not use it because it contained mastic which would burn.

We went into Banjul again. Another heavy thunderstorm came over and we ended up cowering in doorways or walking ankle deep in floods. I took off my shoes and socks and walked through the streets bare footed, stupidly reasoning that with so much clean rain arriving and draining away it was not so dirty, despite the uniform brown colour of the floods. We did not find exhaust repair bandage, but at least I was able to sort out my cash card with a fax to my bank in the

UK. The cash card problem happened each time the bank sent a letter to my UK address and the marina staff, having forgotten me returned it to sender.

Back aboard Storm Petrel we wrapped the exhaust pipe in kitchen foil again, this time adding thick layers of denim from old jeans and many tight lashings plus three ties of a braided webbing material. The exhaust included the engine cooling water so the denim would remain wet and hopefully not burn.

## Banjul making for Dakar

The exhaust repair seemed to be effective. We departed Banjul at 7am. By early afternoon we had left the Gambia estuary behind in the haze. We had full sail set with a westerly wind of force two to three at a speed of 2.7 knots.

Thursday 29 July 2004. The wind was strong under thunder storms. Buba was sick. At 2am the previous night the wind had fallen and a fleet of six large pirogues were anchored near the entrance buoy for the Senegalese River Saloum. As often happens the group of boats and Storm Petrel got closer and closer until I had to start the engine to motor clear. Buba slept away his sea sickness. I pondered a long line of bright lights, stretching over 2 km, coming over the horizon. After an hour ten trawlers, working together, ran parallel to Storm Petrel 2 km away. When we reached the vicinity of a wreck described on the chart as "Position uncertain" the trawlers curved away to the west and I was left to peer into the darkness ahead looking for tell tale breaking waves should the wreck be on our course.

By morning the wind was force seven from the north, the direction of Dakar bringing heavy seas and water sluicing along the side decks. Water and diesel cans worked free of lashings and it was a wet and frantic job to re–lash them. It was hard enough already with Buba sick and hard weather, so we decided to head for Dakar. I was concerned about Buba's health as he had thrown up everything he had eaten since leaving Banjul. I fed him sandwiches, biscuits, water, tea, soup, mash and fish and nothing stayed put. For the last 30 km we motored directly into the wind towards Dakar, with the mainsail reefed and the foresail rolled away. I hoisted the yellow "Q" flag, requesting clearance for a vessel arriving from a foreign country and the Senegalese courtesy flag went up to say we would mind the laws of the country despite being bound by the laws of the vessels home country. At 7pm we anchored among the yachts off Hann Plage, Dakar. After settling the boat we hailed the yacht club tender and went ashore to enjoy a double whisky in the Cercle de Voile de Dakar. Buba had hardly ever travelled out of Gambia before and was astonished at the (two euros) price of a measure of whisky. His culture shock began in earnest.

Friday 30 July 2004. We slept comfortably and awoke in a calm, sunny Baie du Hann. I was concerned at the thought of the journey from Dakar to the Canary Islands – a long slog to windward and I was trying to look for ways out.

## Dakar making for the Canary Islands

Sunday 15 August 2004. An hour after setting off Saturday part of the rigging failed. The cap shroud had pulled up out of the deck and the mast was curving to port like a taught bow. We were just 6 km from Dakar, luckily, and motored back. Repairs consisted of two bolts fixed through the hull side to hold the chain plate. The 4mm thick stainless steel plate needed drilling for the larger bolts which was done by a local blacksmith. We set off the following day at 11.30am, rounding Cap Vert in a difficult lumpy sea. We could either make way in the direction of Brazil, or on the other tack, towards the surf wrecked cape. By late evening we were still working northwards with Dakar glowing orange on its peninsular. Buba was sick during the night after a meal.

Monday 16 August 2004. Both of us became ill and sick. We were only just able to manage the boat. There was engine oil on the floor and we worked the bilge pump every half hour. Much water came in through the repaired cap shroud fixings. My quilt was wet and the locker below the chain plate was soaked. It was hot, so hot, and my head ached. My head ache bloomed and I grew nauseous each time I moved from my wet bunk.

Somehow I kept altering the sails and adjusting the wind vane to drive the boat northwards. After every task I lay down sweating in my heaving bunk or on cushions out in the fresher air of the cockpit. Buba was an impeccable crewman and each time I crashed out in my wet bunk he went to keep watch, steer and tend the sails even though he too was ill. I did the same every time he came in looking like he needed to crash on his bunk too. We travelled 80 km by the next morning.

Tuesday 17 August 2004. I set the storm jib on the inner forestay making Storm Petrel a cutter. Things improved, the wind gave us a northwards heading and the self steering managed to stay between north west and north east. I had not much experience of windward sailing under self steering. It was quite difficult to find a groove to keep the boat in. During the periods when Storm Petrel sailed well alone Buba and I lay resolutely with our health improving, or we were just getting used to our situation. Day temperatures were dreadfully hot, although night time was deliciously cool. This day we travelled out of the ITCZ – the Inter Tropical Convergence Zone. The ITCZ is associated with the rainy season with thunder cells, much cloud and very hot sun – the monsoon. We sat in the cockpit feeling pleasure at being out on the ocean, with shoals of silver flying fish whizzing across cobalt coloured waves. As I relaxed into the voyage more I made mental forays into problem solving. This yielded some good results. To lessen the amount of water coming into the boat I greased the stern gland. Pumping the bilges became essential to keep the water and oil from sloshing over the cabin floor. I crawled along the side deck to the repaired chain plate and packed it with mastic tape. To protect my bunk I fixed a plastic bin liner sack against the locker where the chain plate was leaking and this reduced the amount of seawater coming onto my quilt. My drenched quilt was spread out in the sun over the tiller in the cockpit. All we ate was boiled fruit sweets and a tin of peaches and we drank cups of tea. Storm Petrel was 150 km north west of Dakar, well out into The Atlantic Ocean now, the wind firm from the west.

Wednesday 18 August 2004. The forecast on Radio France International was north west Force 4–5 with a rough sea. I had difficulty with the French words for east and west – "est" and "ouest" sound the same, particularly over short wave radio, both sounding like, 'sst'. I decided the forecast was for ouest, a west wind. It blew from the south. By late afternoon the GPS indicated all forward motion had ceased. The wind was almost zero. I later discovered my old GPS cannot indicate velocity less than 1 knot, despite the coordinates continually changing in the thousandth of a mile scale, so we may have been making a quarter of a knot or more.

The engine started after I topped up the oil, but with much reluctance. It fired up but then died with copious black smoke from the exhaust. I used "Easy Start" to get it going again, but it took five minutes of turning over on the starter motor. I knew it would proceed to leak all of its oil into the bilge over twenty four hours so I could not run it for more than twenty hours without stopping to replenish oil. I bathed and changed my clothes. Buba ate noodles but was debilitated from two days of sea sickness, although he reassured me he was gradually improving. Five dolphins stayed with the boat for an hour while we sailed slowly, but starting the engine drove them away. We ran the engine for ten hours during which time the exhaust continued smoking and emitting oily soot. I tried to pick words to describe the shoals, or flocks, of flying fish. I came up with, "Wet silver linnets take flight amidst blue meadows", I had been sick and sorely tested during the past few days and therefore my poetic flights of fancy must be seen in context.

11 December 2004. For much of the twenty seven days it took to reach Gomera from Dakar, sea water and leaked engine oil had free reign in the bilges. Hourly, Buba and I worked at the bilge pumps, but sailing hard on the wind was wet with the boat heeled at 20 degrees as she clawed to windward against the north east trades. An unbearable slosh of oil and sea water had spread onto the cabin floor and made its way into lockers holding food and clothing. Buba had suffered sea sickness over the first seven days. I was sea sick for three days.

At the time Buba could only eat one thing, a packet of boiled fruit sweets. He threw up everything else, even water and sea sick pills. I was relieved to see he was at least getting a little sugar. After the sea sickness we both suffered a feeling of listlessness with nausea and exhaustion. Any activity was followed by the need to lay down and recover. Even though the wind vane was handling the steering Buba slouched at the tiller, a point furthest from the rancid, heaving cabin. He often twisted sideways and wretched over board. We agreed the main water tank was foul. After Buba had stopped drinking tea for several days we also agreed the main tea bag store was spoiled by a strong odour, as well as the digestive biscuits. I made the connection when I deduced the tea and biscuits had been stowed in a snap lid plastic bucket for at least six months. All the food in that bucket had soaked up a smell from a plastic pot of minced garlic, which sounds trivial, but they were unusable. The water problem was solved by using the many separate containers stowed about.

We had eighty litres on deck amidships, lashed to the shrouds – 50ltr on deck, abaft the cockpit; a 25ltr can; 5 x 5ltr cans; and 10 x 1.5ltr bottles stowed inside the cabin.

With the changed water source we gradually regained our vitality and with this came increased joy.

We were away from almost all danger. There was only the wind and waves and Storm Petrel. Each day I would optimistically call out the kilometres left to go until we reached the Canaries. After we had spent a week battling up to just north of the latitude of the Cabo Verde islands I happily declared, "Only 1118 km to go!" These declarations were met by Buba with an incomprehensive smile. We had departed Gambia in the rainy season and I hoped to take advantage of "the south west monsoon", caused by low atmospheric pressure over the Sahara desert, which sucks in the north–east trade winds so they blow from the south–west off the coasts of Senegal and southern Mauritania. Another feature of the season were tropical revolving storms (T.R.S.), thundery depressions which tended to move from near the Cabo Verde islands westwards towards the Caribbean. A T.R.S. Developed nearby the Cabo Verde Islands on the day we left Senegal. It was forecast as moving westwards at around 20 km/h. One result of it was a day of southerly winds. We marvelled at sailing down wind, sails spread eagled, on a northerly heading. I listened to Radio France International's daily weather bulletins for the Atlantic on short wave radio. A new TRS appeared at least weekly but, thankfully no closer than several hundred kilometres away. I listened with interest as a T.R.S. 400 km to our West grew and grew until it blossomed into a hurricane and was named Ivan and was one of the most destructive storms ever – Hurricane Ivan destroyed many thousands of yachts and buildings in the Caribbean.

In the hope of keeping the cabin floor dry I had purchased a piece of plastic flooring in Dakar and fitted it like linoleum, with tacks all around the edge. The bright blue and silver design looked very smart and cheered up the cabin. After a week or two of bouncing and plunging to windward the oily bilge water underneath the plastic made it slip around and tear. This became a worry because we had not enough Fairy washing liquid to clean up the mess should the floor covering fail completely. We both trod like fairies on the plastic, but it was extremely difficult because the plastic was lubricated by the black oil underneath. It was also necessary to keep sponging up oil and water which came through the splits in the disintegrating plastic. My sleeping berth and quilt had become soaked with seawater and stowed items were ruined as the locker below the repaired deck fitting daily seeped a gallon of water. An air tight plastic box full of twelve volt electrical spares filled with salt water. I accepted the wet bed but was very anxious in case the oil spread there too. Relentlessly I sponged oil off the floor, worried it could become unmanageable and calling myself foolish for not buying two extra bottles of Fairy washing up liquid. Seawater and Fairy liquid worked well, but without the Fairy liquid engine oil was impossible to remove. There were other options such as shampoo and washing powder. But not much of either. During the journey we pumped the bilges every hour. Water was entering through the stern gland and via several leaks in the front cabin. The fore peak (front cabin) began to reek, so I opened the fore hatch and just let the waves come sloshing through – at least it was clean water and the tropical air did more good than the bad done by sea water and the dinghy was upside down over the fore hatch which deflected spray and waves, even so occasionally a cascade of water came in.

From Senegal to the Canaries Storm Petrel tacked way out into The Atlantic Ocean in a series of zigzags, each taking a whole day. The route took us 300 km away from the Sahara Desert, a vast ocean of sand dunes and rock which could swallow the entire north American continent.

We saw ships only every couple of days and hardly any aircraft, maybe one a week. One night I noticed two large fish swimming beside the boat. They showed up as sinuous silver lattice works in phosphorescent cloaks. When it was light they were still with us. Buba watched them for hours, captivated by the sight of these beautiful blue finned tuna, around twenty kilos each, swimming just out of reach. The fins and tail were electric blue. Other times we saw tuna with brilliant yellow fins. Each morning there were up to ten flying fish dead in the cockpit. All over the boat were silver scales left by flying fish impacts. Large flocks, or shoals, of thirty or more, flew on whirring wings 1–2m over the waves, over 60–100m distance. Buba filleted some and I fried them. They were not really very enjoyable – I should have crisped them up a bit more, but our appetites were less than hearty.

A pair of swallows spent the night inside the cabin. They chirruped at each other to make sure they were together. The following day one flew away. Sadly the other died in the very hot sunshine. It had been so pleasant to see those tiny balls of feathers perched over the galley, silhouetted in the moon light, squeaking at each other. Maybe they had been blown off course – we were 300 km from both the Cabo Verde island group and African shores. Eventually we arrived into the vicinity of the Canary Islands. We sailed in from the west between the two islands of El Heirro and La Palma. Buba could not believe his eyes when he saw the mountains with houses and roads snaking up them. At night the valleys glowed with orange lighting like lava pouring down to the sea – as it must have looked when the Canaries were still forming. A series of strong squalls from the east pinned Storm Petrel over making progress very slow. Each time the wind calmed it left heaving waves and we could hardly get going. It was another five days since sailing into the Canary Island group before we anchored off Valle de Gran Rey, Gomera.

The guide book said this was the most spectacular scenery of the whole Canary Islands. Buba just could not understand why anyone would build a house in the sky, while I found majestic scenery intimidating and all I wanted was to cap our arrival with a coffee ashore. Even then we could not approach the harbour because the engine was not working and a strong current ran against us. Buba and I paddled Storm Petrel but gave up after we entered shallow water with rocks rising clear under water and even sticking up 100m further on. We waited till night time in the hope of finding a night breeze and when we awoke with the anchor dragging we decided to set sail into the safety of the open sea. San Sebastian de La Gomera was 20 km around the island but the light wind and strong current prevented any progress towards it. So, we headed around the long side of the island out towards the west where the wind would be stronger. This meant we were sailing all the following day off the disturbingly spectacular coastline. Tenerife appeared as the majestic peak of Teide plundered the sky at nearly 4000m height and Storm Petrel dived into the straits between the islands of Gomera and Tenerife. Finally we rowed her into San Sebastian marina at first light – twenty–seven days after leaving Dakar.

The first night in San Sebastian de La Gomera we slept like lead weights. We had managed to get enough sleep and waking at sea was mostly as light as a feather. The slightest change in conditions and the pattern of noises the boat made had one or both of us out into the cockpit. The first morning after arrival we both felt stiff, heavy headed, with aches and pains from dozens of small bruises. Our very bones needed rest and recuperation. With many of my clothes ruined and Buba having hardly any to begin with it was fun to introduce Buba to European shopping after we'd arrived. I taught him to pick up goods, feel the quality, see the price and compare between several different stores, although he knew how to shop already and I was just being over enthusiastic in showing Buba my culture.

This drawn out process of finding good value was voided for several weeks by a lucky find. One evening as we were strolling around San Sebastian de La Gomera we noticed piles of clean blue plastic sacks full of freshly laundered and immaculately folded clothing and shoes. Buba and I were both tall and slim and most of the clothing fitted us both. We took two sacks each back to the boat to choose the best bits. Buba looked really fine in almost new condition t–shirts and sweat shirts by Nike, Benetton, O'Neil, plus there were Levi jeans as well as Adidas and Nike trainers. I found a lovely pair of raspberry red flip flops with rainbow embroidered straps. If those bags of clothing had been transported to the markets of Banjul or Dakar someone could make a living for months. Even better they could be donated to a village such as Buba's home of Kemoto where they would be highly appreciated. I pondered this but the transportation costs were the problem. Buba was learning the lessons of a consumer society in which waste of resources was intrinsic. Even we threw out bags of clothing we did not like, it was unavoidable. In Gambia even the blue plastic waste disposal sacks would have been salvaged and sold in the market.

*27 days slogging northwards from west Africa to the Canary Islands. Buba was an impeccable shipmate.*

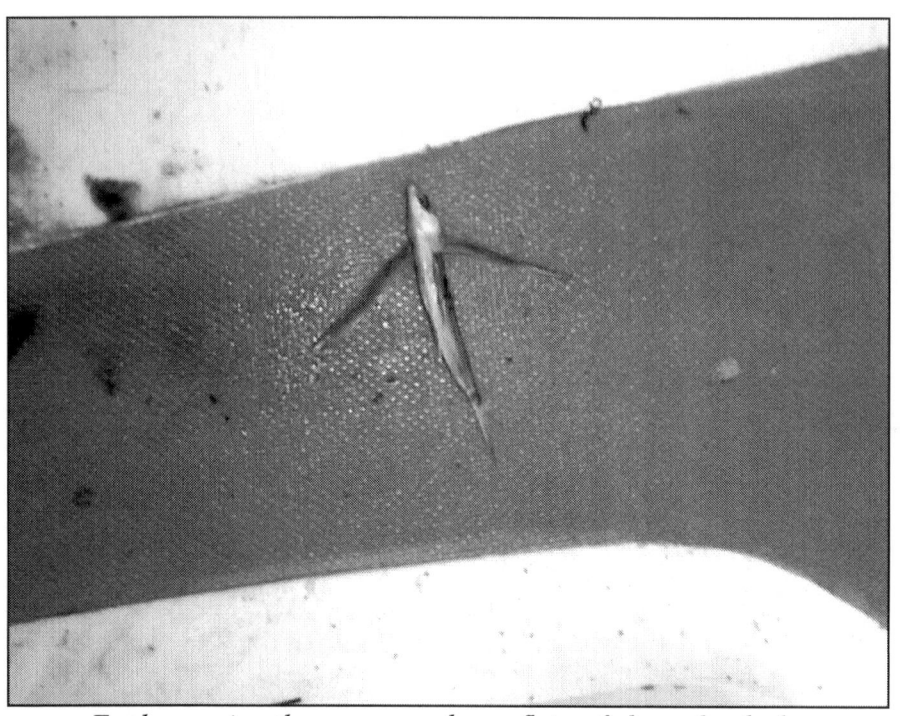

*Each morning there were a dozen flying fish on the decks*

*Nearing the Canary Islands after 21 days at sea, Buba looks like he feels.*

*Gomera from five miles off*

## How I Lost Buba to the Twin Stupidities of Family and Immigration Officials

For eight months Buba had lived aboard Storm Petrel, but he became stuck in Gambia after the Spanish consulate refused to issue a transit visa. He insisted on flying back to go to Kemoto in Gambia over Christmas in order to annul a ceremony in which kola nuts had been passed around the village thus binding him in marriage to a childhood sweetheart. When an African travelled to Europe it was viewed by those at home as equivalent to having won the jackpot in a lottery. Many who'd left Africa and were successful in establishing a new life in Europe never saw their family and friends again because so many unreasonable demands were made for a share of the apparent new wealth. Buba had told me when someone purchased a sack of rice from the village store, it would not be carried home until after dark because other people who saw the rice would ask for some and Gambians almost always shared food when asked. Having fallen out with family members over the marriage by proxy Buba was then prevented from using the return flight to Las Palmas by the obfuscations of the Spanish embassy staff in Dakar. I even employed the authority of a Las Palmas shipping agent, a sort of nautical solicitor, who spoke angrily in Spanish to the Embassy in Dakar, explaining Buba was invited to return to his position as crew aboard a British yacht, but to no avail. At that time the Spanish government were about to announce an amnesty to eight hundred thousand illegal immigrants working and living in the country, thirty thousand in the Canary Islands. One consequence was an outright refusal of the Spanish consulate in Dakar to consider new visa requests by Africans, even a transit visa, to let Buba travel from the airport back aboard Storm Petrel, which was not Spanish territory. Before Buba had gone I told him they would not let him back into Europe but he insisted he would gain re–entry and that he absolutely had to sort out the family matter in Gambia.

Thursday 16 December 2004. Las Palmas became sunny and warm after several days of wind and rain. Christmas shoppers had made the city centre over crowded. People became ruder and inconsiderate, their bags of purchases sticking into me at road crossings and shop entrances. I began to get used to being alone again. A beautiful morning at the north beach – 100m offshore a rock reef ran the whole length of the bay, low tide had left the reef exposed and the incoming waves fell on it in a bright white ribbon and a calmer stretch of water rested between the reef and the beach, where people swam – I was captivated by the sight of a model yacht sailing along there. At the far end of the strand I re–entered the streets and to my delight came upon a charity shop. Even though I bought nothing, everything was priced low, just one or two euros This was real shopping, my first rummage through second hand goods for a year, I could have had anything I liked. A pile of plastic, leather effect trousers got me interested. There were amazing styles – purple snake skin; orange shiny; black shiny and they all seemed to be my size.

Charity shops give the pleasure of temporarily extending ones wardrobe because everything is equally affordable. There was verisimilitude in the careworn patina of the second hand goods. I would feel uncomfortable with a brand new hand bag yet a used one would fit my style. I did not find a hand bag because I wanted a brown one in a simple design and there were only black ones like that, the brown ones had too many frills and panels. I was then chatted up by a sweaty man from Mauritania. When he said he was from Mauritania I guessed the city, Nouhdibou, first time. The conversation then became an attempt by him to take me for a coffee. He said he liked me very much and that he was a business man, which I saw as a strong reason not to drink coffee with him. After I repeated, "No!", several times he hovered about staring at me until disappearing. No charity shop is really complete unless accompanied by a lecherous man, but the golden rule is – if a lecherous man is hovering around you, never bend down at the shoe racks.

Friday 31 December 2004. On New Years Eve shops were loaded with shiny gold card and furry novelty hats, just like at Christmas, but Santa Claus caps had been replaced by golden dunce cones – crackers by party poppers – silent golden balls had become rockets and Catherine wheels. Las Palmas had a shop selling fireworks which remained open all year round and I'd seen these shops in Peterborough and Bristol, in the UK – it seemed life was one big celebration in Europe.

The number of people swept to their deaths by the tidal wave in the Indian Ocean had reached one hundred and twenty thousand. A report on the BBC World Service said in a wildlife reserve where around forty people died, no bodies of elephants or rabbits had been found. The instincts of animals were so attuned to the world in which they lived they were able to sense danger and make their way to the safety of higher ground.

*Illus. Maps - Becky Gilbey*

# Chapter 3

# Loba Joins the Voyage

Sunday 12 January 2005. The New Year rumbled away from the start line in third place. In first place was the Asian wave – one hundred and fifty thousand lives and rising. In second place was the chance of a new engine for Storm Petrel. My parents were worried about the mounting problems I faced with the Volvo Penta MD1, for which spares were almost non–existent – worries exacerbated by stories of how the engine had only just started in time to take Storm Petrel away from some particularly looming bit of spectacular scenery – such as a scary moment when Buba and I had arrived at the vast Puerto de la Luz, at the city of Las Palmas on the island of Gran Canaria. The harbour wall had been difficult to make out in the dark, the engine was not working and we found ourselves lurching around a few metres away from the black concrete on the exposed seaward side. I realized a boat could more easily be lost at the seemingly safe edge of the sea rather than in the wide open spaces. Again Buba and I rowed Storm Petrel 3 km to the marina while giant ships steamed past with rolling tugs taking up protective positions.

But now I was almost alone again – almost, I went to an animal rehousing charity and picked a little black dog called Loba, which in Spanish meant – she–wolf – I had wanted a little dog for a long time. I made severe conditions for myself about the type of dog I would be prepared to take on. It had to be very small, black and female. I went just after Christmas to the animal rescue charity shop, but they told me they did not let any animals go in January because they wanted to avoid people wanting a Christmas present. I left it a couple of weeks until a peculiar dream in which I rescued a hamster from a wooden casket inside a wood stove, removing it and blowing on it to cool it down and revive it. This animal presence dream alerted me to the idea of looking for a dog and I got up and went straight to the animal rescue charity shop.

I sat down and described my tight requirements, it must be small, very small, black, and female. Immediately the man smiled and picked up the telephone, saying to me, 'There is one you can look at, like you ask.' I tensed at the sudden reality of an actual dog being summoned from a nearby volunteer who was looking after it. But I thought it was only my choice and I was under no obligation, so I waited fifteen minutes until an old man bought a stinking, panting nervous little runt of a dog, in on a lead. Immediately I disliked this scruffy mut, which was hauling back and forwards on the lead with no attention to anyone else in the room. But she was female, she was black and she was small and I felt I was trumped by my own tight requirements which had been precisely fulfilled. Without even petting and meeting this dog, just having turned around to see the animal and still sitting at the desk I found myself saying OK, I'll take her.

The proprietor was very pleased and loaded me up with a sack of dog biscuits, a pile of English magazines, a lead, collar, dog bowl, some toy animals and balls, all from the charity shop stock. The price was a donation of 60 euros, so with all the extras I thanked him and gave 100 euros. He offered me a lift down to the harbour as he was shutting for lunch and I sat in his car with this smelly black mut still panting so hard her nose was clicking, while the shop was locked shut. I avoided looking at the mut because I thought it may be challenging to stare at her, but one quick glance and she also glanced up at me from between my feet. Within this half second of eye contact I saw an intelligence and alertness that filled me with optimism about Loba's future. We arrived at the harbour. I lifted Loba onto the foredeck where she stood stock still and shuddered, being unused to the movement of a boat. The charity shop man and his assistant left us alone together.

The next few days were fraught with Loba pulling heedlessly on her lead and barking uncontrollably when I sat down to rest with a cup of coffee. I took Loba into the marina showers and washed her with shampoo, things improved without the mutley smell. The first night aboard she would not go to sleep and instead panted with her nose clicking and tried to get to the hatchway, which meant jumping over onto my bunk, clambering over my shoulder and head, then whining at the hatchway, while trampling on the top of my head. I was quite intimidated by this and found myself wondering if it had been a huge mistake. I even wondered if should take her to the harbour mouth and dump her in the Atlantic, put it down to experience. In a few days I was happily strolling around Las Palmas with Loba off the lead, crossing busy road junctions with her at heel. I made sure each time we crossed a road I stopped at the kerb, made her sit and wait, then went over with her close at heel and stopped on the other kerb to praise her with words and a few strokes on the back of the neck. Loba responded so easily to this freedom with rewards for doing as I wished, we were soon relaxing together and enjoying hurling high bounce balls across the expanses of smooth concrete in the pedestrianised zones. Loba had a thing for high bounce plastic balls and we began visiting the Chinese shop were she would run in and select her ball to the delight of the Chinese family serving. I bought several balls a week as most ended up down drains or in the sea, taken off by currents towards west Africa.

I would bounce these balls almost anywhere in the city with Loba crazy to catch them, but once she ran out between parked cars after a ball, straight into the middle of a busy road. I realised this could not continue, for I had really got to like Loba by now.

After a Canadian oceanographer gave me a pair of running shoes which he had used in the Montreal and New York marathons I tried jogging but it only lasted for a couple of weeks. I managed 5 km per day on a public running track. Loba gave up trotting with me and waited at one end of the track for me to go half a kilometre up and back. She sniffed around happily off the lead, occasionally meeting strangers and charming them with her intelligent demands for attention. In this park I saw several other dogs which were identical to Loba, so much that I thought they must be family. She is a cairn terrier, which is one of the oldest strains of the Scottish terrier breed. Cairn terriers were used for hunting under stone piles, hence cairn terrier.

I spent far too long in Las Palmas de Gran Canaria, eight months, but I loved being in that city and Las Palmas seemed to like having me around – I was a vital vitamin coursing through its streets.

The Spanish couple on the boat next door owned a pharmacy in Britain. Their big old wooden sailing boat *Illusion* originated in Cardiff and was opening up at the seams as the planking dried out in the sun. Ignacio and Delphinia made me feel somehow necessary to the place. During this time I hammered, chiselled and used an electric grinder to sever the old oily diesel engine and its mounting structures. For days at a time thick smoke and fibreglass dust belched out of the hatches and my neighbours gave subtle guidance as I emerged from the cabin still gripping a hot grinder, covered head to toe in white dust. Delphinia would look over and say, "Tranquilloooo", gently. When Storm Petrel was hauled out of the water for a few weeks Ignacio insisted I return to the berth next to them assuring me he would defend the space until I got back. In my absence a German yacht had met with Ignacio's embargo and while I found it pleasant to feel looked after, I was slightly ambivalent in the face of Ignacio's victory. A replacement engine arrived and I hauled it down into the cabin, fearful it might be stolen. It sat there for two months while I built the new mounting beds. The first morning I awoke next to that brand new shiny red diesel engine happened to be my birthday. The installation was an adventure into a new world of mechanical skills I never knew I had – epoxy glass construction, drive shaft alignment, renewal of all the systems – fuel (a new feedback loop installed), electric (complete rewiring of batteries and selector switch), cooling water (New through hull and sea–cock), exhaust (moved to other side to match engine and devised an air lock relief tube), gear and throttle control (new lever and control cables) and ignition panel.

While fitting a new shaft and propeller the shaft bearing was found to be entirely missing and at the same I found a serious fracture in the rudder. Hauling out Storm Petrel gave me the opportunity to put three good coats of anti–fouling paint on the hull and also to repair a gash made by a wreck hit off Banjul. While I gained intimate knowledge of stern glands and cutlass bearings, my sponsors kept abreast of the money it was all costing. After relaunching Storm Petrel the engine was set on the new beds, for the hundredth time, and everything connected up. Friends, Ernie and Joanna, guided me through the commissioning process, commenting on my handiwork in that special Dutch accent of reassurance and rationality, "Ahh, det's good, yah, it looks good." Until one day Ernie turned the ignition key – to me, an impossibly audacious action – and the engine started. Sea trials gave over six knots for half an hour. Storm Petrel was again ready for sea. Joanna and Ernie were so fond of Loba that a couple of years later they too acquired a little Cairn terrier called Quirky.

I was keen to leave on a Thursday to avoid the negative connotations of setting to sea on a Friday – with a long North bound voyage ahead things like this were important – but a fish supper offered aboard Morgan, with Ernie and Joanna and their urging me to stay just one more night to share the large fresh grouper they had been given by a fisherman after going with him to study the local fishing for their documentary film – persuaded me to forget the coming voyage for one more night. So I left the following morning, into the teeth of those relentless northerly winds flowing all the way from mainland Europe – a couple of weeks slogging to windward.

I sailed 450 km to the north. I had set out planning to go to the Azores on a much longer voyage but the loss of a rigging screw forced me to divert to Madeira. This was for the best as I had strong doubts about the sense in sailing such a long distance within the Westerly wind regions north of the Azores, late in the summer (August).

Madeira was dripping with mountain waters and deep green sub tropical plants. The first day or two in Funchal I wandered around drawing in the smells and sounds of trickling streams overhung by flowering vines and splayed ferns and palms. Little lizards glittered on stones and walls. I wanted to shout out to everyone I knew in the world, "Come to Madeira, now! It's the most beautiful place on earth".

After the third day my perception had adjusted somewhat and I noticed apartments, tourists, dolphin trip boats and cruise ships. The industry of tourism was dominant over the charming island and I realised there was little left to look at or do which was not a pre-arranged "experience" within that industry. My disenchantment allowed me to get on with fixing Storm Petrel. A Canarian in Madeira would be on safari in the exotic north and Canarians do take holidays in Madeira, I was told this by an Azorian time–share seller. Christiana said just call me Anna, she had lived in Bermuda for a while and she kept referring to it as *Your island* although I felt no affinity to the island or the idea of Bermuda. I was by this time beginning to lose sight of my affinity with that other Atlantic island *Great Britain* although the latest voyage was a strongly focussed drive to get there. The Atlantic islands were slightly breathless places, unrefreshed by the new oxygen exhaled by the great European forests. Islanders lived on well travelled maritime air which was like living on pickled food only. Gran Canaria and Madeira were two contrasting peoples. The Canarian face had inquisitive, fishy, beady eyes, set in slumping–cliff faces with volcanic textures, done in thick wide brush strokes and oils. The Madeirans wore thoughtful faces, drawn in pencil, alert, intelligent eyes, like those of wall lizards in a sketch–book, hung over by finely wrought–iron balcony eyebrows.

As well as the rigging screw replacement, there were other jobs to get done. The mainsail needed repair. The main water tank was finally abandoned as useless – purchased brand new in Portugal and fitted with care. Two window leaks needed blocking. The cockpit floor leaked. Wooden bungs in the anchor navel pipe and an unused aperture had swelled and jammed, making the anchor impossible to use until the bung was chiselled out. The rigging wire bottle screw was replaced with a new one and the rig adjusted a little tighter. Four water containers, each of twenty litres, took the place of the discarded tank after it was found to have a chafed hole in the inner bladder where it was creased. To help the cockpit leaks, two bungs were fitted to the drains, where most of the water was entering as the boat heeled over, and then found its way through the rubber seal around the cockpit floor. On the way to Madeira water slopped around the cabin floor, a combination of clean seawater and leaked freshwater from the tank. This was much less of a problem without any leaked engine oil and the new engine had borne Storm Petrel to Madeira after the rigging had failed. Erich had sailed to Madeira from Cape Town in South Africa several years before. I told him I understood the need to stop for a while and he said the real reason was there was nowhere left to sail to. I think his main problem was the run down state of his boat after laying unused and unlived on while he'd moved into accommodation ashore. Erich did sail repairs and my mainsail was given into his care while I sorted out the other jobs. The initial enchantment of Madeira evaporated further as I realised my time on the island was severely limited by the fairly high cost of the harbour and the need to move on before the Atlantic became autumnal. Each day a replica of Columbus's Santa Maria, built out of a tired old diesel trawler, ploughed about in the azure offing laden with young couples brandishing total block sun cream. Peruvian bands swung pan–pipes at children and clouds, a crow–like money collector picked through the crowds of enraptured lobsters. Despite evocative soaring wind–pipes and impeccably shaken rain–sticks I grew impatient towards the same music played every day and night.

Funchal sold shoes, but not cheaply. One store was unusually bright and virtually empty of things for sale – orange industrial rubber flooring and two huge white doughnut settees were the sole furniture – it was another shoe shop, but this time modernity had swept the decks clean of such a passé shoe shop feature as a cash register. Instead two DJ record decks were set up. Perspex tabs around the white walls held designer shoes, the kind disc–jockeys might like – unique, different, over–styled, over–expensive, but I enjoyed the white space and orange floor. It was like being in a small modern art gallery in Amsterdam. A beautiful young thing engaged me in conversation, she told me the shop was a design concept of a guy from Amsterdam. She told how another shop keeper who ran a store crammed with the usual tourist gifts kept telling her she must stock her shop with more things. The beautiful young thing laughed wisely saying this was the new way to do business. It was not about shoes really. The shop was a statement about modern style, personal space and identity. Subtly on offer was the possibility that this space–for–space's sake could graft itself onto ones own world – to buy those shoes would be to buy into a world of bright, clear modernity and as soon as those new shoes were set down in the household of the purchaser they would begin to change the room around them and to clone the culturally encoded information of that white and orange consumer space onto the buyers home.

She said the shop had been open just three months and I couldn't help thinking it must fold after another three months. This particular version of the store may, or may not be sustainable – not once did she wave a hand at the shoes – the sole topic of conversation was about design concepts and open spaces – but I knew that beautiful young thing would prevail in her modernity. This was the point. In the future, shops would no longer sell *things* – in the future, shops would compete to claim the zenith of modernity.

In the afternoon heavy black clouds whipped over–head while the wind screeched around the marina. I walked around the harbour to a recently arrived Dutch yacht to ask them for a weather forecast. Most large yachts had marine weather forecasts via high frequency radio broadcasts. The forecast was ideal for a departure towards Europe and so, despite the off putting screeching of the wind, which had lessened a touch, I left Funchal.

I had carefully weighed up my options during the week in Funchal. The outcome was a change in the planned route. The route back to England was altered from a long ocean passage via the Azores, heading instead to the Mediterranean Sea in order to enter the French inland waterways. Both routes were over 3000 km but the Azores way would have meant a long leg in the north Atlantic during late summer with almost guaranteed strong weather in cold seas. Yuk! I shivered to think of it and Loba provided a perfect excuse to avoid such pelagacity. The French inland waterways had attracted me for a very long time and again Loba clinched the decision to head that way – the thought of being able to stop each evening and take walks in woodland paths and small villages and even the occasional large town – was irresistible.

*Loba arrives into the voyage*

*Loba at sea on the 7 day passage between Madeira and Cadiz*

*My hand built wind vane self–steering device I named the 'C Vane'.*

## Sailing from Madeira to Mainland Europe

So, we set out towards the Straits of Gibraltar, 952 km east of north east. After 7 days the continents of Africa and Europe appeared on the chart, like a gaping, 250 km wide river estuary and the two land bulges felt like the cheeks of some great river mouth. 90 km from the Straits of Gibraltar the wind got up and blew really hard, with heavy seas and Storm Petrel pinned over like a moth specimen on a collectors board, for twelve hours while she was heaved–to. It was interesting how the blow had within it intervals when the wind fell to a breeze and everything became quite quiet, hope of an end to it began, but then it squealed again. This noise was soon followed by wave crests walloping against the boat with the impact of dead cattle fired from cannons – Crump! BoooshSSswissssshhhh. The boat lurched and then the sound of water pouring from the cabin roof and around the decks. In the morning I chose the nearest port, Cadiz at 40 km away and motored straight at it. By mid–day I had moored in a marina and was happily walking the ancient city walls into central Cadiz.

A Spanish sailor in Cadiz later told me he thought the trick of sailing was simply not to be scared and this was exactly right. Each moment a little action could be done to improve the situation, and to break the tension of such alertness, to slump in a salty, wet bunk for half an hour of forgetful abandon. Being scared takes up lots of energy and when riding out hard weather it was most important to rid the situation of fear with many small organising actions to reduce the disorder, both inside the cabin and on deck. At one point I had to put on the safety harness and reef the main sail. It took an hour to plan all this and about twenty minutes to do it. Afterwards I knew the boat was prepared if the wind got worse and there was nothing else to be done apart from keeping a watch and plotting the drift course on the chart.

## Cadiz to Gibraltar

My fastest passage ever was Cadiz to Gibraltar in 13 hours. 104 km in 13 hours meant Storm Petrel managed an average speed of 8 km/h. I saw 14.4 km/h on the GPS for a while when the strong tides of the Gibraltar Straits peaked. Of course the new engine was running continually over the trip, to reach Gibraltar in the most efficient way because I was afraid of meeting another Levanter, the strong easterly wind. A Levanter within the Straits would not only be unpleasant but dangerous.

The first impression of Gibraltar was of an unhelpful, grumpy harbour complex. No berthing in any of the three marinas was available and I sensed the marina industry was pandering to large rich yachts only. I did find an old derelict marina with decrepit vessels and plenty of space, but this turned out to be a limbo–land in an imminent development of, so called, luxury apartments and connected marina. Someone warned me about thieves and how it was forbidden to moor there. After talking with the other marinas, on the ships radio, I was as disappointed as they were with the situation. Once they found out the diminutive size of Storm Petrel nothing seemed possible and I decided to anchor next to the airport runway, the last free space in Gibraltar.

The noise of airliners landing and taking off 100m away took a little getting used to and the dinghy row ashore took me and Loba around the end of the runway where we had to time it between planes as take–offs ripped up the water surface behind the plane.

Gibraltar felt like walking in any British town. British tourists trolled around British shops buying Lacoste T shirts and other tedium. The Burger King was popular as were the pubs with sticky carpets, English newspapers, and gloomy walls. I found a web café costing £2.50 per hour. At three euros and fifty cents hourly this seemed quite expensive so I went off to find a cheaper deal. In Cadiz the web café had charged one Euro and twenty cents hourly, about ninety UK pence. The thing was I liked to spend a couple of hours online so a good hourly price was twice as important.

I took a photograph of a woman in a hijab talking, inside a

quintessentially British, red telephone box

The trip from Cadiz had been overnight, without sleep and with several patches of disturbed waves and heavy shipping in the Straits. I was tired. Loba was rearing to go and we walked along the main shopping street of Gibraltar in a dazed but serene state of being – like a funny dream of England. I ate in a café owned by a woman from Yorkshire. *The Penny Farthing* Special Pie and Chips was mediocre – the pie consisted of three samosas containing an eggy, crumbly stuff. Loba was given her own free plate of chips but she threw them up later. The table next door found a maggot in the salad. It cost me £6.50p and everything in UK pounds sterling seemed just too expensive. English bobby's posed smiling for photographs with kids. The throngs of UK tourists were sprinkled with Spanish visitors looking bemused at this petri dish culture of Britishness. The crowds were up–tight with holiday shopping as if the only difference between here and home was the extra holiday money held back then released on touch down at Gibraltar airport. A subdued animosity in the posture and movement around me struck me as the essential difference between British and Spanish people. Back out at the anchorage Loba and I slept and slept.

La Linea was a town butted against Gibraltar, formed out of old defence lines for the treasured and disputed Rock. La Linea was proper Andalucian Spain and it was with relief I walked Loba over the open border from Gibraltar to La Linea. I was in search of reasonably priced internet services, as in Gibraltar prices were six times what I was used to paying. British tourists slouched grumpily around – why did they appear so angry? A majority of Spaniards made me feel at home again.

Shopping for duty free goods in Gibraltar was a waste of time. The duty free prices were hardly cheaper than anywhere else and some things were twice as much, such as a wireless network card for my laptop, 25 euros in Las Palmas and 45 UK pounds in Gibraltar, (so 63 euros). The Asian vendor was curious to know the difference in prices with goods available in the Canary Islands.

In a bar some Spanish visitors to Gibraltar exclaimed at the price of a beer, "Two pounds twenty! Ah! That's three euros for a beer! Surely no?" The bar woman just laughed, "That's Gibraltar for you."

I saw a tired–out community somewhat withered by annexation from mainland Spain. The most popular marina with long term cruising sailors had been mostly dismantled to make way for an upmarket apartment complex with attached marina berths. The old liveaboards ousted and scattered to make way for the other type of yachts, usually brand new and willing to pay large marina fees. Long term liveaboard cruisers were much too skilled at stretching small budgets – meagre earnings over many seasons, or limited pensions – to be of interest to developers as a customer base. Gibraltar was an empty symbol, a possession gripped strategically and relentlessly by the United Kingdom, at the 15 km wide straits separating Africa and Europe. I imagined the local scene in 25 years time being dominated entirely by massive apartment complexes and high–end marina developments.

The border with Spain had to be fully opened or the Gibraltarians would wither on their precious rock – a reproduction of Englishness – a reconstruction of a shopping street in Bournmouth, or Hitchin. With those carnivorous men, so distrustful of vegetables. So many shaven heads, baby faces and flabby thighs and bellies made me wonder at the wisdom of heading back towards Britain. I was accustomed to the Spanish and now these Brits seemed disappointing. I overheard an English man and his son discussing a dolphin watch boat trip, how they'd rumbled around the bay aboard a motor yacht, a crew with binoculars struggling to spot dolphins from the cabin top. They eventually saw four dolphins, which was lucky, but the man said he thought £20 was quite expensive, while his little son was charged £15 in addition. The sailor I was with at the time exclaimed it was extortionate as dolphins were such a common sight to yachtsmen, but this missed the point because a tourist on holiday would see a dolphin sighting as very precious, unlike us sailors who were used to dolphins playing around the boat for hours on end, like starlings in the shrubs next to your home.

My sailor friend told me about the time he spent in the Caribbean, blagging identity wrist–bands from all–in–package–deal holiday makers at the end of their holidays. The plastic identity bracelets enabled free drinks, swimming pool and access to buffets for days on end. Other tricks were robbing dozens of litres of rum from a beach bar and carrying out backpack loads of meat and cheeses from hotel self–service restaurants. I was glad to have not gone to the Caribbean.

The most impressive thing my sailor friend told me was how he had steered his boat from the Caribbean to Gibraltar without a wind–vane self steering, or electric auto–pilot, by just fiddling with the sails until the boat was going somewhere near the right direction and at any speed above three or four knots. This was an insight to me because I had spent so much energy devising ways and means of getting Storm Petrel to steer herself, yet this guy actually with much less experience than myself had crossed the Atlantic with careless abandon and no more than a backed foresail as steering. This method was somewhat like being heaved–to, but with more forward motion while maintaining the directional stability of heaving–to. Thus if the desired course was within a heaved–to sector of movement the boat would continue as long as the wind blew. My sailor friend impressed me again with many stories from overland travels in Africa, by land–rover and even by Fiat 126 from Plymouth to Dakar, with the roof of the Fiat cut off. This last, most surprising trip was in a rally known as the "Plymouth Dakar" after the "Paris Dakar Rally", but with a single rule of participation that the vehicle must not have cost more than £300.

My good friend Buba managed to email me for the first time from Gambia. I had been out of contact since sailing from the Canaries and the absence had provoked Buba to use an internet café. I was pleased he had used email because it showed he was prepared to learn new ways of communication which improved his chances of one day being able to come to the UK.

I played my saxophone in *the tunnel,* an entrance–way to the town through the deep, fortified boundary wall and a few people seemed to like it because they gave pound coins, but mostly I earned copper coins in UK, Gibraltarian and Euro currencies, an untidy handful of coins. I learned to play on the street solely for pleasure, even if a few pounds or euros were useful. A penny whistle player sat hunched in the tunnel and the music sounded tuneless and rambling, with no feeling whatsoever. The whistler reminded me too much of my own off days.

The world's biggest cruise liner arrived in the bay and a couple of Australians cruising aboard the Queen Mary II told me they were on the way to Southampton via Lisbon in Portugal. One said, "I still haven't found my way around the ship, I keep getting lost, it's so huge." The ship's 345m length was impressive and so was the height of the ship above the water. As I rowed my diminutive orange plastic tender, with Loba standing up in the bows barking at everything, Queen Mary II passengers were being ferried between the anchorage and the town in the ships lifeboats and they peered and smiled down at us. Later when I rowed out to Storm Petrel the Queen Mary II had gone and another swish liner taken her place. These cruise ships brought up to 5000 visitors into the town on a single day – a large economic input. Even so my saxophone playing only brought in a pocketful of small change, perhaps the cruisers were so well fed and entertained aboard they only wanted a stroll ashore with a sniff at the local fare. In a way yachties were similar with most yachts being replete with food, music systems, DVD films and laptops connected to WiFi networks, so there was often little desire to look for shore–side entertainment, apart from the pleasure of wandering around on terra firma after being at sea.

Eventually I decided Gibraltar felt like being in a tourist camp, so I sailed 194 km eastwards along the Costa del Sol. It was strange no longer being in the Atlantic Ocean, like changing the person you live with after several years getting to know their foibles. I only knew rumours about *La Mar*, the Mediterranean Sea, the Spanish either choose the feminine gender, *La Mar*, or masculine, *El Mar*. She was known for having either too much wind, or not enough, being enclosed by hot lands and mountains. Her waves were described as short and steep. One experienced sailor described it as 'lake sailing' – where the winds were dependant on the nearest coastal topography. As the land heated up during the day the air over it would rise and draw in a wind off the sea, a "sea breeze". Mediterranean sea breezes extended up to 80 km from land and could be strong, around 40 km/h was common. The sea bed sloped gradually toward the shore and coastal passages would often be in water only 30 to 60m deep and plagued by rough seas. There was the likelihood of a one knot current against me all the way up to France and the wind too was likely to be against. This all meant the 1000 km voyage between Gibraltar and the French inland waterways would not be easy.

Already Loba and I had reduced the undesirable figure of 1000 km down to 800 km. Two days sailing in the new sea had partly confirmed the rumours by being mostly windless. The new engine bumped Storm Petrel along relentlessly at around 7 km/h while I steered around ships as they arrived, first on the radar detector and then, in darkness, as pin prick lights on the horizon. This went on until I fell asleep for the hundredth time and nearly fell onto the cockpit floor. Then I stopped the engine and drifted a couple of hours to take half–hour naps in my bunk.

Ships arrived in packs of two or three for several hours, followed by almost nothing for the next few hours and my napping periods took these quiet patches. At 4.30am I looked at the chart and chose a port I could reach by the following afternoon and laid a course towards it – Almerimar was 60 km away, I could be there in daylight. The problem was hardly any wind for the wind–vane steering while the electric auto–pilot had done what electric auto–pilots do best – stopped working. The only choices were hand steering with the engine on, or drifting nowhere with the engine off, or a combination of the two. Then I remembered my plan was to do only day sails, to head for a harbour each evening and stop treating the voyage as great blocks of days or weeks out of sight of land and so by late afternoon I was drinking a pint of Guinness in Almerimar. My new relationship with *El Mar* had begun.

Almerimar was an urban complex of water front apartments built around a large marina with a thousand boats. It was named after the city of Almeria, some 50 km to the East. Almeria–on–Sea – although Almeria was actually on the coast too. I was allocated a berth, but with the explanation they had no small berths available so I would have to occupy a 10m berth (Storm Petrel was 8m) and I was asked to pay an extra 2 euros per day at their convenience. A UK sailing boat next door told me how they had been allocated a 12m berth when their boat was 10m and then when they found an unoccupied 10m berth they'd insisted on moving into it. The same thing happened in Cadiz where I was told – Well you can have a 10m berth for a week or an 8m berth for a couple of days, it will only be a couple of euros extra per day – I told them I was happy to occupy the smaller berth and to move if and when it was needed. 2 euros per day was equal to my total budget for using internet cafés and I liked to maintain it, thank you, grrrr.

On Sunday, stalls appeared beneath the arches of the surrounding apartments, English and German people offering bric–a–brac. I bought a book called *Trance Formations* about how to hypnotize people to enable desired change. The subtitle *A work book in neuro–linguistics* caught my interest as I wondered about the intrinsic links between language and consciousness. On the cover was a fantasy woman wearing long robes with deep mysterious folds. As she formed a rainbow door with her wand through which an enchanted cobblestone path led over a pool and away into grassy hills and further into a golden sunrise behind distant mountains. Fairies flew around the magical portal and small dragons hovered like dragonflies over the pond. I was captivated by the picture as it impacted directly on my idealistic and childish side – a book about hypnotism had me hypnotized. In Gibraltar I'd met an actual stage hypnotist, who told me about working in Liverpool theatres and working men's clubs. I tried to pick up some hints about performing and audience dynamics. Meanwhile Paul and his brother Phil fed me delicious curry wraps and we talked into the dewy night aboard Phil's boat, but I was none the wiser about performance techniques, apart from it being a matter of being able to fool some of the people, some of the time. So when I saw the book about hypnotism it stood out. How strange, I realised, as hypnotism was defined as literally make–believe in the book which claimed hypnotism had been scientifically defined as nonsense, but what an effective tool it was in helping people get what they wanted from life. I was interested to learn how I represented my world mostly in aural – rather than visual, or kinaesthetic themes – for example I might describe sailing using the sounds of water pouring around the decks, preceded by the *Crump! BoooshSSswissssshhhh!* noises of waves crashing against the boat. Another time I wrote about, 'a great, silent, calm ocean', and I became aware of some of the inner patterns and links between the real voyage of Storm Petrel and the written account of it, for if I had a tendency to describe the sound of the voyage then there must be unused creative potential in other modes of description, maybe I could acentuate the aural descriptions to good affect. Anything which increased my pleasure in travel writing was worth attention. In writing The Voyage of Storm Petrel I had often left out what I personally felt about various situations.

It was by now the beginning of the end of summer, the following day was the first of September. I had 800 km to sail before I could amble through the French canals, passing between leafy glades and stopping to let Loba scamper ashore. There would be the added charm of knowing there was only one bit of sea separating me from the UK, family and friends, the Dover Straits would be a mere 4 hours motoring across the 35 km from Calais to Dover. The European inland waterways not only could deliver me to within sight of the white cliffs of Dover but could be followed to other destinations such as Paris, Amsterdam, Germany with its castles and vineyards, on to the River Danube, Eastern Europe and the Black Sea. The European inland waterways offered a virtual ocean of cruising potential but with walks ashore a constant option. I was headed towards a remarkable and most pleasant position, especially with my trusty black terrier and brand new diesel engine.

At the same time I lived with a vague and persistent sense of discontent – a mood of dissatisfaction about the Mediterranean which had already proved itself an overwrought tourist trap and the sailing was decidedly uncomfortable. The weather was too hot and the flies too careless, they would just keep landing, relentlessly, heedlessly, fatalistic, like bored, tired children running into walls to get attention. The sailors I met were either too naive, having just began voyages away from the UK, or too cynical, having voyaged far from any possibility of contentment or adventure. The tourist complex of Almerimar was probably culpable, being a huge, stupidly arranged leisure machine, consisting of apartments staring out over yachts and bars and restaurants watching over declining seasonal visitor numbers. Free newspapers lay in heaps outside bars and stores which had gone out of business. They published letters from fearful ex–patriot retirees who had been mugged or burgled and the classified sections were full of Senegalese ladies, and Spanish chicas, wanting to massage and be penetrated for euros. Big articles suggested one use the more expensive chemicals to keep your swimming pool from killing the grand children on their visit. The bull fight, while being somewhat unfashionable in Barcelona, where it was banned by the local council, was however a fascinating cultural tradition down south – said the free newspaper journalist – and you will want to know what to wear when you go to the bull fight. For me the real news was that the Canary Islands had also banned bull fighting. The weasel brained article went on, an Englishman from Huddersfield who had became a professional matador in Spain bleated, "It's not cruel like fox hunting, it´s just you with a cape, against the bull, you have no weapons."

Banning bullfighting was widely considered a form of cultural castration and it would thus be many years yet before the cruelty was stopped.

On the web I read an account of a French inland waterways cruise by three American women which made me crave to be over with the Mediterranean voyage and setting off into the bucolic trance of inland France. It was this yearning to be somewhere other than where I actually was that produced my discontentment. I was now precisely half-way between Gran Canaria and the UK. On first entering the Mediterranean I had intended to go headlong up to the French coast but I realized this new sea was not to be dismissed so easily. A sailor, called *Sharky* because one of his legs had embedded shark teeth from an attack while he was a teenage sea scout in Australia, told how he had attempted to go around Cabo Gato four times and been beaten back. A chart seller warned me about Cabo Palos, further north, where two weather systems meet, how there were hundreds of wrecks littering the coastal waters, making it popular with scuba divers and inversely, notorious amongst sailors. One of the major lessons of cruising afar was how locals perpetuated heroic images about their locality. It was likely Cabo Gato – the Cat Headland – would be purring in my lap as I rounded it and Cabo Palos would pale into insignificance as Storm Petrel fresh-motored towards the French canals.

And they were.

## Lingering Along the Costas

Sunday 4 September 2005. Almerimar had been good for second hand stuff and I bought a pilot book and two charts. Then at the Sunday market I bought five more charts, for 4 euros the lot. I had almost everything necessary to navigate the 800 km between Almerimar and Sete, the entrance to the French canals. Almerimar was typical of the Costa Del Sol – a bland soulless surface, arid mountains, spiky ground and dull and ignorant tourists auto–indoctrinating via the tabloids. The uncomfortable heat of the sun was hemmed in by overbearing voids of empty apartments. A hotel offered double rooms with self catering for 24 euros (12 euros per person – £9 per night. A bargain if you could bear it.

One whole block of the hotel was empty and retail spaces at the level of the street remained bricked up to save paying for glaziers. Some units had the tumbling, dusty remains of stock from abandoned enterprises. Building went on in expanding bands around the waterfront. West African steel fixers prepared the structures of swimming pools and apartments, dressing sites for all–night concrete pouring. DIY (do it yourself) was prohibited in the Almerimar boat yard, yet many UK yachts chose to spend the winter because low season berthing prices were very cheap, but a boat is a shed – cosy, intimate container of gestalt anarchy and quirky DIY. Imagine buying a garden shed with a contract attached to it forbidding DIY.

The owner of The Irish Bar had set out from Eire with a dream of sailing around the world. Reaching Almerimar he dreamed again and bought a bar instead. One evening there was a family group and a couple of other individuals who I did not know so I sat alone. I treated myself to a Magnum ice cream from a vending machine and had a pint of Guinness. The family group sat glumly enjoying their holiday – two gangly teenage boys with their parents – and when they left the taller of the lads accused his father, "Well I didn't know it was a GAY bar!" I laughed inwardly – this li'l fella's got a long way to go.

I left Almerimar to it's feeble merriment and creaking building site cranes. Luckily the wind had turned favourable, although gales were forecast in 48 hours. I hoped to round Cabo Gato before then and gain the lee of land. If I kept going at 8 km/h I could reach Cartagena by the afternoon of the following day. I paid the bill and exited the marina. On the way out Storm Petrel, with her young engine, raced a family motor cruiser with youngsters sprawling on the front. The little boat wallowed in the sudden unreasonable space beyond the harbour mole, like a canary ousted from its cage. Storm Petrel was spellbound beyond the horizon. 6 km out to sea from Almerimar the coastal plain, backed by mountains, showed as hundreds of fields enveloped in white plastic to retain moisture in vegetable crops. The region was one of the most arid in the whole of Iberia. Storm Petrel was guided by the engine and the wind vane and I turned my attention to the second hand charts – examining the contours around Cabo Gato to choose how close the waves would let me pass – I marked a point much further in than my earlier cautious route and was pleased with saving several kilometres. A bit earlier and a bit nearer would give me a good sight as I rounded the cat cape at sundown. I would then move further out from the coast for a night passage north. The sea was easy. I worked at the GPS making a route based on notes taken from digitized charts on the laptop. I used electronic charts only in marinas where there was an electricity supply. Only rarely did I boot it up out at sea to use the two hour battery capacity. I had seen enough of life in the sun – I was migrating towards the cold north – it was time to be on my way. These thoughts were suddenly disturbed by the appearance of a ship passing 300m away on an opposite course. I had not seen it until it was abeam. Either the master had carefully steered past or we passed at that distance purely by chance.

 Cabo Gato was gentle and as hoped, purring in my lap. It was a smooth, feline, humped ridge, stretching its back at the sea. Mountains behind loomed black and flared with the prolonged vivid flash of sunset. Small fishing villages twinkled. Another yacht made its way into a bay several kilometres inshore, seething in reflected tangerine sundown, like a spaceship entering a star, through the compression effect of binoculars. Night fell. I steered a little further to seawards for a safer offing. The shore looked welcoming in the distance but I knew there was nothing to stop for – the usual fish restaurants, marina apartments and holiday makers grazing on pizzas and beer. Then only the stars, car headlights zigzagging between coastal bars with pink and green neon bar signs. Around midnight I was left with only the discreet flashing of distant lighthouses and aqueous black night.

Dawn came 80 km further along the coast. A pod of pilot whales wallowed around, one with its rounded squeaky black fin hanging out of the sea. The course converged with the coastline towards Cartagena past a series of rocky headlands. The lay of the shore, now neared again to about 4 km distance, was obscured by morning fog, out of which emerged a high, sand coloured cliff, topped with a lighthouse. A string of fishing boats came into view with a solid wall of cliffs 2 km behind. Several anchored ships affirmed the presence of a major port. Finally at 10am. I saw the deep cleft leading inwards towards Cartagena with a Spanish navy destroyer standing grey guard against the cliffs at one side. The moment of arrival bought relief and by 11am Storm Petrel was secured within the Club Nautico de Cartagena. Immediately Loba was lobbying strongly for a walk ashore and I too was as enthusiastic as a Scotty terrier, or a Cairn (but definitely not a Schnauzer), to explore the streets.

Cartagena's main shopping street was thick with chain stores – everything over priced and over styled – walking past a MacDonalds' I let out an involuntary, "Yuk!", in protest, after I'd seen a film about someone who ate nothing but MacDonalds products for one month and the resulting negative health effects. A music shop gave me directions to a partner store which stocked soprano saxophone reeds, but when I reached the second store siesta had imposed its embargo. People gathered in puddles of shade on café terraces to chat and smoke relentlessly. I walked Loba around looking for somewhere to reflect, pack away, forget, and relish last night's sail. An internet café, relaxing bar, or a tranquil square, but I found none of them. The internet café cost too much and would not allow Loba in. The bars had waiters with white cloths over their arms looking formal and uneasy. The squares were not tranquil enough. Later, after a sleep back aboard and a shower I went walking again and found a different part of Cartagena, away from the chain stores – where many north and west Africans and small businesses flourished. I found a telecentre with internet for just 1 Euro per hour. This was an area of squalid and neglected buildings housing mostly north and west Africans.

The following morning I looked out of the cabin to see a white cruise liner towering above Storm Petrel with rows of windows showing hushed movement – a thousand cruisers taking breakfast – a strong aroma of fresh toast and soon they would make their way into the over stylish shopping streets and eat at the overblown MacDonalds, "¡Yuk!"

Cruisers walked off the ship dressed in pressed and ironed shirts, shorts and blouses in light, clean, colours. I imagined strolling ashore after a good nights sleep in crisp linen and breakfasting on fresh toast, but I thought I would not enjoy being surrounded by waiters with white towels over their arms. But I would enjoy having fresh toast and boiled eggs set on a table each morning. A table would be a good start I thought as I scoffed a bowl of porridge oats and milk held on my lap. Then I took Loba to follow the steady trickle of cruisers making their way towards the shops.

Cartagena was surrounded by mountains but the valley floor it occupied was quite flat – a natural harbour enclosed by rocky headlands. Something inside me resented the containment of looming mountains. I preferred more open views and did not feel like wasting more time in Cartagena.

On the way from Cartagena to Denia I was sheltering from hot afternoon sun, working out courses and destinations, when I heard *BUMP!* I thought it was the sail filling after a collapse but I was shocked to realise Storm Petrel was motionless against a network of ropes, buoys and black tubing. We had come to a dead stop from bowling along at six knots. Storm Petrel had ploughed into a fish farm. Dozens of black rinks, to contain the fish, were anchored in an area covering about 500 square metres. The jib was still pulling hard and gradually the pool rotated until Storm Petrel sailed free from the leeward edge. The wind vane steering rudder mounting had snagged and before I could get a pole and push the warp down around the auxiliary rudder it's bracket flexed and the line twanged free. Nothing fouled the propeller. I had instantly put the engine into neutral. I gibed out towards a space through the the field of inflatable pools. Numerous yellow special–mark buoys boldly declared the existence of the farm – I had been absolutely negligent. A fishing boat was now trundling around the perimeter towards my position, but a good 100metres away and just then the radar detector began beeping – I thought at least they had only just switched on their radar, so had not seen Storm Petrel actually stopped against the fish pen. If the radar of the guard boat had been switched on as I approached my radar detector would have alerted me and I might have looked up earlier.

Afterwards I nervously popped up to scrutinize the sea every five minutes although there was nothing but empty space again. I imagined the difficulty if Storm Petrel had breached the half metre high inflatable rubber pen, pushing it downwards and sliding over into the inside to be trapped as the walls popped up behind. There was not much danger apart from the liability I would face in extricating the boat and compensating the fish farm for damage. It was solely my fault for not keeping sufficient watch – a constant problem for the single hander. There were many other fish farms to come but I managed to avoid them.

## Cabo Nao and Loba's Argument to Remain There

Cabo Nao stood bluntly out to sea and made a sharp corner in the voyage. In morning calm I was able to motor close, within 10m of the cliff face with the lighthouse almost directly above the boat and I took photographs. I wondered about going on to Barcelona from this point – two or three days at sea would get me to where I really wanted to be – Catalunya and beyond there, the French border. I was tired after steering all night but I reasoned being well away from land would give plenty of opportunity to sleep. I also knew the wind could be too light to self steer and there would be heavy shipping taking a similar path across a wide bight. Alternatively the port of Denia was just 10 km from Cabo Nao and I could be supping coffee and playing ashore with Loba by lunch time. I asked Loba what she would like and the answer came in a wag of her tail – a walk ashore of course. Cabo Nao became the Cape of Now, the image of a little ship permanently rounding a headland – a metaphor of living, to remind me life happens in the present. With the metaphor the insight – If I had sailed straight across to Barcelona – a 200 km bight – there would soon be a new set of headlands in front. Guided by the small black terrier wisdom, Storm Petrel turned away from the superficial horizon and in an hour or so arrived at Denia. After twenty four hours I was very tired.

Hot sun by day, largely windless calms by night and a route staying quite close to the coast – fish farms, trawlers, other yachts and the coast to hit. The radar detector often buzzed but Storm Petrel was inshore of the shipping lanes. Larger vessels crossed between major headlands bypassing the myriad of bluffs and twists of the coast. Large scale charts showed only grand turns and majestic curves. Small scale charts were like fractal progressions towards the real thing. Other yachts, far inshore, appeared to want to penetrate the shoreline. I needed to view both the inshore yachts and the coastline – by sailing further offshore, but it was amusing to pass close by other yachts and I waved, genuinely pleased to see other people. This produced some amusing responses in the Mediterranean Sea – where there were so many yachts the marinas often turned boats away – as people realised they did not know anyone with such a far out little yacht and the waves were often returned in flaccid, curtailed ways. It was odd to see yachts towing their tenders behind – in the Atlantic Ocean a towed dinghy would be thrown onto the stern or flipped and spun until the rope parted in a squall. Depths in these coastal parts of the Mediterranean were usually 50m or less and this must have been the reason why Mediterranean waves had such a threatening character – waters hemmed in, turned neurotic and rancorous under superintendent mountains.

El Elefante was a rocky ridge with a long grey trunk of rock extending from the bulk – the elephant. I visited family friends whose home overlooked Denia and the sea from half way up El Elefante. Wendy and Bill asked if I intended to write about them in the Voyage of Storm Petrel. I could only say I write whatever comes to me at the time. Wendy had recorded many hours of conversations with her mother in law who'd lived in the same house for one hundred years. Family members complained when their grandmother called their childhood home a "slum". Fear of rifts halted progress with the biography for several years although the audio recordings still existed. Wendy had recently bought an Apple iMac with a view to resuming the work. Bill asked me what I would do with my life when the voyage of Storm Petrel was over but I had no answer because I felt like a child being asked what I wanted to be when I grew up – if I had answered I didn't believe in reincarnation, the question would have as much answer as I could give.

When I went to check out from the marina I became quite angry. They refused to give back berthing fees I'd deposited. When I had arrived they asked for three days payment in advance – because several boats had left without paying in the summer – and I paid the advance money in good faith. It had not been discounted for paying more than a day at a time. A second grievance was because I had arrived a half hour before noon I was being charged for the previous day, they told me if I'd arrived just a half hour later my bill would have been twenty euros cheaper. Two unjust exactions. I now distrusted a further deposit on water and electricity services which I had not actually connected to and I would not be confident while Marina de Denia held any of my money in lieu of services. At least the services deposit was returned, but the pre–paid days were not, so I stubbornly remained in the berth for the two remaining paid up days.

Then I moved from the Marina de Denia to the Club Nautico Denia – 50m across the harbour – but a sea change in customer relations and ambience. Ten times more friendly, the environment twice as pleasant, the distance into town was halved and to crown all these benefits it was 25% cheaper. The whole environment was more user friendly, there was no piped music in the showers and no electronic access cards for toilets, pontoon water and electric supply. Marina de Denia was modelled on a business class hotel and had drifted far from the notion of providing a safe and amiable haven to mariners. To take a shower in marina de Denia a plastic card was used to activate the services in individual shower suites – only then would the lights switch on, the toilet cistern fill, the shower and sink taps function – and they knew who was there and what they were doing – each and every time and motion left a data trail for the company to scrutinize. If there was a spy camera peering into the suite I could have hung a towel over it, but this bar coded card was coordinated and logged into my customer account and afflicted my sense of privacy and autonomy.

Another UK sailing boat had met a problem with Marina de Denia when they checked out just after noon and were told to pay for an extra night. They argued and moved to the Club Nautico Denia where they paid ten euros less per day. We agreed it was much better in the Club Nautico de Denia. I showed them photographs I'd taken in Africa. She was a ballet dancer, he a session drummer. Their son Joe, recently graduated in zoology, played something intricate and classical on his guitar. They were on a voyage to Italy.

A few days with torrential down pours held me in Denia longer than expected. The weather report spoke of thirty millimetres per square metre which when it arrived was torrential. Deep purple thunder heads grazed along the trough between El Elefante and the sea. I found a friendly café where Loba was allowed to sit quietly at my feet while I sheltered from the rain – the onset of autumn.

70 km north from Denia was Saplaya, a terracotta coloured apartment complex in the shape of an octopus with boats moored in the arms, overlooked by seven and nine story balconied flats. Storm Petrel was allocated a berth right by the entrance so was spared the overhanging gaze of flat dwellers. Despite costing 18 euros per night there were no toilets or showers. The surrounding urbanization consisted of a bland commercial centre – a supermarket and cheap clothes and gift shops, all very down market. Further along another large warehouse with a DIY superstore. When I paused in the entrance to eye up the wares a security guard advanced wagging his finger at Loba. I could see the "No Dogs" sign and only wanted to get a look from the lobby. The security guard remained close glancing sideways at me as if my bitch and I were going to make a rush into the store.

I left and entered a café at the edge of the shopping centre next door. It was 'Self Service' which meant selecting tray, cutlery, paper napkin and bread roll, followed by a choice of fatty fare – I hungrily picked grilled white fish pieces with roast potatoes and my coffee slopped messily into the saucer as I carried the tray to a shaded table outside where Loba was tethered expectantly. The fish was white oily rubber and I tried to reduce the portion by feeding bits to Loba but she sniffed it – took some in her mouth – dropped it – and began rolling in it.

The third largest city in Spain, Valencia, lay temptingly just 6 km back along the coast. The previous days sail from Denia had passed Valencia but the city marina was too expensive and positioned deep within a huge harbour, far from shops or city streets and the pilot book said it was easier to visit Valencia from Saplaya. I was now in a dilemma, it would be pleasant to take a train ride and look around Valencia, particularly as I spent several weeks busking there in my late teens. Naively I half hoped my Valencian friends would still be selling hand made mobiles of painted glass fragments. I could almost imagine walking into the street where they worked to see the large umbrella hung with colourful, tinkling mobiles and Aurora, long black wavy hair with strong blue eyes, smiling there. Aurora and several friends lived in a large town house with blue tiles covering the interior walls. "Azujello" – blue Valencia tiles. Some made up epic scenes taking up whole sides of houses or rooms, while others were curlicue motifs. But that was all 25 years ago and I would not see the smallest shard of my friends if I went looking for them.

I knew Valencia would be an endless array of cafés, shops, and monumental squares. I asked myself did I want to spend money on trains and in cafés amusing myself, tiring myself out. The marina was already costing 18 euros, way above my total daily budget (+/– 15 euros per day). I was not on holiday, I was not a tourist, despite this easy life along the costas.

Actually with the Sahellian dust and Atlantic salt still ingrained in my psyche I did not look anything like a tourist. The friends I met in Denia had remarked how my sun tan looked the weather beaten sailor rather than the sunbathed tourist. Another couple said I looked like a pirate after I stepped ashore in Cadiz, 8 days out from Madeira. I had on flared corduroy trousers, brown leather brogues, a long sleeved, worn out, T shirt, with a green silk scarf tied over my hair and flowing around my shoulders. All this was to keep off the sun at the shadeless helm. The couple asked if they too would look like pirates after a couple of years sailing in 'The Med'. I told them I was just trying to be feminine.

People who move long–term to other countries for a better lifestyle defend their decisions with opinions about the places they left. They say the UK is freezing cold, windy, wet, dark at 4pm and the people glum and eccentric. The people who remain in the UK and show deep affection for their country, describe it as – freezing cold, windy, wet, dark at 4pm and the people glum and eccentric. People organise life's chaos around these myths. Denia, being north–west of Cabo Nao, I was assured, had one of the most healthy environments in the world, due to its position on a headland sticking out into the azure blue Mediterranean Sea and washed by winds untrammelled by industry, nothing for hundreds of kilometres inland apart from villagers eating home grown garlic, bell peppers and potatoes. But, a mere day's sail up the coast lives the monster in this idealistic myth – the city of Valencia with massive industry and heavy pollution of air and sea – prevailing winds and sea currents flow from Valencia straight to Cabo Nao.

## High Bounce Balls

Las Fuentes was a bit further up the coast. The voyage was reaching a travel weary phase, one I knew well by now – each new harbour a potential winter haven. Las Fuentes held me safe while vicious winds screamed overhead. On a Sunday stroll after the wind abated I explored the town. One gift shop sold net bags containing six, high bounce balls for seventy five cents. At that price I could buy high bouncing balls enough for the next six months. Alas, Loba destroyed the first in five minutes. The second disintegrated in under four minutes. Compared to these rubbish balls, the previous batch had been a pack of three in Almerimar which, upon opening the package, I almost returned to the store to complain about them being riddled with deep cracks. But instead of getting a refund I threw one around the grass between some apartments. Loba liked this particular batch. One was quickly lost in a thick bushy tree and I felt like a vandal gripping the trunk and shaking. The two others remained intact, cracks and all, despite hours and eventually months (and the green one prevailed as Loba's favourite ball even a year later – a truly remarkable durability) of concentrated gnawing by Loba. Perhaps it is the same with people and things, the deeply flawed can be more dependable than the superficially flawless.

A new sense of joy entered my days with cool air reminding me of my favourite places. Winds flowed from distant mountains, scintillated with aromas of twiggy herbs, crumbled villages, crumbling peasants, streams of olive oil and dark red wine meandering across the coastal plain by the lorryload.

"Vinaros, or Vinaroz, it's up to you, a young guy with a mullet hair style smiled as if to say, 'stay in the Club Nautico Vinaros all winter, we're friendly here and look, the winter season berthing charges are excellent.'

Vinaros. The name chimed promisingly. I had visited many years previous but could remember nothing apart from the name. Vinaros was a friendly and homely seaside town. The Club Nautico Vinaroz charged half the price of the previous three harbours. Mornings became distinctly and deliciously chilly then climbed to 23C by noon. I made the decision to stay in Spain for the winter months and go into the French canals the following spring, to avoid the winter closures when the locks, tunnels and canal banks were repaired. Vinaros was the first really serious candidate for a winter berth. The word – winter – took on significance and depth as I relished the thought of it, even after evading the cold for three years in Portugal, the Canary Islands, Senegal and Gambia. A mountain range to the north sheltered Vinaroz from the dreaded Tramuntana – a violent and prolonged mountain wind. The sailing pilot book warned of the region a little further north – Tramuntana blows up to 200 km/h and was common during the winter months when Tramuntana could be expected four out of ten days. A train had been tipped over by Tramuntana. This may have been on the radio news, it may have been a worse case illustration in the sailing pilot book, or it may have been part of the mythology of Tramuntana.

I reasoned there would be five clear days in any ten and with the new engine Storm Petrel could travel 80 km during daylight so I would be able to zoom past the Tramuntana region. Trouble was what lay beyond – another wind – 'Mestral' in Catalunya – 'Mistral' in the Golfe du Lyon. Mistral was far worse than Tramuntana and unlike reality where things get smaller the further away they are, myths get bigger with distance.

There was progress, a sea change, long ocean passages had turned to coasting. Further in and higher up lay the French canals and I so wanted those things absent out in the Atlantic seascapes and islands. Vinaroz had a music shop where I tried out a digital delay sound–effect unit which would enable me to overlay saxophone sounds almost indefinitely to make metaphorical seas of squawks – carpets of shrieks – multiple layers of honks. I played with the unit in the shop and discovered it suited precisely my musical ideas. The long haired guy in the store smiled approvingly as a multiple helix of ascending fifths was displaced by a sea of major triads descending in fourths – I knew his smile was about the approaching sale – that music shops suffer endless strings of musos trying out effects pedals. Nevertheless, I left the shop vibrant with musical inspiration, and for a while freed from the decisions about where to spend winter which constantly occupied me and scared me a little. Vinaros offered a safe, affordable harbour for Storm Petrel and the town itself was attractive and unpretentious with a small, well–to–do manner. The weather had turned unusually tranquil and I let these late September days, the hushed commotion of a dying summer, ease my stress. What a beautiful month is September – hints of harder times to come, birds migrating, 'V's of flamingoes flying sun–ward. Maybe people deliberately strengthen their love for one another a little in the dwindling light of the hardening season.

    I was relaxing at the end of the push north from the Canary Islands. I sat in café terraces – observed and wrote – thinking about what I really wanted – to learn more how to capture in words the interactions of people. One morning on a sunlit, cobble stone terrace with overhanging trees and water–fountains swishing in the background, the warm Mediterranean sea blueing up between shops, I knew for sure that of all the experience of travel – sitting doing nothing, was the best of it.

    I managed to note down tiny threads of observation, but much of it went by unrecorded. Ladies, wearing fuchsia, violet and cream, chatter–marked the times, exclaiming, "¡Hombre!", each time they touched on something vital, that ragged edge of reality. A magenta coloured plastic lipstick tube wielded by the fuchsia lady – her olive mottled hand trembling the cosmetic up to her mouth. The violet lady wore block heeled fashion shoes bound to her ankles with thongs. They nested at the table at the correct time, 11.30am. A small coin glowed momentarily in the tip saucer at the height of noon when the women headed off into an hour or two of shopping before the metal shutters of siesta were dragged down. A group of Netherlanders came pushing bicycles. They wore subdued tones, colours on the verge of camouflage, clothes fit for multi–activities, shopping, café terraces, rural hiking or cycling in the hills. Instead of ladies clasp bags they wore fanny packs (Bum bags in the UK) and rugged style ankle boots by Sketchers or Kickers. They seated themselves matter of factly around the table, relaxing and optimising the time on the terrace, a large golden coloured beer for the man and Fanta orange for the women. One woman popped across the road to buy postcards while the rest sat stretching their healthy legs.

A group of young Spanish talked onto the terrace. Cigarettes, cellphones and sunglasses dominated. Their children played on a wooden platform with a slide and a climbing net. A boy pushed a girl, she fell sideways like a doll into soft sand. Havoc from the adults, who were no more than twenty three years old. The boy was smacked. He argued his point strongly between tears and was smacked again. He looked angrily at the angry parents, unable to express his reason. The girl cried and pouted into space, with a faux–broken neck, on her mothers lap. Father spoke rapidly through mouthfuls of croissant. The boy who had pushed went to play with a second girl who wore pigtails and shorts and was more competent on the climbing frame. Having eradicated the naive, younger, girl, the boy now played keenly with his preferred friend.

Vinaroz ended in a "z" or an "s" with equal prevalence. I liked both equally. A prominent feature of Vinaros were banners hanging on buildings with the words, "¡NO EL PARC EOLIC!", which puzzled me for a week. I chewed around the words until the meaning of "eolic" breezed into view – it was "wind" as in "aeolian harp" – a wind harp hung in a tree so the wind blew through the strings to produce a sound. I followed the meanings, "parc" meant "park", aha, wind park, that's it, "parc eolic", a wind farm.

¡NO TO THE WIND FARM!

Associative thinking was much more fun than using a language dictionary, although when I found a scruffy old Spanish/English dictionary, language did become even more interesting when words could be looked up. The protest was against a planned wind farm. Wind farms were the sailing boats of energy generation – I liked wind farms – the sight of sixty wind turbines atop a ridge with clouds scudding through was like seeing science fiction, but I suddenly understood the local protests when I saw a poster giving details of two hundred and fifteen turbines each of a height of 100m, set in ranks directly offshore of Vinaros. Fishermen and the towns people treasured the clear blue seascape beyond their golden sandy beach.

## Harbour Neighbours

October 2005. "Storm Petraal, hellooo!" A woman's voice hailed me from the pontoon. Wearing a straw sun hat she quickly assured me her interest was, 'solely in animals, not people'. She stood like an orator, hands clasped and swaying side to side as she spoke. She was a retired dancer.

"How is your little angel, I heard she was ill last night?" I told Virginia that Loba had improved.

"Of course it was white foam, dog vomit always is like that, I have three dogs. And a parrot."

I was thinking about how I raised a jackdaw from a nestling which lived as part of the family for fourteen years. I wanted to reminisce about my two green iguanas but stuck to, "I have often fancied having a ships gecko," But the loneliness of solo sailing made it hard to stop talking, once I'd begun. I went on, "Parrots are so funny, there was one in a café I went to regularly in Portugal and it would wolf whistle and talk away all day".

Virginia evaded the gecko because it was really me talking about me. She knew her parrots.

"Was it an African Grey or an Amazon Blue?" She enthused,

"Mine's an Amazon Blue and he's green. They are you know." I thought about a similar contradiction in the naming of the yellow wagtail which was grey and the grey wagtail which was yellow. Parrots prevailed.

"The parrot watches television with me. Sits on my shoulder while I read a book and while I play my guitar. I'm only interested in animals, people are not nice," "I love the smell of my dog's paws, they are very pungent, you know." The conversation continued about Vinaros and local vets. That odd refrain.

"I'm not interested in people."

Each time Virginia met Loba she exclaimed, "Ahh, my child, you sweet child." Virginia saw animals as people and people as animals. Even so I found her and her partner really friendly and interesting. Loba had eaten something unsuitable the previous day and been ill throughout the night. I had been on the verge of contacting a 24 hour vet, but her breathing was relaxed and she was not looking too distressed. She was listless and wobbly on her legs, while refusing food and drink. The main sign was her lack of interest in her ball. I drove away fears of waking up to find her dead and decided to wait to see how she went. In the morning she had improved and after a walk seemed almost entirely OK. I had experienced many losses of family pets in the past – ferrets, rabbits, guinea pigs, gerbils, mice, hamsters, spaniels, grass snakes, a quail, canaries, Muscovy ducks, lambs, hedgehogs.

There were numerous others. All passed away to be buried in the back garden apart from Cocky the warrior like bantam who was carried away by the Valkyries to Valhalla, well actually it was St Ives cattle market. Jacky the Jackdaw did not die either, she flew away. Jacky used to roam the local villages, but grew increasingly frustrated at longer captivity after my family moved to a more built up area and she made an escape while on a boating holiday on the River Thames. One of my favourite voyaging books, called Jack De Crow (Auth. Andrew Mackinnon), mentions a tame and slightly injured jackdaw which found a home on a barge on the River Thames. Jack de Crow's arrival was within a couple of years of Jacky's going off. An appealing possibility – did Jacky fly off into literature?

# Chapter 4

# A Braver Coast: The Costa Brava

October 2005. Two beggars sat outside a supermarket. They were scruffy and smelled of alcohol. I asked if they would hold Loba's leash while I went inside to shop but they started to get up and leave. I realised they thought I was telling them to shove off. They were from the Balkans, one with a mohican the other a bobble hat. Twenty, maybe twenty five years younger makes people smaller as if looked at through the wrong end of a pair of binoculars. They sat down again after the bobble hatted one spoke a little English and understood what I was saying. I gave them fifty cents and they were pleased to look after Loba. I met them a few days later in the same place and they got fifty cents again.

I saw the bobble hatted one with a larger group of friends one Saturday night sitting in the town square. I had noticed some travellers occupying a wooden bench and the surrounding pavement as I passed to listen to a recorder player busking in a side street. Having observed the musician and given one Euro I went to look at the travellers. There were three young guys sitting in a line and a fourth stood stirring trouble with the one seated at the far end of the bench. A girl sat on a heap of rucksacks on the ground. The bobble hatted one was in the middle and somehow I trusted them. Loba moved in to meet their tall white dog.

Bobble hat boy recognized me and his friend spoke to me explaining they were from Yugoslavia.

Meanwhile the aggressor had flung his coat off onto the pavement and began fighting with the one at the end of the bench, flooring him and then more punches thudding weakly as they grappled drunkenly on the path. The fight was contained so I remained talking. The girl lowered her mass of braided hair down onto the rucksacks to sleep without having said a word. One young guy was similar to myself at twenty years old – tall, skinny, naive, intangible, but positivist.

He transformed a handshake into a gentleman's hand kiss. In a brief moment he seemed to have grasped the complex story of how I got from someone similar to him to someone like myself.

Meanwhile the puncher and his target got off the ground and sat on the bench talking together as if a point had been made. I couldn't imagine what life must have been like to be twelve years old during the Balkans war. Travelling away from the remnants of those times, with a bunch of friends to live rough and drink alcohol seemed perfectly understandable. At twelve years old I lived in a United Kingdom, in a rural county, where a simple village named Folksworth included a pleasant house called 'Rycotes'. Walls, alcoves, seating and a hearth were built from local stone. A black wood stove, with fire gold curves of flame visible through mica windows, stood on dark slate. Life was characterized by the certainty of security. The only threats in my world then seemed to be Russia, a long way away in distance, and Germany, a long way away in time.

The next day I was waiting on the step outside a pizza come kebab takeaway, trying to prevent a small horny dog from impregnating Loba. Despite waving my arms and repeatedly rushing at the dog as if to beat it, it sidled up to me with a glint of the eye and said, "Give 's a stroke, uh?"

This particular dog was well known and locals greeted him with much affection as he trotted around the fishing quay and its hinterland seemingly unrestrained by owner or lead. I too felt unbound inside Vinaroz harbour. The boat was lighter than ever before and the new engine gave me the assurance I could be home in time for tea. The flat harbour waters and sea breeze was ideal for sailing, just for pleasure, just to sail, the first time in years. But I wanted more. Vinaroz had given a month of rest but that was all it had to give.

The Swedish couple moored next door became good friends, but soon left, to winter further south. The two remaining cruising couples flew away to the UK for Christmas, leaving me and Loba alone in a sea of empty boats. I decided to try the life in Tarragona, 89 km to the north. One small but strong reason for moving along was a particular mosquito borne virus, which was dangerous to dogs, was incurable and resulted in sores and lesions all over the body. It was local to the River Ebro delta and there were often mosquitoes biting during the night despite my mosquito net and spraying with insecticide. I often heard the sound of Loba's ears flapping as she shook off mosquitoes.

A French sailor told me Vinaros was the best harbour in the world because it had a micro climate, being protected from the north winds by a mountain range. I knew it was time to leave, before this strange form of xenophobia – a fear of other weather systems – got me too. So rather than pay another months mooring I set off northwards again.

After a few hours Storm Petrel reached the Ebro, the largest river in Spain, flowing into the sea over a tongue of mud and silt sticking 14 km out from the coast. The flat delta was quilted by fields of vegetables and rice paddy with a fringe of industrial salt lagoons. At the tip of the tongue we sailed in waters just 7m deep amongst hundreds of fisherman's pot markers. Eventually the course led back in towards the main coastline, across a wide bay backed by mountains. Beyond that, still invisible, was Tarragona, a major port which also served a number of oil rigs situated 20 km offshore. Thunderclouds streamed out to sea from the mountains and I reefed the main sail and put on wet weather gear, expecting a squall and sudden rain. The soft wind became a breeze and the scene turned ominous and dark, but hardly any rain fell.

Two dozen ships were anchored outside Tarragona. A fleet of activist fishing boats were blockading all commercial ports south to Valencia. The embargo did not concern yachts.

I anticipated being in Tarragona in a similar way to Vinaroz, there was something desirable about the name. The kingdom of Aragon united with Castille in 1479 to form Spain after the marriage of Isabella and Ferdinand. In 2005 Spanish same sex couples were given full marriage rights. In 1981 a portrait artist and two budding musicians spent Christmas in the house of a Catalan couple who lived in Tarragona. We had played music in the bar they ran. We lounged around in the spacious, modernist style home, savouring big books of painting and photography. Having been left to ourselves for a few days by the owners, we lit a crackling fire in the hearth, but an expensive glass fire screen exploded and the snow white mantlepiece was licked with smoke marks. The couple arrived back and were angry that we were so naïve.

25 years later I was back again in Tarragona and couldn't help looking in bars hoping to come across the one we'd played in, but as my busking friend, Tijn, had often said, *You cannot stand in the same stream twice.*

Busking in Tarragona was good. I found a busy market and played my saxophone nearby. I was handed a double dog bowl and a bag of dog food, although I would have preferred being given the choice of a couple of euros. I enjoyed playing until someone parked a car over a zebra crossing and drew the attention of the police. I continued playing while the drivers' family and friends argued against a fine. The police attitude to street music would need to be tested before deciding to overwinter in Tarragona, but they turned to me and told me to stop playing, or my saxophone would be confiscated. That evening I came upon a clarinet and accordion duo busking. The cheery, sentimental sound enhanced a beautiful city. The musicians told me they had applied for a licence over a year ago and were still waiting. They said it was very hard to avoid the police in Tarragona. I could not understand how they had kept their instruments.

The following day I came across the same duo, near the market and I sat for over an hour to observe them. I was hoping the police would pass by so I could see what would happen. An Argentinian woman sat on the bench next to me and told how her two year old grand daughter was born in Germany and lived in Spain. She said Argentinians were much better people than Spaniards, and besides, she said, Argentinians love jazz.

The marina in Tarragona housed a crowd of night clubs. It was difficult to sleep in a sound–scape of thumping dance music until 5am. At first I thought Tarragona was a beautiful city, enriched by Roman architectural remains. 600 year old foundations clustered upon 900 year old walls built from stone taken from 1000 year old temples, dedicated to goddesses 300 centuries old. Ruins had been incorporated and exposed ingeniously amid modern architecture. Ghostly ancestors floated in and out of shaded fissures in stage lit ruins of old Tarragona.

Alleyways harboured shops with antique style goods asparkle and aglow. So many ways to fill a stylish home with the type of expensive objects children and dogs love to knock over and break. Polished brass, lacquer and wood oil; velveteen and quilted textiles; sparkling dangles and giant glass bowls, as big as a dinner plate looks to a child. Giant ornaments to put in clean spaces. This style mimics rural poverty, inverting the artefacts and tools of agriculture into unusable ornaments. The possession of such objects and the sheer space needed to house them are signs of being monied.

Tarragona flowed upwards into the past in backwards streams of cobbled streets and alleys, until a cathedral jutted, like a volcanic core out of the cone of the old town. Back down past the glassy and oblique architecture, across the Rambla Nova – the new walkway, and down the straight, shop–lined hill to the harbour, was Storm Petrel and my dog–eared travelling life. The streets were not so pleasing after I found busking was discouraged. I found the marina over–demanding of licences, certificates, registrations and other bureaucracy. I only had the bare minimum – while I had been sailing with ancient sharks off Mauritania or recharging my wooden shaman's stave with earth energy in the stone circles of Wassau, and swimming with Nile monitors in the River Gambia – most of my official papers, and status, had lapsed, along with the so called real world. Faced with the excuse of my insurance certificate being, "swept away about 1000 km back", bought a demand to get my insurance company to fax a new copy. This was impossible, my whole life was water damaged – that was the point of sailing away. No underwriter would take on a lone sailor going out beyond the lion and the unicorn, the pillars of Hercules, to the dragon lands – not even 3rd party only. The world beyond Gibraltar was a terrifying place for insurance clerks in Surrey and Reading. It would have been easier for me to get a "letter of marque". In the 16th century, piracy was used as a tool of statecraft. Queen Elizabeth viewed English pirates as adjuncts to the royal navy and granted them "letters of marque", now called privateering, or piracy, a "letter of marque" was a commission to harass Spanish trade.

The inconsiderate Tarragonense police and over–controlling marina made me uncomfortable. Instead of a winter home and a rich chapter in the Voyage of Storm Petrel, Tarragona was officious and patronising.

## Storm Petrel Hits a Tree

Barcelona was a day sail away now, so I headed out to sea and turned north. On the 80 km between Tarragona and Barcelona Storm Petrel hit a tree. It was floating low in the water off the estuary of the Rio Llobregat. The boat lurched and cranked around as if hitting the bottom and almost before I could react a 6 metre long bifurcated tree trunk twisted to the surface in the wake. It was huge and must have weighed a few tons. Younger boats are built much lighter and easily holed in similar collisions. The wreck back in Banjul, gave Storm Petrel a 30 cm long, 25 mm wide and 8mm deep gouge, but would have torn the bottom out of most fibreglass boats built after the 80s. Builders might claim their products are not designed to sail over tree trunks or hit sunken trawlers, but this is what a boat must occasionally withstand.

Barcelona was replete with huge and astonishing architectural spectacles of which I saw nothing, because they were much too must–see. Friends who visited recently described the famous Gaudi park as "tacky" and every must–see place was over–run by crowds of tourists. Tourist sights are marketed as astonishing, impressive and stunning by making everyday things seem ordinary and uninteresting, but they are not and I find constant fascination in everyday things. Port Olympic, built for the 1992 Olympic games, attracted hordes of people who consumed shoals of charcoal grilled fish. Runners paced the sea front and cyclists wobbled around excited dogs. Storm Petrel bobbed among 700 other boats for just under 10 euros per day, a surprisingly reasonable berthing fee.

As a couple came into view of the fine sandy beach next to the marina a British voice exclaimed, "¡This cities got everything!" For a while I gleefully thought I would spend the winter in Barcelona. I made some money with my saxophone in a park near a concrete hairy mammoth standing in the trees. I played in a bandstand where the sound was intensified by an acoustically crafted roof. Nearby was a cascade guarded by large stone dragons. I enjoyed being in the park and the thought of being surrounded by all that wonder, Barcelona in

2005, I was sure I was going to do well there. My Barca dream ended when I found out the marina had a waiting list of over 100 boats. The next blow came when I talked to a street artist, an Asian looking woman who painted peoples names with intensely coloured picture writing. She was standing with her portfolio but not set up to work. She told me I could try, but the police constantly moved artists and musicians on. I came to the conclusion there were too many people in Barcelona with not a niche for one more musician or her boat. Establishing oneself within a new city is a process of grooving in despite the slots all being taken up, but I lacked the competitive spirit to groove myself into Barcelona.

Adam, a British sailor and his wife, had lived in the marina for 8 years. They had travelled through the French canals and sold me the pilot book they had used. They told me about the mosquitoes in the Camargue where I was also thinking of spending some of the coming winter. One day their retriever dog had been covered with around 400 mosquitoes. The mossies bit right through clothing. I was a little put off the Camargue by this information.

In the morning I left in search of my own road, my own space, remoter, wilder places promised by the next costa – the Costa Brava. Offshore, the view of Barcelona was an encyclopaedia of Spanish modernity. The spiky and knobbly Gaudi cathedral overhung by extremely high cranes, a work in progress for decades to come. A silver grey tower looked like an airship standing vertically. A gaping mouthed, wire netting abstract fish sculpture, rusted like an abandoned trawler in a ship breakers yard. The city scape had a recurring theme of spikes. Three towers topped by giant prongs impaled the sky line on the shore further along and then a large rectangular roof appeared to be sliding into the sea. Gradually the two tower blocks at the Port Olimpico, crowned with autumn mist, mulched down into the increasing distance. The coastal slop of reflected waves gave way to a heavy swell from the east. A bank of fog reduced visibility to 100m for several hours. But I was well offshore. As visibility improved a jagged white line of waves breaking vertically against rock cliffs developed like a colour photograph out of the paper white scene and I was alarmed at how much nearer the coast I was than I'd thought, 500m rather than 3–4 km and just ahead a rocky headland bisected the course line I was on. I had been heading for the rocks. I had no chart for this stretch, only a tourist guide to the marinas along the coast, a glossy handbook containing maps oriented so the shoreline ran horizontally across each double page spread and so the north alignment of each map varied. Instead of the usual studied safe route, this time I was using the GPS to indicate only the relative bearing of Palamos. My navigation practice had grown lazy – this was only a daylight hop along the coast and when the coast disappeared in fog I felt the bearing on Palamos was a suitable course to follow because we were far enough offshore for it to be an acute enough angle. This was wrong, the bearing cut through several headlands as it neared Palamos.

The first mate ordered the bosun to kick the deck watch who accused the navigator of spending too much time wagging with the ships dog. The captain looked across the water at forlorn cliffs – it was just another landfall – nothing to get worked up about – the crew had been listening to too many stories about the "Brave Coast", named after its jutting rock–strewn headlands and vicious winds. While the crew were frightening themselves with legends and rumours the captain had been reading the true story of the naming of this coast – the 'Costa Brava' was in fact a tourist device. The original Costa Brava was a particularly hostile coast on the north of the island of Majorca. Then a section of the Catalan coast was named after the Costa Brava to capture some of the drama for artists and other visitors. Subsequently as tourism grew, the whole coastline north of Barcelona and south of the border with France took on the name Costa Brava.

The nearest beach to my near miss was called Playa de Tossa, which despite an unfortunate name was a very popular tourist beach. The name of that beach reminded me of a comment somebody had thrown at me, several hundred kilometres back in Denia, a singularly ignorant British holidaymaker said loudly as I passed, "What the f*ck is that! A f**king man or a f**king woman!?" I wondered if he was spending his holiday at Playa de Tossa.

The Costa Brava was a rock strewn coastline blown over by the formidable wind called, 'Tramuntana', but worse than the rocks and the winds were the frighteningly high berthing prices. A boat called "Vindleka" was asked for 65 euros for one night in Porto De Aro. Of course they left to find another place.

## The Braver the Coast the More Sheltering the Haven: Palamos

I passed a couple of bays with harbours nestled inside but, with an onshore breeze, waves pouring inwards and rocks everywhere it all looked unsavoury. In falling darkness having travelled 80 km I made a clear, safe approach into Palamos and moored in the darkness, fearful of what it may cost.

I reckoned between 20 and 60 euros The night staff helped me move to a visitors berth but could not tell me how much the berth would cost. I would have to wait until the morning and the cognitive dissonance was unpleasant but I decided I was going to rest for the night, pay whatever it cost in the morning and then leave. The morning arrived with a gift. The daily charge was high but not terribly, at 20 euros, so I went into the town to play saxophone and earned the marina fee back. The best thing was finding out the winter rates, paid monthly, would be just 7 euros per day including electricity, hot showers and water. I spent the next couple of days busking in Palamos to find out the attitude of local police to street music. People liked it and I saw no police.

The musician throws up new things out of thin air, wondrous, exciting, strangely pleasurable things which contrast strongly with the mostly disappointing goods all around in the shops. A Sarajevonian said on the radio, 'Don't change the world, just change the square metre that you're standing in', which I thought applied well to busking because the essential message of street music is that individuals can create stuff that money can't buy. The sound of free music on the street enhances shopping but also critiques it. The consumer can only choose products, or dream of buying things they cannot afford. No wonder the police suppress unlicensed musicians. The next pleasant surprise in Palamos was the marina had a free WiFi network, so I bought a WiFi card bus for my laptop and was able to use broadband internet without time limitation and at no extra cost, from inside the cabin of Storm Petrel. With a fan heater and internet connection I felt set–up for winter.

Each daily walk with Loba revealed more of the town and its outskirts. A coastal path took us around rocky headlands and sandy beaches. I discovered a tiny cove occupied by fisherman's cottages built into the cliffs with painted wooden boats pulled up onto the sand in front. There were bushes laden with juniper berries, pine trees full of cones and abundant wood mushrooms in dewy grass beneath the moist greens of this pleasantly northern landscape. In sound of a waterfall hidden in woods we picnicked on cured cheese, an apple, a clove of raw garlic and smorbrod with curry sauce poured over.

Back in the town a sign pointing to – Policia Locale – the local police station had been altered to read – Policia Loca – the idea of "Crazy Police" made me laugh because it was not funny. I went into a dated and small butcher's shop to get a bone for Loba. Nights had been quite chilly and I was concerned about keeping the ship's dog warm and healthy because being a Canarian she was not used to the northern climate. A bone would keep her happy if not healthy. I am convinced happiness is the primary cause of healthiness. The butcher was aged late sixties, less than 1.5m tall, wore a white, bloodstained apron and thick black eyebrows. I waited as another customer nattered on in Catalan and the butcher gently trimmed and sliced. I had a peculiar impression of the butcher, that he was not a cruel man. A pregnant woman came in and sat down caressing her bulging belly. The ceiling was painted a very light green and the colour tone reminded me of the very soft light green I would like to use inside Storm Petrel. I chose a couple of large sausages for dinner and was given a couple of spare ribs, "par la gos" (Catalan – "for the dog"), for free. The sausages cost half as much as I expected so I asked for two more. The gentle butcher and his small, simple, uncluttered–by–overstock shop made me feel gentle, small and uncluttered. Even the door handle was a smooth curve of rounded metal which felt pleasant and familiar, to my hand with no twist or wrench as the door swung on oiled hinges and the latch clicked with neither weight nor force. Such peace in butchery.

## A Music Student and His Teacher Take a Coffee

Brown corduroy jacket, brown trousers, brown and cream check shirt. His long silver hair in a pony tail, silver beard, cigarette in mouth, unlit. Sun glasses held as pointing tool. Student carrying soft guitar case, about 18 years old, very long and thick shiny black hair, wearing a black jumbo–cord jacket, blue jeans and brown leather trainers. Tutor imparts little asides, sometimes with a touch of the students elbow, who sits straight–backed in his black jacket, making small movements, like a model with her photographer. The duo have an aura of shiny lacquered pianos, chromed music stands, bronze wound guitar strings, turtle–shell plastic plectrums and acoustically considered rehearsal rooms.

New cafés brought new faces, attitudes, views outside and interior aesthetics. One echoed, with sharp edged metal arm rests on curvy laminated wood chairs. A hard café named after the hard regional wind – "Café Entrepaneria Tramuntana".

Young feminine waitresses made everyone happy somehow. People like being approached by a young smile. The dynamics of femininity were more complex in another place, named "Café Rustic", after the natural tones of light, wood flooring, terracotta floor tiles and wall hung plates depicting village stereotypes – women in long skirts pressing olives, decanting red wine and chewing garlic cloves under curing hams next to piles of pig–blood sausages, with olive trees leading away to distant hills. The pretty young waitresses in Café Rustic frequently touched each others hair, shared stolen kisses and pouted at one another. The owner looked around 50 years old, a man doing so well he only watched the dance of coins into the till, thank goodness he failed to notice Loba close on a tray–full of fresh warm croissants. The reason she did not have one in her jaws was her utter surprise of arriving at the brink of such an abundant array of crisp, warm, croissants and that gave me a momentary chance to pull her away.

The Café Entrepaneria Tramuntana allowed Loba inside. Useful to know for when a bolt hole was needed on a rainy tramuntana–wrecked day. Actually tramuntana is a very dry wind, A llevant, from the east, brings rain, because it comes in off the sea.

Civil unrest troubled several French cities in late October. I was glad to be in Catalunya, rather than moored in Lyon, Avignon or Marseille. The French border was just 70 km north. For a few days I noticed more police on the streets of Palamos so I tuned down busking to avoid being banned as an anomaly in the business–as–usual they were there to maintain.

*Loba riding in the basket on my bicycle*

*The coast of Girona, Catalunya.*

## The Turning of The Year

On 21 December I lit a wood fire in the small stove aboard. An English friend had given me a bag of cork oak bark. I placed bits of bark into the fire then removed them to spread the fabulously scented smoke through the cabin. In the morning a post winter solstice sun seemed to rise a half a second earlier and half a degree higher.

A few days later I popped up out of the hatch to look at Christmas day morning, I was enthralled by the utter calm. Not a breath of wind and no clouds in the blue sunny sky. By 10am this rare mood had foundered on the shores of the commitments of people in cars. Loba and I went for a walk by the sea. I wanted to note down the wind directions as written in Catalan around a particular, gushing, fountain. The eight directions were:

tramuntana – north
gregal – north east
llevant – east
xaloc –south east
migjorn – south
garbi – south west
ponent – west
mestral – north west

I liked the wheeling motion of this octet. In a different order the four quarters draw a cross:

tramuntana – north
migjorn – south
llevant – east
ponent – west

Interesting how this particular emblem, the cruciform, lays within the maps and compasses of exploration, discovery and domination. The wind rose was a predecessor of the navigation compass. A wind rose is a radial diagram marked with directions of various winds. Tramuntana, the north wind, was marked with a T and the Fleur de Lys is said to have evolved from this T. Fleur de Lys is commonly used on maps as the symbol for the north. Spanish explorers, conquerors and discoverers carried their tramuntana wherever they went, although tramuntana really only blows in the north west Mediterranean. The word means "from the mountains", so it will almost certainly be used in other places but not all mountains lay to the north of a given place.

The easterly Llevant (pronounced ye–vant) was marked by a Maltese cross, indicating the direction, from western Europe, of the holy lands.

The compass of Storm Petrel is set out with eight directions over a scale of 360 degrees. It is a globe floating in a bath of alcohol (to prevent freezing) within a transparent acrylic dome. A third part floats in correspondence with the scale to indicate the bearing on the globe even when the boat heels. The trouble with a spherical compass is the way it wobbles and slops around with the heaving of the boat, like some great whales eyeball lolling at you. I found focussing into a rolling, pitching ball of numbers inside a transparent sphere of liquid can be nauseating and relied more on the hand–held GPS with it's rock solid digital read–out.

I thought all the cafés would be shut on Christmas Day, but I found one open and very busy. In England most people stay at home at least until after the ritual dinner. By mid morning many people were strolling about the town. The weather was unusually calm – cold but with warm sunshine. The long stretch of winter was half done. I knew the second half would both drag and fly by.

## Thoughts of France

Near Cap Creus where the seam joining Spain with France reaches the sea a cave allows entrance in one country and exit in another. I wished to reach Avignon and Lyon in March to avoid strong currents on the Rhone caused by spring melt–water from the Alps. At 9.7 km/h, nearly full throttle, against a reported current of 5.6 km/h, progress would be slow. Lyon was over 300 km inland, so the Rhone would take at least seven days. Already I was challenging future obstacles, designating itineraries and preparing for struggles. I wondered what had happened to my plans to lazily drift through the canals, stopping at villages to buy fresh baguettes and croissants, drink wine, walk Loba. I recognized I was emotionally structured to live life as a mountain to climb. Even the difficulty of reforming this inner drive, to a more tranquil way, was yet another personal mountain. In my log entries made hundreds of kilometres from land there was a certain point I consistently arrived at, that I strongly disliked ocean sailing. Untrammelled, lurching handwriting in my log book declares, "I just want it to stop, I want to be on land, I do not want to be out here". Without those field notes the discomfort would be forgotten and I would repetitively sail away into those disagreeable spaces. So the "sea change" plan was set in motion but even now, on the very brink of reaching the leafy tracts of inland France, I already regarded the open sea with a sense of loss and desire. Time to take notice of the small, black, bundle of joy that was Loba, whose wisdom had no heroics or great journeys, only the chasing of the ball and the joy of the moment the ball was seized and a reward due for dropping it at my feet. Or the cuffuffle as a group of ladies on a café terrace gave Loba delight, strokes and chunks of croissant. With Loba on deck–watch the best bits along the French waterways would be sniffed out. With Loba as navigator she might lead Storm Petrel around, rather than against, my personal mountains.

## Winter Brings Back–Pain Brings Introspection Brings the Cure

With an aching back I tried to dive down inside the pain to enquire about exactly where, what and why it was hurting. An image entered my thoughts, of a heap of rubble, like a waste tip on a building site and so the pain could be caused by a build up of detritus from wear and tear as well as poor sitting posture aboard during long winter nights.

I relied on my walks outside to relieve this chronic back stiffness and the cabin fever of over–wintering. The cliff path around the marina was thickly coated in greenery – winter flowers, stalks, bamboo, cacti, pines and cold, wet grass. The sight of Loba plunging in and out of foliage, tail a–wag, hunting the ball, was my favourite. A thick bank of soft yellow trumpets made me think a second image of my back pain, not as a rubble heap on a building site, but a sea cliff, covered in flowers. The back pain couldn't last long after such a transformation of its metaphor.

A friend sent a parcel from the US. It was exciting to get a real postal packet. It contained a present of two books I had heard friends describe in awe as, "these books will definitely change your life".

The Celestine Prophecies impressed me as a self–help guide set in an adventure story and today, along the same flowering cliff side, I stood staring at the greenery trying to see nature's life force, central to the book, around me. The sun's energy was certainly there. Loba nuzzled amongst yellow daisies, delicate intense purple splays of miniature flowers. The Celestine Prophecies offered an interesting psycho–economic view, in which individuals take energy from one another in repetitive learned behaviour. To transform these negative patterns one must learn to live with the abundant energy of the universe. Perhaps the books will change my life and the story herein as I am guilty of pulling–in the energy of others instead of relying on the abundant but subtle resources of the world around me. Isn't that just being human though?

Web blogs on the internet show a way of writing using shorter informational comments, in the style of a diary. This brief but intimate style is appealing because it leads the reader onwards over a terrain of personal details without setting up any particular viewpoint. Web blogs are often candid and heedless of intensely private information. This makes people slightly more reckless and unpredictable while less fearful and controlling of their identity. The Celestine Prophecies and web blogs both encourage openness and sharing, but I was not convinced the book, or most blogs I read, would change my life.

Preparing For Incompetence

The International Certificate of Competence (ICC) is mandatory for a British vessel using the French inland waterways. I did not have one. The cost of an ICC was £250 but that would be only the test. A 3 day pre–test preparation more than doubled that, so I joined several online boating forums to discuss the ICC. I had originally thought I would not be asked to show one, despite it being mandatory and I wanted to find out if this was the case. At first I made a mistake by asking the forum community to email me a scanned ICC so I could make one up on the computer. This brought a swift and hostile response in one case with threats to report me to the authorities. The idea seemed innocent enough considering my experience which was a thousand fold that required by the ICC. Having been within the real sailing community, in the Canaries and Africa, people with a powerful respect for each other from sharing the integrity and knowledge of their real voyages, people would always help each other, by lending charts to make copies or suggesting ways to get around certain officious rules which would otherwise entrap those lacking resources. The forums on the other hand had members who were without any experience and totally lacking the sensibilities of the actual voyagers. It seems a high proportion of internet forum members are those who aspire to joining the group but have not begun to participate in any way apart from peddling assumptions and wielding stereotypes within the web forums. I realized that my generosity in adding my experiences to the forums was like casting pearls before swine.

My stress about whether I would be prevented from passing through the French canals lessened after I contacted a marina at the entrance to the inland waterways by email and their opinion was I would not need the ICC because the canal officials did not ask to see it. This information gave me back the carefree hope I would be OK just turning up and I decided that was what I would try. In the summer the Mediterranean would become overcrowded and horrendously expensive. For example Palamos marina cost 7 euros per night for my winter stay but in the summer the same berth would cost 65 euros per night. The only good news was the marinas do not have berths available in the high season and it would not be unusual to be turned away from a marina. Photographs of the numerous coves and bays during the summer showed boats crowded together, so I really had to make sure of escaping the Mediterranean before the winter ended. In the canals mooring is abundant and often free so the thought of not being allowed to enter and being forced to remain in the Mediterranean tourist trap was deeply unsettling.

Once I had contacted a marina at the entrance to the French inland waterways and found out the berthing prices would be reasonable for a few days while I lowered the mast I felt much better. Preparations began for departure towards Port Napoleon, at the mouth of the River Rhone, nearer the end of February.

## Choice is the Crown of Life: A long Wish to Sail to Sete

February to April 2006. The answer was no. The question – can I busk in Palamos. The police had stopped me after three months of uninterrupted street performance. It was the first time any police had passed. I should have left as soon as I saw a tow away vehicle with orange flashing lights patrolling the roads nearby. Two policemen arrived with wagging fore fingers. They told me I had to apply to the town council for permission to play music. I did, but after daily visits the only answer I could get was "tomorrow". Two weeks of this led to me being told licences were only issued between June and September.

Palamos had turned its back on me and I felt like leaving. The north wind was bitingly cold although sunny days had grown brighter and warmer than in January. February mooring fees had been paid but even so I could leave any time the wind set in from the south for a few days. Storm Petrel was nearly ready to leap even if a few more weeks would make a pleasant difference to the temperature. The wind pilot charts gave more or less the same likelihood of meeting a gale right up until April, with the Mistral harassing the Golfe du Lions on 4 out of 10 days. I watched the weather like a hawk.

For two nights I enjoyed rich colourful dreams, although, upon waking I could remember almost nothing of them except a sort of aura, like looking at the cover of an unread novel. My will to travel again uncoiled gradually from hibernation causing eddies of anticipation, apprehension and excitement about the coming journey in my imagination.

There had been no opportunity to gain an International Certificate of Competence (ICC) in Palamos. Most people who had been in the French canals said they were never asked to show it, only the "Vignette", a cruising licence. I worried the vignette might not be purchasable without showing an ICC. I could become stuck in the Mediterranean by bureaucracy, with the breathless heat of summer and all the marinas treacherously sliding into "high season" prices. Anchoring too, was widely prohibited, most bays and beaches being buoyed off in summer to create swimming zones for the precious tourist industry, jet skiers and sailboards. Cruising yachts anchoring in these sheltered coves and bays would be fined for so–called illegal anchoring. I really wanted to continue the voyage back to my family and friends in the far north again.

In February Palamos marina unexpectedly hiked up the price by 25%, but several days of screeching winds followed by a cold snap made me cringe at the thought of the rough windy sea and abandon immediate plans to leave.

End of February 2006. Oh no, carnival time again. If a nagging headache was captured in a test tube, then a spectral analysis made of it and the results somehow played as music, it would make carnival music. Palamos carnival style was a truck wheelbase with a concert hall sized public address system and a crowd of high–camp but motley looking dancers strewn over it and sporadically writhing. In between the blasts of humiliation and chaos caused by passing carnival trucks I noticed a black man looking with fascination into a baby clothing shop at a black baby mannequin. He appeared thoughtful and I guessed he would be pleased to see an African baby and at the same time unsettled to see an African baby and he was likely taking a moments contemplation to forget about the absurd false joviality of the carnival trucks.

Eventually carnival was dragged off into storage until the next year and the cross–dressers went back into their closets. March came with beautiful sunshine mixed with wind and rain. I finally assembled a bike from discarded parts and finishing touches from the bike shop – a new basket to carry Loba, a bell, a lock and mudguards. We found coastal paths and coves and shared picnics made of cheese, raw garlic, banana, apple and chocolate, eaten simply with a penknife sitting on a rock overlooking the sea.

Richard, the English sailor with a boat in the marina almost got me to make him a wind–vane steering device. I spent several days working out how to adapt the idea to his boat and made a list of materials. The momentum was lost between my determination to sail away by the end of March and Richard's hesitation to buy a sheet of plywood. I think he wanted me to create one from found materials, as I had done so with my own wind–vane. The cost is minimal in money that way but it takes a lot of time to come upon the right bits, so with April fast approaching I cancelled the project despite reassurance I would be paid to make it. Palamos marina fees were due to increase by 80% on April the first, I'd be a fool not to leave by then, so I finally sailed away from the winter refuge, in company with the French single hander, Marita, on his little boat, *Iguana* to reach Rosas, 6 hours up the coast. At the point of setting out he was celebrating his departure in the marina café, but I slipped away with no goodbyes. He came running out demanding, "Aren't you going to take a coffee first? Are you in a hurry?" He made me feel slightly foolish but imagined the silly scene inside the café and I dislike big goodbyes, so chose to continue on my way. He slunk back to his coffee. Outside the marina entrance I put up the sails and tidied away ropes and fenders, always a tense and mildly shocking time, particularly after over–wintering. Shortly a mast came hurrying out, it was Marita, now rushing to catch me up and we set off north together.

Rosas was a pleasant town where I was able to replace a diesel filter which had corroded and leaked. The corrosion was due to water in the fuel so I bought an expensive additive to absorb water and protect the engine from corrosion.

Rosas was replete with shoe shops. I bought a new pair having worn my soles through over the winter in Palamos.

A few days later, in absolute calm, we rounded the great and viciously regarded Cap Creus. In two weeks time a catamaran sailing yacht would be wrecked here, with the loss of four lives, by the sudden onset of a tramuntana.

The village of Cadaques revealed a large white concrete egg atop the former house of Salvador Dali. We passed the Spanish/French border ahead of schedule and passed Port Vendres, our planned destination, moving on in the fine weather. As the afternoon wobbled past the Pyrenees mountains swivelled incrementally by as the next few harbours came and went. Leucate, where I failed to see the cliff side road described in, 'A Ship of the Line', C. S. Forester, one of the Hornblower series. In the story Captain Horatio Hornblower anchors off this coast in full view of a column of French soldiers and armoury travelling towards Spain to join forces against Britain there. Hornblower knew the unsuspecting enemy had no idea of the destructive power of a 100 cannon broadside. The horses, field guns, artillery units and foot soldiers are cut down by cannon balls, trapped against the cliffs on the coast road at Leucate as Hornblower executes his duty with typical callous efficiency. At Leucate I was pleased to see there were actually cliffs, but there was no evidence of a route exposed to the sea.

Back in Rosas the entrance to the citadel was a stone portal with a draw bridge crossing a moat. There was an impact crater in the left side of the door arch. It looked as if a cannon ball had hit and fracture cracks radiated from the football sized socket blasted in stone blocks. I wondered if this enigmatic feature had been added by the tourist authority to bring drama to the place. In the same way an antique dealer cuts a wooden chest with an axe to render it characterful with a look of past drama.

Over 100 km of coasting in a single day, left me keen to find a café. I was now in Gruissan, in south west France. In the chosen café a certain table had iron legs and a marble top, marked with deep scratches and cuts filled with a black grime, or polish. Near one corner a letter had been cut skilfully into the marble. An "A" giving an impression of the idle, but artful cutting of a mason's apprentice, but was probably recently added to enhance the table.

I took Loba in the bike basket to explore Gruissan on the fourth of a week of windy days. Wind blown etangs, shallow saltwater lakes, interrupted by light coloured rock ridges and skirted by neat vineyards were rendered dreamlike by the wind. Occasional small flocks of flamingos flew over.

Mallard ducks stood outside café doors in defiance of the famous Languedoc/Roussillon regional dish, "cassoulet", duck and bean stew. The approximate ingredients are – white haricot beans, mutton, onion, goose fat, goose or duck, bacon, salami and two hours of slow cooking. Cassoulet is a typical rural stew made of odds and ends and left–over cuts and sausages. The French single hander said while in Spain he had not eaten cassoulet for four months. He resumed by eating several large size tins of duck stew in that first week. The Lidl supermarket sold cassoulet for a third of the usual price. I was squeamish about "confiture du canard" – duck jam? – but I tried some and found it a rich, buttery stew, if a little over salted. I learned later it was "confit" not "confiture", the difference being fat instead of jam, but the idea of duck fat made me as squeamish as duck jam.

A breakfast of pain au chocolate and two croissants, taken on a bench in the sun. The cold, irrepressible, wind made for short bike rides. It would be easy to roll away downwind across the flat salt pans but struggling back against the hard wind in first gear was slow and hard.

Several of the yachts along the row where Storm Petrel was berthed were occupied, but only one in fifteen of the apartments which overlooked the water. A huge black dog lay sleeping each day just along the way. Usually he awoke as we passed and tried to mount Loba. The French single hander remained ensconced in his boat and those talkative, relaxed morning coffees in Palamos were now replaced by a patronising condescension and a defensive and insensitive attitude The first night we arrived in Gruissan I had been tired after sailing over 100 km but he tried to jostle me to leave with him early the following day. I pointed out a gale warning but he made me feel stupid for scrutinising the weather forecast and tried to make light of the intended passage by saying Port Camargue was only 50 km. Later I looked at the chart and was annoyed to find Port Camargue was in fact 80 km, not 50. Two other ports lay ahead and I was keen to visit them, Cap d'Agde and Sete. In the morning I kept my cards close to my chest to avoid criticism of my choice to remain in Gruissan for the time being. We went for a coffee together, but his company was spiky and I grew angry. Later he swallowed his pride enough to admit he was not leaving straight away and had decided to moor his boat in

Gruissan for an extended period while he visited friends in Paris. In a road services café I looked at a motoring atlas and mentioned the nearest large town with a main railway line was Narbonne. Telling a French man about France was a mistake and we squabbled about Gruissan and Narbonne being either 8 or 11 km apart.

The weather forecast was strong winds for the coming week and we helped each other move from the arrival berth to our allotted marina berths. I would have preferred to do it alone with no wind to ruffle the move but for the sake of fraternité I accepted the French single handers help. I began untying Storm Petrel's mooring lines but immediately he treated me as if I was stupid and told me to do it his way. I was now angry. Ordering me about Storm Petrel was his big mistake. Boadicea with sword flailing swept in front of the terrified Roman soldier, "No! I will say how this is done." Then in the new berth he told me to swap two ropes over, because one was slightly longer, but I would not let him. We then shifted his boat and as he came towards the quay he told me curtly to take the bow line ahead, whereas I was prepared to hold his bows off the quay. As I followed his command the boat bumped on the quay, as I knew it would. I just hated the stupid situation. If I had needed his help I would have asked and I resented being drawn into so called co-operation and end up frustrated and resentful. Our boats were now berthed apart and I grumbled and cursed to myself every time I remembered the mornings antics. The next few days were full of cold and wind but I found serenity in taking Loba in the bike basket through the surrounding landscape. The French single hander stayed in his little boat watching satellite television, pleasuring himself with tin after tin of duck stew.

He was older than me and he had sailed his little yacht for 30 years, but I had voyaged 8000 km in Storm Petrel plus a decade of cruising in Juggler before that. I was not going to put up with being made to feel stupid. I was able to recognise our communication problems were probably due to similarities rather than differences, but I did not offer this insight to the French single hander.

Gruissan marina was endowed with three ship chandlers in a large technical yard where many yachts were shored up for work. In each shop I was handed a thick A4 glossy catalogue, adding up to around four kilos of paper. The books were profoundly interesting particularly for planning repairs and maintenance. After extensive browsing I decided one of the chandlers was cheaper and with more integrity than the rest and so gave away the three other catalogues.

In the chosen chandler, Accastilage Diffusuion – AD, I found a sewing awl. It had a bobbin of oiled yarn, a wooden handle and a chuck holding a grooved needle. The yarn passed along the needle and through an eye at the sharp end. Pushing the awl through the material forms a loop of yarn through which the other end is threaded, in the same way as a sewing machine but with the manual intervention of threading the loop, to make a lock stitch. It had a natty name, 'Speedy Stitch' and was excellent for sail repairs, awnings, cushions, tarpaulins, spray dodgers, seat covers, clothing, rucksacks, in fact anything. I bought one and repaired three split cockpit cushions to try it out. Most sewing work aboard ship is tough, often requiring pliers to push the needle through heavy materials. The sewing awl is easy to push and twist through with a wooden handle and a sturdy triangular needle. Everything I ever stitched by hand has remained intact. A common problem with factory stitching is running too close to the edge of the material, which frays and pulls apart. My hand sewing is quite brutal, but I see only the permanence and strength of the stitching and there is beauty in function. Often out at sea I have smiled as my eye wanders over hand stitched repairs which seem only to improve as they weather and become integral to the material, holding as fast as the day they were done. I use sail repair twine for almost everything, including clothing and bags, it is waxed and as strong as wire. I found the Speedy Stitch a most satisfying tool.

AD also sold a diesel additive – to absorb water and protect the pump and injectors – thankfully at a much more reasonable price than the tin I'd purchased in Rosas. Instead of nearly 20 euros to treat 50 litres of diesel this product cost 18 euros to treat 400 litres.

I asked about changing the cassette filter in the fuel/water separator and was surprised to be told to change it after just 50 hours use. Storm Petrel's new engine had done three times that since leaving the Canary Islands so I bought a replacement. Meanwhile I was trying out cheap Lidl supermarket fare, mostly the range of tinned mackerel and smoked herring in various sauces. The tuna was also very good value. The tinned salmon was not nice and had obviously come from farmed stock, because it was dry, flavourless and indigestible. The tinned crab was cheap and also a complete waste of money.

Meanwhile it had become difficult to make a decision about which port to head for which would be suitable for lowering the mast and entering the inland waterways The French single hander was single minded that I should enter at Port St Louis du Rhone, but the headstrong single handed sailor I was, made me want to follow a different route. I could go to Port St Louis du Rhone, as long as it was my choice. Choice is the crown of life so I chose Cap D'Agde, the largest naturist resort in the world, as my next stop. Curiously, there was situated the largest naked population on earth. It even had it's own harbour, Port Ambonne and I imagined sailing into port to be greeted by a smiling, naked harbour master, but the naturist harbour was too shallow for Storm Petrel and I went instead to Cap d'Agde, the main marina complex nearby. I planned to lurk in Agde for a day or two and discover how I felt about naturism, but the naked zone was gated, with a daily entry charge. Intuitively I sensed I would find the whole experience tiresome, so after enjoying the idea of it for an afternoon and being disheartened by the general tourist ambience of Cap d'Agde, I made plans to sail to the good old, workmanlike, fishing port of Sete.

The weather forecast warned of a fierce tramuntana wind which would pause on Thursday. I had meant to go to Sete since first taking to sailing boats with dreams of going through the French canals to "The Med" and so I wanted to fulfil this 16 year long wish of arriving at Sete.

I made a passage plan to sail to Sete where, if I chose, I could lower the mast and enter the inland waterways. But the sea had become a dwindling realm of freedom and space and I was also tempted to sail further east to Port Camargue or, even further, to Port St Louis du Rhone, 130 km away. The risk in going inland was an early encounter with the authorities and demands to view my non–existent ICC. There were numerous entrances now, into the inland waterways, linked with the various etangs of the Camargue, right along to the Rhone valley. It would be prudent to avoid tangling with officials earlier than necessary at locks and lifting bridges, when I could be coasting all the way to the River Rhone.

Cap d'Agde was very busy with boats and the streets thick with holiday makers. The water and electricity supplies were in disarray while a man who obviously wanted to finish work for the day hooked up several connections in such a temporary arrangement of plugs, extension leads and adapters I saw no hope of linking in and I resigned to a night without power. After travel I usually go to bed at nightfall so would not miss it. First Loba wanted a walk and I wanted to go and leer at the border of the nudist zone to see if the image I held in my imagination was anything like reality.

The streets near the marina were crammed with shops full of excited tourists and I plunged unselfconsciously into the their midst. By now the thought of quiet countryside on the imminent journey inland had become a holy grail. I followed the flow of excited tourists towards the naturist zone, along a multicoloured gorge of shops. Individuals with radical body piercing, tattoos and severely shaven hair cuts moved amongst the more conventional holiday makers, standing out like initiated monks in the streets surrounding some great temple. I found myself labelling some as being naturists with their clothes on, out of the nudist zone for a break and this was the mood all around. People were titillated, grasping at each others elbows and sniggering as another queer looking couple black–swanned past in a bra–less leather waistcoat. When I reached the naturist zone I managed to glimpse neither freedom nor joy around the place, just a little–used shallow harbour with a bland complex of hotels and dry scrubby land and a squeaky gate with a sign warning non card carrying naturists to keep out. On the way back towards the marina I took a wrong turning and got lost in some outer suburb of Cap D'Agde with endless rows of holiday homes, a tennis complex and pine trees coveting dog dirt.

The following morning my shower was disturbed by a rude woman who wanted to point me towards the men's block. I ignored her but she involved a cleaning operative who could only tell me the dog was not allowed inside the shower rooms. This was fair but I was disturbed by the rudeness and aggression of being so ignorantly tapped on the shoulder by the nasty lady.

The rest of the huge marina complex, with four thousand boat capacity, was busy with entertainers, strumming and singing pop in neon fronted bar/restaurants while holidays played out amongst the flashes of digital cameras and shrimp flambés. After putting into Agde under a forecast of strong winds, the new weather update gave one extra day before the bad weather. The hard wind would come in the evening of the following day and I managed to make a snap decision to get the hell out of Cap D'Agde, clawing back a second days marina fees paid in advance. I was very grateful to them for giving me back my money.

Sete was just 16 km further along the coast. I needed to avoid several areas of protected marine environment, marked by yellow buoys and guard boats, each around 4000 square metres in area. They lay in a row about 4 km offshore and occupied the space between Agde and Sete so I headed seaward of them, glad to have seen indications of the zones on the chart rather than entered and been hassled out, or fined. It is interesting to see the division of the right of passage into zones of permission. The protection of some areas of the marine environment from sports fishing, divers and fleets of leisure sailors is an inspired policy but this zoning and restricting of the sea has become ubiquitous in most traditional anchorages in the south of France and Spain. Swimmers, board sailors and inflatable beach toys are overseen by lifeguards and fenced in by strings of yellow buoys excluding cruising boats entirely from the shelter afforded by beaches and bays. I foresee the future zoning of the entire ocean regions by GPS co–ordinates with access and permissions of various vessels restricted and controlled throughout.

Storm Petrel made way under engine in hot sunshine and in the distance a low, long mountain marked the location of Sete. I would be glad to leave this hot, windless sea where Storm Petrel had motored over nearly 1000 km. When the wind had blown I was usually cowering in port because it was too strong. Perhaps the Irish sailor in Ipswich at the time I bought my first yacht, 16 years previously, had been right when he declared, "Oh, y'll never mek a seeler".

Later in the canals of France, when I met boats packed full of the dream of going down to 'The Med', I maintained a carefully guarded secret – the fact of 'The Med' being over–hot and packed with tourists in the summer and decidedly cold and violent in winter. I too, had nurtured the same dream, like a swirl blue marble in my coat pocket, while bashing around in the silt brown waters of the Lincolnshire Wash, the East Coast Rivers and the Thames Estuary.

Finally nearing Sete I took a photograph of Mont St Clair and pondered the fact that this would be the last sea for a long while. Arrival into the harbour was absolutely calming. Something old and ruined embraced Storm Petrel as she moored at a rough pontoon in a windless late morning hour under a hot sun.

Loba instantly liked Sete and so did I. People walked around in a calm of respect and pleasure in the old port town.

I walked ashore, suddenly tired, as the sea slumped out of sight like a collapsing stage set, weighing on my shoulders more as I turned my back on it and during the coming week in Sete I was almost loathe to turn my gaze over the harbour wall, at the sea, out there. In three and a half years of voyaging I had learned one prime lesson – that I had been very lucky. In the yachting press I saw a photograph of the catamaran shipwrecked on the rocks near to Rosas by the sudden onset of the tramuntana wind, killing four sailors. The skipper, who perished with them, had 60,000 km of seagoing experience.

After repeated visits to a nearby boatyard I failed to meet the manager in charge of the crane. Storm Petrel's mast was bigger than the one on Juggler, which, although with considerable effort I used to raise and lower alone. I decided I had to stop pushing and go easily through the next few days. Otherwise I was at risk of turning the transition, from ocean voyager to river boat, into problems and stress. I had come to the canals as a way to relax and avoid over-stretching my luck. One way to relax was riding my bicycle with Loba in the basket and no particular route in mind, just wander around as free as a paper bag in the wind.

One evening I found the offices of Voies Navigables de France. The following morning I entered the V.N.F. Building to test the waters by enquiring precisely which documents I would need to produce if I wished to purchase a cruising licence. They needed the ship's papers but said nothing about a certificate of competence or the obligatory CEVNI test certificate (an additional canals test). My dry run was very hopeful so I returned to Storm Petrel to collect the fee of 113 euros and my ship's papers and went back to buy it. I cycled through Sete happy with the new vignette in my bag, it had all turned out well and I felt the pleasurable texture of easy going cruising was inherent in my choice to travel inland.

I met three musicians playing hot club jazz on three guitars, one singing too. In the effervescence of hearing street music with my new vignette I gave them a Euro and they invited me to play with them.

Under the scruffy charm of Sete my mood grew buoyant as a new risen star. My star brightened with the arrival of a yacht called "Aurora". They were raising the mast after arriving at the sea from the canals and the boatyard had given us the same time to turn up beneath the mast crane on the same day. We swapped things – a book about the French canals, two iron mooring stakes, a temporary marine radio transmitter antenna, books about sailing the British coasts, with comments, "Were not sailing back that way again."; six motorcycle tyres, ideal for protecting the protruding ends of the lowered mast. After Aurora had raised her mast and Storm Petrel had lowered hers, we moored back in the marina next to each other and a day of sorting out a grand mess of rigging now lying all over the decks followed.

The evening before I began the new journey Aurora handed me an envelope. In the peace of the cabin after organising the standing rigging, running rigging, boom, solar panel and mast top electrical cables, I opened the envelope to find a pair of silver earrings shaped as rain drops.

*Approaching Sete, anticipating my entry to the French inland waterways*

*At Sete the sails were removed and mast taken down in preparation for the French inland waterways. Loba had achieved her wish to go inland, away from the interminable ocean.*

*Illus. Maps - Becky Gilbey*

# Chapter 5

# The French Inland Waterways

On the 22 April the Marrakesh Express ferry, connecting to Morocco arrived with foreigners smoking cigarettes on the bows holding stances of arrival into a new culture and Storm Petrel entered the canal system. Large fishing boats with Moroccan names in Arabic script lined the town docks. Storm Petrel was able to pass beneath the low town bridges ahead of official swinging and lifting times but the bridge near the railway station was just 2.2m and I stupidly let the wind vane grate and bend as Storm Petrel slipped underneath, thinking, well I have all summer to repair it and I hardly need it to cross from France to Britain.

The Etang du Thau (pronounced tong–toe) opened up like a sea. I panicked in the open water, having only a faint idea of the direction to steer to reach the opening to the Canal du Rhone a Sete and having little idea of what the entrance to a canal from an inland sea would look like. It was only necessary to cross 2 km of the eastern corner of the etang. I headed cautiously into the wide flat lake before spotting the rough concrete arms of the canal entrance, helped by two canal cruisers setting out to transit the etang and looking nervous in the open water.

80 km lay ahead from Sete to the Grand Rhone across the Camargue. I passed several boatyards on the banks and in one I noticed a yacht ashore which looked like a Folkdancer 27 (Storm Petrel is a Folkdancer 27), so I moored and went to meet the owner. The boat turned out to be another type. Eight men stood laughing between two propped up boats over a board laden with a picnic. I was invited to join them in wine, pate, sausage and cheese. This was at 10am. We chatted, swigged wine and scrumped on pate, sausage and baguette as they laughed and joked and amazed Loba with French fare. The Setois people were open and friendly.

Sun blanched salt marshes with tatty fisherman's shacks, or houses, lined the banks of the canal as it headed between crumbling walls and embankments built across salt water lakes. The canal was barely separated from the lake with frequent gaps and small footbridges where currents flowed in or out according to the tide, giving glances of terns, swallows and black headed gulls.

Frontignan was the first town I reached. The bridge was in repair. I thought Storm Petrel would pass beneath the bridge without it opening but navigation was halted for 6 hours. The amazing difference between setting out to sea and setting off on the canals struck me – Loba had her third walk ashore of the morning and I felt totally relaxed. In the centre of Frontignan, where a Saturday market was full of 5 Euro blouses, 10 Euro fashion jeans, hippy clothing and free samples of German pate.

On the Frontignan quay a collection of liveaboard yachts looked dilapidated and way past seaworthy, such as the English plumber's yacht. It had been in the canals for 17 years and was once crushed by a barge. He'd built extra headroom in the repair to the split cabin upon which he sat slicing open oysters and quaffing them as we chatted. A big dog and cat stared patiently under a tent of tarpaulins and I noticed the rigging wires had been used to moor the small yacht, a sure sign of it never going to sea again.

The Canal du Rhone a Sete continued parallel to the Mediterranean coast with the sea never visible.

Les Cabanes was a collection of fisherman's sheds evolved and evolving into small houses. Trees in white blossom, pretty rickety fences and endless variations of little boats tethered to makeshift planking piers. As promised in tourist brochures pink flamingos and white horses appeared. Frogmen stood about in the lakes beside the canal, chatting in the unusually hot sunny spell we were having, about the price of the oysters they were harvesting. Around 6pm, the last mountain bikers trailed off towards the low, salt grass horizon and hundreds of large mosquitoes arrived. Loba hid under my legs looking up me with a pleading expression. We were being invaded but we suffered not a single bite.

I stopped for the night at Maguelonne, an islet between three etangs and within sound of the surf of the Mediterranean Sea somewhere over beyond a low strand of bleach grass and sun warm sand. I was utterly disinterested in seeing the beach, just elated to be away from the humping and jolting of the waves. I took Loba for a wander along the hard earth and wind hiss of the canal path, next to shallow waters with fish flopping at clouds of mosquitoes. The track led to the gates of Villeneuveles–Maguelonne, a cathedral mainly hidden amidst trees, with a dozen small fields surrounding it, the sum total of the island. Maguelonne was once a community of Protestants and was razed, except for the cathedral, by Catholics. We got back at nightfall. A huge barge, some 38m in length, arrived and squeezed into the gap between Storm Petrel and a German motor yacht moored 40m away. I resigned to my fate as the black bows slid slowly into place high above Storm Petrel while I rooted through a delicious supper of fried beef liver, onions and boiled potatoes.

The next day I arrived into Aigues Mortes under a medieval stone bridge. Someone waved down at me so I waved back but it was a ploy to get good video footage. Moorings were all crowded out with hire boats and exhausted live–aboard yachts. I left Storm Petrel on the arrivals pontoon and walked into the town to see what all the fuss was about. Inside the stone walls were cobbled streets splayed with restaurant terraces and shops strung with medieval style trinkets and mass produced artisan products. I escaped into the back streets to look for intrigue and fascination. More restaurant terraces, quieter but continuous while smaller artisan–mass–produced goods jangled under awnings.

Like a rejected organ I popped back out of the entrance portal, an impressive port cullis, or perhaps grand wooden doors with beaten iron hinges and hasps, I failed to look as I'd had enough of Aigues Mortes and hurried back to Storm Petrel to move on before she incurred harbour dues. Nice boaters who had taken my lines on arrival and were now anticipating news about the voyage of Storm Petrel tried to persuade me Aigues Mortes really was lovely – later in the evening, after all the tour coaches had left – but I was compelled to leave regardless. Someone had mentioned a free mooring next to UMart, a large supermarket far from the medieval bit. I found the UMart but Storm Petrel ran aground so could not approach the bank to moor up. I decided supermarkets were boring and went on to rejoin the larger canal, as Aigues Mortes was on a diversion arm. It was signed as having 1.6m depth but Storm Petrel's keel pushed through soft mud all the way back to the Canal du Rhone a' Sete. In late afternoon a pleasant mooring appeared near a bridge at a village called Gallician. I took a tiny, strong, black coffee in a roadside café, then went to speak with the owner of a Storm Petrel look–alike. The Folkdancer 27 type boat was a "Regent" constructed by French boat builders Jouet. The owner, a photographer, gave me his card and showed me an article in a French yachting magazine about his yacht.

I cooked fried eggs, with baked beans on toast and felt happy, but then unsettled by local boys peering down at the boat from a bridge. I might have been paranoid but thought I heard one say, "British, huh, easy, a Molotov cocktail straight into the cabin." After a couple of hours I was unable to put the comment out of my mind, so just before dusk I chose to leave, knowing I would sleep uneasily with such a weird thought, as waking to a blazing cabin. Beyond Gallician, the deep wilderness of the Camargue was a profound chorus of frogs and with evening the song of nightingales was relentless while swallows drank water in flight, wings in a V, like butterflies. I tied to a tree next to a reed swamp and a stone bridge harbouring more youths who were fishing. They had lit a fire up against the buttress and I thought that is the way to destroy the stone bridge, but I had no paranoia here, as earlier. After a while they all zoomed off on scooters leaving the air filled with croaking frogs. Nightingales continued singing and the low sound, like blowing over a large bottle, of bitterns booming. Again mosquitoes smudged the failing light and were polite enough not to take a single bite.

I awoke with daylight, now early at 4.30am with the ship's clock still on GMT and set off on the voyage. Mist blew slowly along the water with the smell of herbs de Provence and silence from the frogs, nightingales and bitterns. After an hour alone two German motor yachts came around a long bend in the opposite direction. Both shouted something, although none of us throttled back to establish proper communications. Both also gestured with their hands like anglers, "It was really big, this big!". I called across the water ripped up by our colliding wakes as if I had received the message loud and clear and they slurped off around the bend towards the Med. Wondering what, "It was this big, really big!" could mean in the context of a canal voyage suddenly a behemoth of rusting plate steel appeared around the bend ahead. It was a big one, a huge barge propelled by a push tug. I nosed Storm Petrel into the shrubby bank to make room. We passed without stress.

I reached the end of the canalised section at L'Ecluse de St Gilles, the St Gilles lock led onto an offshoot of the Rhone, called Le Petit Rhone. A friendly lock keeper asked my name, departure port, destination and did I have a vignette. I said, "I'm going up to Calais. It's nice there you know." He was cheerful and had no interest in seeing my actual vignette. In the bowels of St Gilles lock was also the same German motor yacht seen in Fontinelles while waiting there for the bridge and we spoke briefly. They were heading up the Rhone and they enthused we would meet again certainly along the long route northwards. When the Petit Rhone, a free flowing river, opened up ahead the German yacht met the current with powerful engines, while Storm Petrel slowed to 5 km/h (from a canal cruising speed of 8 km/h) and I knew the other vessel would leave me far behind.

The Petite Rhone was as much like the River Gambia as a girl could wish. Thick bushes and trees lining the banks, islets prowled by birds – a jackdaw and crows pacing across mud banks, kingfishers straight blue flight along the river, buzzards collected in twos and threes in the fresh air above high trees and picnickers waving floppy hats. Recent floods had left branches, and tree trunks entangled against red and green channel marker posts. It was a most beautiful river.

20 km further up the Petite Rhone Storm Petrel arrived at the Grand Rhone. The current had been strong, but now it was shocking, not only was speed reduced down to 2 km/h but a wrenching and sluicing motion gripped Storm Petrel making steering a tense occupation. Any lapse in concentration and the boat slewed across the current and lost

all forward motion as she careered sideways and progress tumbled towards the ripped trees and torn rock banks.

As in Aigues Mortes, everyone had told me I simply must visit Arles, another medieval walled city with stunning tourism. Trouble was Arles was 3 km back down the torrent of the Rhone and I was only just making way with nearly 300 km of this tumbling melt water off the Alps to make way against. With the disappointment of Aigues Mortes in mind I made a decision to evade Arles, with the proviso of a certain halt at Avignon, a couple of days further up.

One bridge at Tarascon had such a strong current beneath that Storm Petrel, at full throttle, a generous 11 km/h, only just crept through, held almost stationary with the engine roaring and a foaming bow wave but nearly in still motion.

Heavy laden barges hurtled downstream with white heaps of water in front, even though they were running downstream with the formidable current. I looked through binoculars into the wheelhouse of a barge of 150m length, to see the helmsman who was a pretty blond woman, hair in a jaunty knot, with a small boy standing beside her in the huge barge riding down stream.

A new southerly breeze blew millions of white fluffy seeds along with Storm Petrel. Spiders came aboard floating on the wind on web streamers. We passed under bridges, avoiding logs and branches. Graffitied trains trundled across bridges and fishermen stared at speedometer floats. A surveyor with a theodolite stood on a sand bank appearing captivated at the sight of the little yacht pushing its way up river. The new engine roared impeccably onwards towards Beaucaire lock. The lock was huge, with a level difference of 12.15m, 195m long and 12m wide. A large hotel boat, designed to work day to day up and down the Rhone amongst those currents, was reduced to what looked like a toy at the far end of a bath. By late afternoon I reached a small port du plaisance, a set of pontoons in a bay set out of the river current and found a serene grassy river bank with a village called Vallabregues behind. In the single store I bought a bottle of wine, bread and biscuits. Back aboard Storm Petrel, with 250 km of the

Grand Rhone ahead, a glass or two of red wine tasted just perfect.

In the village of Vallabrégues I needed some ground to stand on as my mind was swirling from the currents out on the river. Loba was mounted by a large dog while I chose a bottle of Cote's du Rhone to match the region. A young guy kicked and hit the dog, which had begun gripping Loba in the early stages of copulation. I dragged her away but my leg became the object of the dog's desire. The guy beat the dog viciously while I hollered at him to stop. I have often left Loba tied up outside a supermarket, like a sacrificial goat at the stake, vulnerable to passing hot dogs.

Back at the river I met a sailor refitting his yacht. He told me the Rhone had been in spate a week earlier and I would not have been able to make way upstream. Also that Arles and Tarascon had the strongest current of the whole Rhone, so I was glad not to have turned downstream to see Arles and then have to make back those kilometres. I would reach Avignon the following day, with it's appealing name and everything lofty walled and medieval that Arles could offer, but bigger, so tourists would be easier to avoid.

Meanwhile the small village of Vallabrégues was all I wished for in French provincial impressions. A church bell clanged the hours, and boys, scooters, strangers and funny little dogs were captured in the darting eyes of teenage girls.

"I've purchased three houses in the past and each time I've reached a point where all I wanted was to sell the house and get a boat ready for a voyage again", a yachtsman on the riverbank said.

In the calm of darkness scents came over the water, cedar wood? Myrrh? No, the fragrance of distant oil refineries and heavy industry strained through the sigh of night trees and burping frogs. A huge barge hurtled downstream sometime after midnight and beyond its rumbling engines, like radio chatter, squawking, squeaking amphibians sung from the far side of the river.

I ate brine, tabbouleh – couscous with red peppers and sultanas – and savoured a Costieres de Nimes red. The wine set up a mental current to wade against for a few hours of writing before turning into bed, drunk with travel and looking forward to arrival at Avignon the next day. I was intent on evading the 16 euros marina charge at Vallabrégues by leaving at "le bon heur".

In Avignon I played saxophone. Locals paused to listen, wistful and interested. Tourists siphoned by like molecules in a tube. I stood on Loba's lead when she snarled at the French poodles, which I had promised her we would encounter when we were back in Spain.

The architectural grandeur of the Palais du Papes showed the power of the old bishopric. I entered neither museum, exhibition, visitor centre nor art gallery. I evaded the reception centre for the famous Pont de Avignon. SP had floated around it so I could see no point in engaging further. The Saint Benezet bridge, it's other name, no longer spanned the river having been partly destroyed centuries ago. When I arrived in SP I was confused by a sign saying ships were not permitted to pass under the bridge. I could see the boat moorings beyond and the map showed no other access apart from through this bridge. As I got closer I saw one end was missing and realised the navigable channel went around, rather than under, the remaining arches.

On my birthday I went busking with two songs in mind, *Never My Love*, with a compelling and simple melody, and, a song by a French saxophone player, Didier Malherbe, who I revere, from his work with Trio Hadouk. I found an internet café and spent 6 euros, quite a lot for a single coffee and one and a half hours internet connection, but it was my birthday. Later I found another café where I could use a WiFi connection free, with a cup of coffee.

I attempted to save money by avoiding the high cost of diesel fuel sold at the capitanerie and cycling to a garage a kilometre down the road with two cans tied to the cross bar. Loba enjoyed the ride in the basket, but the garage was unmanned, requiring payment by French fuel cards. I went several kilometres in search of other garages. The afternoon was really hot and the roads riven with fast cars. I did not find a garage and got back exhausted by the tricky cycling with two diesel cans and a dog. The cans were still empty so I decided to buy diesel from the river station, but get half the amount due to the higher cost. I checked with the harbour office and then fell asleep. Just before 6pm the harbour master called to say he was closing and I'd have to get fuel in the morning, but I persuaded him to sell me 40 litres straight away. After refitting the repaired exhaust silencer and testing it SP was ready to go the next morning.

The 30 km after Avignon were against less current, about 4 km/h but were also some of the heaviest conditions I'd ever met. A Mistral wind blew waves up to a metre in height and SP cleaved over crests and dropped into troughs, while the wind dashed spray flew over the whole boat. The spray hood windows ran white every couple of seconds and ahead there was endless advancing white horses with the river banks an off white blur to each side. Such conditions, so far from the sea, were humbling. It was not salt–water so everything would eventually dry out properly.

Saint–E'tienne des Sorts, described by my pilot book as a former boatman's village, offered a pontoon mooring. Being on the outside of a long curve in the river gave a long fetch and waves were dancing and slopping against the stone wall, with the pontoon set in the thick of it. A French motor boat I'd seen leaving Avignon was moored there and the day had been tough, so I took the option of a bumpy, wet mooring with the promise of a walk around the village and up into the vineyards and herby hills behind. The French motorboat man took my lines as SP was pressed and butted against the pontoon. Waves washed up through the grating and by the time sufficient lines and fenders were in place I was soaked in all the parts the river had so far missed. Loba was curled up on my bunk looking as frightened as at any time during the 2000 km between here and Las Palmas. She was ready for a walk on dry land.

In my absence the tender broke free and momentarily rioted against the other boat, but just prior to skimming away with the wind, down river into the jaws of a hydro electric power station, was caught by the French motor boaters. A store provided a couple of bottles of Cotes Du Rhone red wine produced organically and later I ate boiled potatoes with Lidl (Lidl – the impressively economic supermarket) tinned herring in a curry sauce.

All evening the wind and waves butted SP outside while inside Loba slept and I wound down with the wine and wrote in my diary. A clay cup with a soft green outer and a yellow orange inner glaze, bought from a Czechoslovakian in the Canary Islands, held a delightful bunch of poppies and small violet coloured flowers picked while waiting for the Caderousse lock (9.6m rise) to open around lunch time. The lock keeper had hollered down at me to put on a life jacket, obligatory anyhow. It was the section of river beyond this lock where the wind and waves had been worst so I was thankful to him for compelling me to be more prepared.

The next day the wind continued and SP bucked against the pontoon with decks wet from wind blown spray. By the third day I could not tolerate waiting in those conditions and I was able to leave in a brief early morning calm on the 30 April.

*Saint–E'tienne des Sorts. Some of the roughest water I have ever experienced was on The River Rhone with a Mistral wind. At this mooring white water was breaking right over the boat.*

*The Ecluse de Bollene raises the river 22m. The lock chamber is 190m long by 12m wide.*

The French motor boat, with ten times the power, caught up after a couple of hours and we went through the Bollene lock together. The Ecluse de Bollene raises the river 22m. The lock chamber is 190m long by 12m wide. SP entered a cathedral of dark slippery concrete with the sky above a forceful rectangle of light. At one end an office on a high bridge over the lock, like a pulpit, from which words of eternal wisdom were again hurled down at me, "Put on your life jacket!"

A shirted figure moved, behind venetian blinds in the control room, watched and pressed buttons to fill the chamber and then open the upper sluice gate onto a new section of the Rhone. I emerged under a strong impression of sailing into higher lands, as trees and villages, tree tops and church spires lay in valleys below the river banks. Ahead distant hills turned upwards into mountains and I wondered how on earth this river would make its way through.

The opposing current required full throttle and ten hour days to make way. A small town lay spread along the space between a limestone cliff and the river. A bridge came slowly along while SP ploughed upstream, twisting and swerving in eddies and slowly the town came abeam. Against a buttress of the bridge sat a frail woman resting her left arm on a stick. She watched the little boat striving towards the bridge. Through binoculars I saw her right hand on her knee gripping tensely, as if willing the boat onwards fearful it might be swept back away from the town. The little boat with the new engine of course reached and passed beneath the bridge, one of dozens that day. After watching this little boat struggle by the onlooker stood up and walked tiredly away.

One eleven hour day had no stop for lunch apart from ten minute waits at lock entrances, During these brief periods Loba ascended the deep embankment up a metal walkway to sniff about in dry grass and thick shrubs. I strolled around on the ground, chucking pebbles and pine cones about. Looking back at the boat was like noticing your own coat slung over the back of a chair with a peculiar sense of seeing it as that of a passing stranger.

I covered 65 km, from Viviers to Tournon. Tournon port had old rotten pontoons with no sense of security. I tried to puzzle out the selection of people hanging along the quay side. There was a cruise ship with a gaggle of crew who looked pleasant enough. A line of camper vans were parked next to the river. A gritted park with huge plain trees and overflowing rubbish bins was a market on Fridays, a car park, a place to play boules and walk the dog. The boat did not seem at all protected so the next morning I left Tournon having realised it felt claustrophobic, being squeezed between the river and a cliff. The surrounding hills were emblazoned with giant lettering advertising the names of wine producers. Compared to the farm houses each letter was higher than the second floor windows. I would have liked to know the price per bottle along with each name, like in supermarkets, where price is integral to the choice.

Each time I saw a river joining the river Rhone with a name I recognized as a wine make I tried that one at the evenings stop. Small village shops had a good range, not as cheap as the 1 Euro per litre I'd been buying in Catalunya, but much more interesting flavours. Corbierres was the cheapest red, but due to the strong sun and relentless winds of south–west France, Corbierres lacks subtlety.

Nimes, Carcasonne, Ardeche, Aube, Aude, Cotes du Rhone. The more expensive, at more than 2 euros per bottle, were Cotes du Rhone Villages and Bourgogne. I found the harsher wine reflected the harsh landscape and therefore was most evocative of my travels in those lands.

One afternoon I walked Loba up into the hills above the river. There were vineyards and ancient ruins. Goggling at the writhing streamer of the River Rhone down in the valley, the distant hills, the deep green clumps of trees, I picked herbs de provence. In the evening a bottle of sunny, hilly, herby, Cotes du Rhone was quite expensive but the only available choice, produced by organic agriculture, tasted so alive. Organic wine leaves no trace of grogginess in the morning. I drank only a couple of cups, as more than two cups risks a heady, blurry sleep and lethargy the morning after.

After Tournon a patch of rocks stuck out of the river to one side of the middle. The reef was easily avoided because it was indicated by a slightly bent iron post with a top mark, but at another point in the river a much more dangerous obstruction caught me out. The pilot book warned of a destroyed ferry wharf on the right bank and to stay in mid channel. SP was actually closer to the left bank and she impacted with a rock groyne right at the bottom of the keel, sliding immediately off and out towards deeper water. Luckily the strong and contrary current meant speed was less, but I wondered how a boat would suffer if travelling fast downstream.

Arrival in Lyon was a major accomplishment. Now my route would turn away from the River Rhone onto 215 km of the River Saone. I moored at the first of several stopping places in Lyon intending to explore the town quays the day after. There were small, stylish and expensive looking restaurants, great open parks full of people traversing and talking on mobile phones. A black man sat on the pavement with a discarded shop display of eye shadows. He slowly dipped a finger in some colour and held it up to me. I did not wish to have my eyes made up, but I offered him some coins which he did not take.

During the night the river rocked SP quite violently as waves funnelled up from the docks and seemed to bounce endlessly back and forth between the stone brick embankments. In the early hours the twang of SPs mooring ropes and feet on deck had me out of my bunk in a shot. I flung open the companionway hatch ready to make jetsam of boarders. A crowd of club goers, already walking away along the quay were just being ironically mischievous. A fight–or–flight reaction had thrown me out of sleep, like a spider whose web had been twanged. A young blond girl looked back over her shoulder, and caught my eye with alarm. Heart thumping with adrenaline, I lay back in my bunk, thinking how I disliked being in a city.

In the morning I knotted a fraying mooring line of the French motor boat I'd been in company with, the owners having left the boat for a few days. After a short walk with Loba to buy a river breakfast, a few snacks to eat under way and departed up the River Saone to look at moorings further along, nearer the old city. I had already seen the best of Lyon in the busy shopping streets and park, the quay sides were rough with suspicious looking characters hanging around. There were no other boats to provide any solidarity, or a helping hand, so SP continued through the city and after a short while the scenery became thickly tree lined and I could breath a sigh of relief. The leafy and charming river still had a contrary current but no stronger than 1–2 km/h.

Feeder roads with unseeing drivers headed into and out of the city past signboards for ELeclerc, Lidl, Aldi and Intermarche supermarkets. Just beyond the first lock a pontoon had been thoughtfully situated near a petrol station on the road next to the river. On the grass between the river and the road a woman lay sunbathing alone. I carried 40 litres of diesel back from the garage and Loba sniffed the bare stomach of the sunbather. A fat taxi driver reclined in his car either asleep or watching the woman who was either a prostitute or an exhibitionist. The place was not at all a sunbathers choice. "Dogging", doing public sex acts, often with strangers, was called that because it was done in the same places where people walked their dogs. Certain common grounds, parks and lay–byes earn a reputation for being hot dogging spots. I think I was passing through a hot spot, just outside a major city, plenty of people about, but the bushes and grassy river banks offering discretion and openings – prospect and refuge. Further along the river another woman lay sunbathing, face down and bare naked. As SP approached she rose stuck her bare bum in the air and arched, like a cat, to stand facing out on the river, at me. Her head remained bowed beneath the only thing she wore, a straw hat. Next along the shrubby grassy banks was a naked man in a deckchair, who waved and called hello with a cheerful smile. The mornings cruise continued past another naked woman and then two semi–naked lovers entwined on a slipway.

Further out into the countryside a motorway crossed the river. Framed by the beige concrete beams a sailing cruiser tacked to and fro against the stream looking just lovely.

Macon was a fairly large town reached via an old arm of the River Saone, while a commercial cut, took barges away from the town. The day was very hot. After walking around the town and finding it unremarkable I returned to the boat. The sun was too fierce and after a brief rest I left the shadeless pontoon. Thin reed tips sticking out of the water mid–stream should have attracted my attention but SP ran aground sliding deeply onto a soft mud bank. Full power in forward or reverse failed and I launched the dinghy after loading in an anchor with 7m of chain and 40m of rope attached. The anchor was dropped in deeper water and the rope led back and attached to a winch aboard SP. I managed to pull the bows of SP around to face the down side of the mud slope and gradually eased her free. I motored away from Macon glad to have extricated myself from both the town and the mud bank.

The satellite navigation system showed the city of Geneva was only 100 km to the East. To be voyaging that near to Switzerland felt quite strange after having a sense of Southing for so long. From Switzerland came groups of men on hire boats. They always overtook at full throttle and left the river in disarray for several minutes until quietness and all the small things emerged again.

Crows, herons and capybara lived on thickly wooded islands. Camouflaged fishermen stood in front of camouflage tents, munching bush snacks under camouflage caps, tending multiple arrays of lines with electronic beeping bite alarms. Often a fish would strike just as SP passed and just as often the fish would shake itself off the hook.

At Tournus a long pontoon, busy with hire boaters, offered free electricity and water supplies. At the Saturday morning market I looked for liver but there was only veal liver which was extremely expensive so I ate cold boiled potatoes, with mayonnaise, onion and tuna instead. Sunday morning a 2nd–hand market, called a "vide grenier" (empty–loft), occupied the quay. I bought three items, a Stanley Fast–Cut wood saw for 5 euros, a small plastic seagull, to grace the cabin, for 50 cents and a book titled, "Systeme D", full of do it yourself repairs and home made gadgets. In the Canary Islands a French sailor was writing a book called 'Systeme D', for sailors. His yacht was built and equipped with found objects, such as the main sail, which made the boat look like a tramp wearing a jacket many sizes too small. Looking at his boat I had reached the conclusion it was a most uncomfortable vessel due to the wide, flat hull and would make for unbearably tedious voyaging. I concluded the only choice with such an impractical ship was to remain in port and try to sell the idea of 'Systeme D' instead of suffering the reality of voyaging. It was interesting to have found the source of inspiration of that French sailor.

In the afternoon two hefty hire boats were taken up by a crowd of teenagers. They sniggered, giggled, smiled and eventually waved as they departed in a chaos of locked knots, over revved motors and hasty leaps over swirling water gaps.

On Monday morning I left Tournus into heavy and cold rain. After 10 km the cold and wet drove me into a marina in a disused lock, hoping to find an electricity point and dry out in front of the fan heater. There was no one to be seen and I gratefully plugged in the fan heater. A kilometre across the fields was a tiny village with a camping caravanning site occupying grounds of a grand old house. Two cottages held sculpture studios with strange figures and designs adorning the eaves and windows.

Loba bounced through long wet grass chasing pine cones until we arrived back at SP to be met by a man asking for 10 euros mooring fees. Ouch! Quite expensive for a night's berthing but the alternative had been to stop along the cold and rainy river banks and stay cold and damp all night.

As the rain and cold continued throughout May, I collected wood and cleared the little stove for serious use. Chalon–sur–Saone passed with a bridge and fine stone architecture. Spires in detailed neat brickwork had shiny dark grey roof tiles. The following evening Seurre was an utterly silent town at 7pm. Some workmen gave me a long wooden plank to use as a fender board. Some locks filled to the brim and the fenders floated above the lock edge so the plank was tied just at the water line to protect the hull.

St Jean de Losne,was strung quite high up on the map of France and held the promise of a pleasant town under that pleasant name. A large marina held a community of liveaboard boats, many British. A well stocked ship's chandler was the first since Gruissan and I bought a spare water pump impeller for the engine. It was a different configuration, having more fins, but the helpful staff explained the hire boat companies all used this one which happened to be half the cost of the alternative and was widely believed to be equally effective. I took the opportunity to remove the old impeller and test the new. It was equally effective and so I refitted the old one, having learned how to change it if need be.

Instead of seeking to join in the tempting friendliness beaming out of the live aboard community in the marina I took the liberty of a free public quay.

Noticing the V.N.F. (Voies Navigable de France) office had a bunch of keys hanging in the door I knocked and attracted the man inside. He reluctantly walked around his desk and came to the door eyeing me suspiciously. I pointed to his bunch of keys but he only shrugged and removed them. I entered the office to ask about the imminent re-opening of the canal ahead following a month in maintenance. The booklet of chomages – closures – showed a further delay near to Calais of four weeks from the time I would arrive there. The future delay was disturbing but I decided to see it as an opportunity to slow right down and linger along the canals and arrive there at the beginning of July in a relaxed and restored state. The return across the Channel to the UK was going to be a big arrival home.

Fortified walls, munitions stores and military barracks dominated the town of Auxonne. Au – xonne means, on the – Saone. Napoleon Bonaparte studied there and would walk by the River Saone. A sluice plunged to one side and above the lock the river went under a stone bridge. A mooring pontoon was placed just up from the bridge. A broad basin stretched upstream towards trees and a bend beyond the town. A wind surfer zigzagged expertly and hire boats came and went inexpertly. I strolled up to a wooden office with maps and leaflets hung around the entrance, staffed by two young people with welcoming smiles where I expected to be told the price of the mooring, but they loaded me up with a tourist information pack and told me the mooring was free.

In the market I bought fresh sardines and returned to cook them over charcoal and bits of wood picked up along the river side. Loba and I relished morsels of the delicious grilled fish. Afterwards the tiny improvised barbecue on the back deck had an hour to burn so I decided to make Gambian tea, 'attaya', as a way to remember my African adventures. The tiny, round, blue enamelled teapot, two tiny glasses and a box of Special China Green Tea were carefully stowed in Tupperware boxes. The word "attaya" pronounced "attire" as in "clothing" and "gear" and "outfit". When tea first arrived in Britain it was so expensive ladies would ask for the tea equipment, the attire, and brew it themselves. The servants were not allowed to handle the highly expensive tea. The term attaya must come from colonial times.

I waited four days for maintenance work on the Canal de la Marne a la Saone, renamed for the tourists "La Canal entre Champagne et Burgundy". In those four days I took bike rides through dandelion and buttercup pastures, past fields of yellow flowers and creamy cows. I rowed the dinghy along offshoots of the River Saone while Loba barked at sheep and swallows inscribed their delicate flickering lives into the hesitant sunshine. I biked along a particularly muddy path leading up to the junction with the canal de la Marne a la Saone, to speak to the lock keeper about the chomages – closures. I walked in Pontailler sur Saone, where SP was moored in a most pleasant side stream. The "Vielle Saone", the old Saone, was a realm of swans, lilly pads and fishing punts. The navigable Saone too was filled with swans, swallows, lilly pad corners and fishermen, but on a larger scale, with the occasional shotgun report and a raucous panic of crows above the treetops, poff!

The Canal du Marne a la Saone opened on Monday 15 May. A couple of barges were waiting but there was no backlog of boats bunched together as expected. When I found out the difficulty in passing oncoming barges I understood why the hire companies do not use this canal. Despite it being the deeper of three possible routes between Paris and the Mediterranean, SP was "dropped" onto the canal bottom each time a barge passed.

114 locks on the stretch ahead was daunting, a stretch completed relatively recently, in 1907, the Canal de la Marne a la Saone was deeper and had fewer locks than on the Canal du Centre, completed in 1790 and the Canal de Bourgogne which was upgraded to Minister of Public Works, Freycinet, dimensions established in 1879.

Over 224 km there are 41 locks ascending from the River Saone to the summit and then 71 locks descending towards the River Marne. The locks on the River Rhone could fit in twelve 300 ton barges but these locks were exactly one 300 ton barge big.

The first lock was attended by a smiling woman who I initially thought was a man. With a measured pace, in baggy slacks and a gardening sweatshirt, she walked around opening gates and paddles and then smiled again as SP set off towards the next lock.

The first day SP travelled 29 km, through 14 locks, in 8 hours. The first night's stop on the Canal du Marne a la Saone SP had to moor perpendicular to the bank due to the shallow canal sides. The 15th lock keeper had closed 10 minutes early to attend to a barge ahead. Working boats were able to navigate one hour earlier and one hour later than pleasure boats, meaning they always got in front. There was no hope of overtaking because, as a barge passed, the water level dropped 15cms. Oncoming barges were a real worry. With so little room beneath a deeply loaded barge the water piled up ahead of the vessel and poured aft along each side. SP was often grounded and leaned over helplessly while a barge passed. In the worst case SP was slewed around on her keel to face the opposite direction. Then like a toy boat she was lifted out into the churning wake behind the barge. Despite the mast overhanging both ends it avoided hitting the barge. All I could do was give full throttle whenever the bank happened to be ahead. Imagining how easily the mast could have been dragged from the deck and left broken in the canal, I grinned inanely and waved at the figures behind lace curtains in the receding wheelhouse. The turbulent wake spun SP one final 360 degree pirouette before I was able to set off north again.

The canal often passed over the River Marne via aqueducts. These water bridges gave views of inaccessible turns and branchings, overhung by kingfisher boughs. Pastoral quiet lay heavy in the wood smoke air of the villages. Pouilly–sur–Vingeanne was yet another tiny village clustered around the river Marne as it dipped and cut under the foundations of houses and farm buildings. An open door, a television, a dog rioting against a fence, impenetrable hedges, barns, log piles, rot, swallow holes and sparrow nooks. All the sparrows of the world live in the Bourgogne. No shops, no bars, just a realm where no cars or scooters appeared and people barely showed themselves outside heavy gated yards and stone houses. Loba found a blue plastic ball next to the little river Marne.

The next day SP travelled 26 km and 20 locks, in 9 hours. One lock cottage, a little old house, was converted for holiday lets. Three German ladies arrived in a car. The water lifted SP inside the lock and as the boat appeared in their front yard they came to look and say hello. In 30 seconds I described my voyage – Bristol, Spain, Portugal, the Canary Islands, Senegal, Gambia and then here, replete with hippos and crocodiles, in front of this peaceful lock cottage. One, about my age, with short blond hair, dreamily exclaimed, "You must have seen many beautiful things."

In late afternoon Villegusien offered a silo quay. Loba led me into the village where a yellow field bled into the edge of the houses. I wished I had my camera as a wide furrow of yellow cut in half an oak wood on the brow of a nearby hill. An old couple sat outside their wood smoky cottage and asked me if I'd come to look at the yellow field. Loba walked through their open front door and scampered from room to room as we chatted. I told them she was looking for the kitchen in search of ham or cheese. The amused woman was bright and engaging – the wary man was weary and receding.

On Wednesday 17 May the Canal de la Marne a la Saone arrived at an ever increasing staircase of locks embedded in woods and cornfields, to the last lock in the ascent up the Vingeanne valley. A 10 km summit level was created by the Balesmes tunnel – 4828m long. I cleared for immediate passage at a VNF (Voies Navigable de France) office next to the lock. A rusty white van had stopped at the lock side and a farming lady stood in the back bent over among tattered boxes of fruit and wrinkly vegetables. I was one of the first boats through for over a month since the canal had been closed for maintenance and she apologised for the disarray. She had no potatoes, so I bought a bag of apples.

The canal entered a narrow brick lined cut between high wooded embankments. Corpses of a small deer, a badger, a sheep and a hedgehog bloated into a spiny ball, were drowned when the canal was refilled with water after the long closure.

The tunnel was cold, dark and dripping with water. I had read somewhere there was a church directly overhead somewhere near the middle. I felt squeamish when drips of water that had filtered through the graves above, fell from the roof onto my face. After emerging into the light at the other end another narrow brick lined cut continued some way through wooded embankments.

Eventually a lock appeared, this time descending, the first of more than 70 along the northern section of the Canal de la Marne a la Saone. Crowning the Langres plateau is a town circumscribed by immense walls. Here Denis Diderot, 17C philosophe, was born. He was one of the French encyclopaedists who believed that representing all human knowledge in text and diagrams meant it could be reconstructed even if civilisation was all but lost.

At 340m above sea level and exposed to the winter winds Langres has a reputation for being a particularly cold place. Sloping hills sweep across the plain, like ocean waves, rising gradually and abruptly dropping at a scarp and Langres was built on one of these crests.

Much of the surrounding land was forest and the rivers Seine, Meuse, Aube and Marne each have their source near Langres. These rivers either flow South down to the Mediterranean Sea or North down to the English Channel.

I had arranged to meet my mum and dad in Langres for a few days. We always kept close contact by email but I had not met them in 17 months. I enjoyed being driven around the region, seeing small villages and woodlands and treated to restaurant food and café stops. In one village a tortoise came running along the path and just as we stopped in some confusion as to what to do, a woman appeared in pursuit. Her expression clearly declaring, "yes, my tortoise".

In the single village store I was amused by a doormat with writing woven into the brush which I interpreted as "Ring the doorbell of this house and change your sex". I should have brought it for its rare humour. The mother and daughter behind the counter were grinning as I heard them exclaim to one another, "Oh la la, that risqué doormat, the foreigner understands".

Loba went bonkers as only a small terrier can, at the appearance of a large black dog, before we drove off in search of a picnic stop deep in the local woods. I was convinced we were bewitched after driving 20 km without finding the place despite numerous signs pointing to it. We found it after driving back into the same village to undo the get–lost–spell and it turned out to be within a couple of kilometres of the shop with the door mat and the large black dog.

Dad, mum and I visited an exhibition of African artefacts held in a tower with a spiral ramp inside to roll heavy guns up to the battlements. The tower was in a camp site we'd stayed at, 36 years previously, on a family holiday. On the short walk back to the hotel my father stopped and began padding and searching the flap pockets of his buttoned up tweed jacket. The belfry next to the hotel was plainly visible above the houses but he was insistent on determining the direction there by compass. His face red and stubborn under a soft green hat with annoyance at my mother because she had let him leave the compass in the car. His grey beard whitened at the scissor trimmed tips. Mum and I walked on, but dad refused to follow and when we looked back we saw him striding like an explorer across the end of the street, without turning to see us, heading the wrong way. My mother called but to no avail, so she went to follow. Just then my father arrived back at the end of the street having made an independent conclusion it was the correct direction and he turned up the street towards us. We arrived back at the hotel within a couple of minutes. I banged my head on a wooden beam over the winding stairs. My father sat on the end of the bed furious and enervated, holding his head in his hands until a glass of wine re–established magnetic North.

The next day mum, dad and I traipsed through the rain towards a café I'd suggested. A handbag on her shoulder in a clean beige coat, strong hair with buoyant grey silver moods in the rain. My mother frowned at umbrellas opening like flack, or at my father's acute questions about responsibilities and practicalities of the voyage of SP. My mother piloted us past the shops, smiling at passers by and at the novelty of walking in France with their daughter. Joyous at my imminent return to the UK, my mother had set–aside euros wrapped in an elastic band in her bag for me.

On Thursday 25 May my parents and I parted and left Langres. After a wet days travel SP was moored in a village called Foulain. To warm my wet cold limbs I walked with Loba. A sign stood where the track turned away from the canal towards a wooded valley. A hand painted pentagram held the words,

"CENTRE LOTHLORIEN"

Lothlorien was the fairy realm of trees in Tolkein's, *Lord of the Rings*. I cautiously and excitedly followed the path beside a stream under raindrop woods.

Centre Lothlorien was a grand mansion and other old houses set by a jade coloured lake in an enchanted valley. Originally a leper hospice, it now offered rest, peace and personal growth. I ascended the stone steps past a waterfall inhabited by gnomes, horned beasts, fairies and elves around a pool of water and reached the main doorway of the grand house. I climbed the steps up to the doors and struck the bell. I wanted to say hello and was curious about the fascinating atmosphere and nature. When nobody answered I went around one side and peered into a wrought iron and glass annex to see a crowd of faces sitting around inside, now turned to look out at me. I saw one leave the room, so I went back to the front door. There I met a Netherlander who explained a little about Centre Lothlorien – there was camping, accommodation, personal growth workshops with individual counselling and tuition in areas of creativity and health. In the wooden floored hall behind him I saw shelves of books, objects and ornaments in casual but comfy disorder and shoes on the floor. There was an openness to the place with no hint of religious or idealistic perversion. The man suggested I take the path leading around the lake and so I did. It was a lush haven of old trees filling a rocky gorge sided valley with the lake held back, near the house, by a dam. At the head of the lake several streams meandered over a green bed of grass and the path crossed over rusty iron walkways to a grove of huge broad leaved trees. Looking straight up to the swaying leaf crown, the light grey trunks and boughs brimmed with life and the sound of water trickling and pattering through stones and leaves held me rooted in a moment of delight and absorption in nature.

Friday 26 May. The next day I left Foulain heading for Chaumont, a large town and then Vieville a village beyond. The densely wooded hills and farmland of Bourgogne altered with the approach of Chaumont. Joggers paced the canal path, unheeding cars sped past on busy roads beyond rows of pine trees. One tree stood out from the rank with a double kink where it must have been bent over decades ago and then continued growing straight upwards. This tree stood out in a line of more than 30 straight pines, each 20m tall. It was slightly stunted by the trauma making it a third less tall than the rest. Exactly at the point when SP drew abeam of the one cranky tree, two other events converged – the lock keeper whizzed by on her scooter and a TGV train hurtled past – a train, an eclusier (lock keeper), SP and the crank pine – happening there in an insignificant coincidence like a knot in wood, or the way light and images are pulled together by a ping in a metal sheet.

The first mechanical failure occurred on arrival into Chaumont after a morning of pervasive unease, an intuition of something amiss. Chaumont quay appeared at lunch time, where I'd arranged with the eclusier to stop for an hour and a half. I swung SP towards the bank while moving the engine into reverse, usually a 180 degree spin and the boat slides to a halt against the quay with perfect, well practised grace. The spin was necessary because the ropes and fenders were arranged for port side mooring. Reverse gear would not engage and SP was running towards the steel pilings of the canal side at 5 km/h Reverse gear stubbornly refused to engage and the bows hit square on with a loud bang. No body came to help although several office workers peered across the marina grass frontage with sorry looks, obviously thinking, 'ah, just another incompetent hire boat skipper crashing into the canal side'. The bow had only superficial marks at the impact point. On impact Loba had been inside the cabin. She leapt out looking terrified and stood next to me quaking with fear. She crept between my legs to look up at me appealingly with her little brown eyes, "Are we really for it now? Will you protect me, please?"

I dismantled the single lever throttle and gear control to find four casing screws had vibrated loose, one of which had jammed the lever. After applying some thread lock to the screws and greasing the workings I reassembled it. Loba then walked me up the hill towards Chaumont. We did not reach the town which was a couple of kilometres from the canal and after deciding not to visit a hyper market we got back to the boat and made ready to enter the quiet of the countryside again. I had read the berthing charges and did not relish paying 2 euros for water, 2 for electricity, 5 for mooring and 2 for a shower. I had been spoiled by the freedom of arriving in Foulain the previous evening in the rain and cold, then sawing wood and enjoying the deep, comforting warmth from the cabin stove, without connection to electricity or the dubious security of a marina berth. Foulain had been a most interesting stop. In the village I saw several wood stoves being used as garden ornaments. One with flowers in was was only as big as a small bucket. The other more elaborate with two doors and a chimney outlet, had been painted bright primary colours and was now a home to geraniums. I placed my eye against dusty web–grey glass to look inside abandoned cottages with slumping roofs. Among old bicycles, sacks of tiles, piles of sacks, farm implements, rotting arm chairs and wrecked standard lamps the occasional dormant wood stove lurked against rotting plaster walls.

The next day I moved onwards to Veiville. The mooring was popular with long term moored boats and several motor caravans sheltered from the persistent rain and cold. The French provide stopping places for boats and motor caravans with electricity and water points, free of charge. This was slightly different as a local restaurant seemed to have assumed an administration role with notices telling me prices and to go to a restaurant in the village to pay. I went and declared my wish to stay for a couple of nights and that I would like to use the electric point. The man behind the bar asked if the electric was working and I told him I would first need to change my plug to suit so I did not know if the supply was switched on. He assured me he would be down in half an hour, on his scooter. I waited for him to tell me how much to pay but he motioned me to do it all when he arrived at the canal. He did not arrive, but the electric point was working and I did not visit the restaurant again so failed to pay anything for my two day stay.

The next day was a Saturday and I took Loba on a long walk up into the surrounding woods and hills which turned out to be 15 km. I followed a path signed with yellow and green paint marks, called the Route de la Roche Bernard, which had promised fine views of the "Roche Bernard – popular with hill walkers and rock climbers". In persistent rain we saw lovely woodland and fields of yellow rape flowers. A couple of times I got lost and had to back track half a kilometre after exploring several deeply rutted and very muddy tracks used for hauling logs. I called a cuckoo, by cupping my hands and blowing the notes. He came immediately grunting and flapping overhead and at one point even struck the tree tops sending a shower of raindrops down onto Loba and I. I recorded the maddened cuckoo on my hand–held Psion 5. Loba happily scampered the whole way and near the end when I felt dead tired, she was still pouncing at sticks I threw. She was covered in ticks for the next few days and I did not know how to deal with them. Then I realised they needed twisting out with no hesitation, but they certainly hung on and I found it most unpleasant to have to touch their grey or brown bulbous bodies.

After a weekend in Vieville I set out for the friendly sounding town of St Dizier. Arriving there Muslim children waved and called hello from a town bridge. Youths rolling joints under another bridge distracted me from noticing the twist pole hanging beneath the bridge. Just as SP emerged beyond the bridge a hooded lanky kid ran from behind the buttress bellowing like a demon. At the same moment I spotted the missed pole and threw SP into hard reverse which somewhat unnerved the stoned youth. The boat arrived backwards under the bridge and I avoided any eye contact as I twisted the pole to open the lock ahead. I arrived next to a car park with aggressive looking cars drawn up in conspirational huddles. Now scanning the embankments for a nights mooring I glanced over at the group of dodgy cars and one kid waved as if we were old friends. In completely ignoring the gesture I managed to front him out and retain my social integrity. Moorings along the canal through St Dizier seemed hostile and grim so I continued out to the far end of the city. A line of big trees leading to a, now closed for the night, lock offered a peaceful enough stop. A walk with Loba and then I built a fire with wood given by a VNF man after I had asked for some of a pile of scrap wood at one lock during the afternoon. The rain and cold was forgotten as the toast warm fire reassured me and dried out my socks and shoes. After a couple of glasses of Bourgogne red wine I slept as SP rested on the stillness of the canal beneath those old trees.

In the morning a thick mist filled the canal. I was hoping to reach the climax of the canal de la Marne a la Saone at Vitry–le–Francois. The locks shut for an hour and a half at lunch time so I walked Loba to a lock cottage and met a father and his son. The little boy had a slightly twisted nose and mouth with round face, chubby but with beady eyes. He caught my attention and pointed to the earth garden along the side of the cottage. In a high, genderless, excited voice, he told the story of a lizard he'd just seen, "It ran along here, behind there, up there, over this, in there, out there along that way and, and," He looked up at me while pointing at the last observed position of the lizard, "it must be somewhere in there!" I was overwhelmed by the sweetness of this little herpetologist. I suggested, partly to his father, he might be a scientist of reptiles when he was older. His father called him in to lunch.

The afternoon was a slow progression over 15 km and numerous locks. Two barges had set off ahead and each lock took half an hour to drop three boats individually to the next section. At 6pm, right at closing time, I passed through the final lock into Vitry–le–Francois. It was now the first week of June.

Architecture, place names, people's faces seemed to have so much more north in them. Temperatures had been nothing but wintry throughout May, with endless days of rain. Strangely the people I met who had travelled down from the north talked about having got away from all that rain and cold in England, to have made enough southing to have escaped the bad weather. I was acutely conscious of having left the warm southern lands far behind to have made enough northing to have escaped the relentless sun. There remained 428 km between Vitry–le–Francois and Calais, and 117 locks. Even so I was certain I could smell the North Sea.

I wondered why, "Tauberbischofsheim – 525 km", was signposted in a medium small town like Vitry–le–Francois and how, to my sun crinkled ears, that Germanic name sounded positively north.

When the end of one long canal was reached I would stop for a day to reflect on the evolving scenery of the journey. Vitry–le–Francois offered a pleasant small boat harbour with electricity and water all for free. I explored the town over two days of fine weather and took the opportunity to buy a new top in a sale and two new balls for Loba. In the evening a kebab shop made me hungry for a bag of chips. I ordered just chips but after ten minutes was given a huge bag with a huge price. I questioned the 4.5 euros as far too much for chips alone. Then

I realised I had been served with a kebab and chips. I said I did not want a kebab, I had asked for just chips, but the phone rang and as she answered it the girl waved the bag at me and said it's OK take it for nothing. I was flustered and wanted to leave the fat bag of food and the embarrassment. Kebabs are expensive at around 5 euros, but also that turning pole of processed meat looked squeamish. I could no longer ask for just a bag of chips and the person serving ignored me while dealing with the telephone, so I left with the bag of food. I found the broad town square with fountains overlooked by a splendid church and sat down on a bench to pick out the chips. It was absolutely delicious, with garlic mayonnaise on tasty slices of meat in a freshly opened pita bread and a mound of chips. In twenty minutes I'd eaten the whole lot and sat burping with my bellyful of freedom fries.

## North Into the Vertical Future

After Vitry–le–Francois the canal travelled past industrial sites where machines on giant tyres moved between graded piles of aggregate. Pigeons occupied disused silos surrounded by broken fences and waste ground. Chalons–en–Champagne eventually appeared with many people walking along the canal path by a tree filled island and the cathedral rising majestically from green meadows. I had no wish to stop at such a picturesque place and continued by. I thought there would be a medium sized town at Conde–sur–Marne with the junction of the Canal–de–l'Aisne–a–la–Marne and in a couple of hours I moored to a pontoon there. A man approached to help me moor and tell me it would cost money to moor there. I needed a free berth and made to leave, but the mooring was then offered free as long as I did not use water or electricity. The man explained the marina was still being built. I stayed although after I saw the pleasant public moorings just up the canal I regretted entering the marina in the first place. I walked Loba into what turned out to be a tiny village and almost immediately I had walked out of the far side of Conde–sur–Marne. A smooth, undulating agricultural landscape flowed northwards towards higher ground in the direction of Reims. The water of the Canal–de–l'Aisne–a–la–Marne was light chalk green instead of the dark soupy Canal–lateral–a–la–Marne. The big city of Reims was within a days cruising and I looked forward to being there.

Some locks were problematic. A sensor at the entrance caused automatic doors to close after the boat had entered the chamber, but designed for working barges of 38m length it was difficult to convince the sensors SPs 8m length was a real boat rather than a passing swan. The trick was to go slow enough to break the infra red beam for at least 10 seconds, but SP easily passed the sensors in half that period. In the first lock in Reims the gates refused to close. There were unfriendly looking people huddled around in the park next to the canal and I was glad the locks were surrounded by high wire fences. I used the assistance phone and within 10 minutes an eclusier arrived by moped. He took pains to tell me SP had not registered with the sensors at the lock gates and how I must check the signal lights had turned to red and if not, to walk to the front of the lock and wave my shoe in front of the sensor for 10 seconds.

It was absurd having to climb up the lock ladder to walk back past the gates, then down the steps to where a metal box protected the sensors. Then a foot was dangled out over the canal to break the infra red beam for a sufficient period – I would have preferred a big green button to press. Often I brought the boat almost to a standstill before a sensor would bother to register properly the problem being SP was also below the level of the sensors for much of her length and only the short cabin broke the beam. The same thing happened on leaving locks. To complete the cycle and prepare a lock for another boat it had to know the last boat had left. The temptation was to move definitely out of the lock but the sensor required an almost full stop otherwise the entry lights would stubbornly refuse the next boat because the system had yet to clear the last boat out.

Several times, having failed to register, I reversed SP back into the beam and then the lock system mistook me for a boat entering against a red light and the necessary combination of 10 second interruptions to convince the system everything was in order became unfathomable. Then a telephone call, a wait and a condescending eclusier would ensue. "You go too fast through the sensor," he would say informatively. "See the lights are still red. Look, OK, then hold your foot out over the canal, like this, in front of the little metal box," I knew all this but he continued to condescend. "And then climb down the slimy ladder, quickly now, before your boat is left hanging on the ropes."

Eventually he would realise there was a technical fault with the lock system and enter the control room to manually press the lock into service. I was always polite and cheerful with the eclusiers and them to me, but some other grumpy and unhelpful British boaters told of grumpy and unhelpful eclusiers. I found the lock keepers polite and cheerful if a bit condescending but the locks were their work and I was just a pleasure boater. At one lock where I telephoned for assistance the voice spluttered out of the speaker phone in rapid French and I could not understand a word of it, so slightly impatiently I asked for someone to come and sort it out. At this particular lock the sensor was 200m before the lock and when the lights had failed to register my approach I'd turned SP around to go back and try again. A couple of sensors could determine the direction the boat was travelling and so I swooped SP at high speed through the sensors, to avoid detection, then spun her in a swirl of impatient water and returned to pass the sensors at dead slow. Of course all this resulted in was a crashed logic system in the lock control box. So I knew the eclusier would have to come and do the manual thing with his official key.

The speaker phone continued in a barking voice and I became exasperated. When I almost demanded the eclusiers attention he responded with, "Vous et Allemande?" Aha, I thought here was a bigoted eclusier who thought I was German. "Non, je suis Anglais," And they arrived within 5 minutes.

At the port of Reims I was charged 20 euros for two nights. I exclaimed at the high cost and was told, "Well, you know, this is the city." It was not at all safe to moor along the canal side with drunks sitting in the park overlooking the canal, eyeing up the boats and tourists. The marina offered no security apart from the presence of other boats but appeared mostly empty and the marina office was unstaffed for most of the day and night.

It was exciting to be in a large city and I walked Loba into the centre. Reims Cathedral had an astonishing façade with rank upon rank of stone figures. At each side of the multi–arched entrance portal two animal heads projected extrovertly out of the grand masonry – a comical rhinoceros and a cartoon donkey – they held me fascinated, then awed and then I laughed out loud.

An English couple had come to Reims after buying a catamaran through Ebay. During the past winter they had travelled to Reims to refit their new boat which was moored out in the canal and they told me how they'd rowed through ice to get aboard. The mast was somewhere in Calais Marina and when they went to claim it they were told to take their choice from a ramshackle pile of masts and rigging that had been laying there for decades.

On the morning we'd both planned to leave their engine was still dismantled and as we talked the cylinder head lay on the floor in a cardboard box, even so a couple of hours later we were both heading north and we met several times on the way towards Calais.

The Vosges contrasted with Burgundy and Champagne with more cars and roads visible through the trees by the canal and those trees were often neat rows of pine instead of oak and other hard wood trees. At Berry–au–Bac a wide basin with moorings was described in the pilot book as, "often windy". I thought how presumptuous, I mean Cabo Sao Vicente, the very end of Europe is "often windy"; The Cabo Verde Islands, laying square in the true Atlantic trade winds, are "often windy"; the Golfe du Lion, ripped by the tramuntana and mistral, is "often windy"; but how could 500m of moorhen and duck ridden pastoral canal basin be termed "often windy"?

The evening was made extra friendly with a glass of wine aboard the yacht of four Belgians. I then walked Loba a kilometre into Berry–au–Bac and found a café where I took a glass of red wine, served by an attractive woman with intense steel blue eyes, framed by yellow smokers wrinkles. A black poodle came around the bar to sniff Loba. Fluffy white seeds filled the wind outside and for a brief moment the four or five other customers in the café all turned to stare through the windows at the fluff streaming by.

The following morning I went for a coffee in the same bar and then followed my curiosity down a back lane called, "Rue de la Ancienne Place", past gardens, houses, bungalows and agricultural plots on one side and the River Aisne on the other. I threw sticks into the current for Loba, but she began treading out into sticky wet mud so I called her back into the fluffy white seeds gathered in drifts and clinging on Loba's fur. A car and an SUV arrived at the opposite bank of the swift little river and some fishermen pegged themselves at the waters edge.

The following day the voyage of SP entered a 20 km stretch of the Canal de la Aisne without interruption by a single lock. In the thick bushes by the canal a narrow gauge railway line twisted and slumped, disused since the time when the canal had small trains to tug the barges along.

Eventually Bourg–et–Comin came along with an electricity hook up point and water for free. Hot air balloons roared peacefully overhead in the calm evening. Several touched the surface of a lake beside the canal, then lifted off again. I took Loba on the bike to see a rainbow balloon which had landed next to the lake. Three cars attended the landing spot and a family fussed around beneath the balloon. One four wheel drive vehicle had a sticker in the rear window, "Cameron Balloons of Bristol". A young girl was allowed to remain in the basket while the adults manhandled the swaying monster to a suitable position for deflation. An older boy looked afraid and would not go anywhere near the basket.

The late evening was so warm I was glad of the electric supply because I used the fan heater on cold to help cool the cabin. There were ten days to wait before the two closed locks near Calais were reopened which meant for each day of progress there needed to be one of staying still. I needed to avoid waiting somewhere unpleasant and I knew the canals and landscape north of here would be increasingly fringed by industry, urbanization and stone throwing kids.

The following day I took a bike ride through cornfields surrounded by poppies. After several kilometres I stopped by a stone wash house at the edge of a village. The sun was strong enough to drive me into the shade of steps leading down to a shallow rectangular pool. A spring flowed in at one end and in bubbling sound and coolness I ate cheese, raw garlic and an apple. I picked a partially sunken margarine tub from the water to make a little boat, but inside was a sodden pencil and paper with writing on, a list of names. I dried out the paper in a shaft of sunlight and added my own note describing the voyage of SP. Then I noticed a type written note on the lid, asking people not to touch the tub because it was part of, "un jeu de piste", a treasure hunt, so I relaunched the dried out note in its tub after removing my addition. Instead I placed my note in a niche in the wall held by a garlic bulb. I had developed a peculiar taste for pieces of raw garlic eaten with cheese, or apple, or other morsels and I always carried a bulb of garlic with me.

The Canal–de–la–Aisne branched into a link canal – The Canal–de–l'Aisne–a–l'Oisne. The first lock was number 13. A signboard indicated I should press a blue button on a remote control lock operation device. The trouble was nobody had mentioned such a desirable gadget to me before and even though I knew some canals used remote controls, there had been nothing to say I would need one until now. An empty lock cottage watched over the unmoving lock so I pressed the button on the orange VNF assistance box to communicate with an eclusier. Several presses resulted in silence, so I went back to where SP was tied to the bank to get my mobile phone, but there was no network signal. Meanwhile Loba stepped onto a carpet of fluffy seeds accumulated in front of the lock gates and plunged through into deep unanticipated water. She swam towards the higher ground of the opposite bank and hung there on the slippery concrete wall while I hurried up the steps, over the gates and down the far steps, to help her out. Once on land she went mad with excitement, jumping, yapping and growling. Another boat arrived from the opposite direction so I thought everything would work out. The other boat entered the lock but after it had been lowered inside the chamber the gates failed to open. I walked up and met the Dutch couple now waiting inside the bowels of the lock. I suggested using the orange communications box, but they wanted to lift the red emergency pole and I suggested it was not a dangerous situation. They agreed. This time the orange button was a success and a public address system crackled into life to reassure us an eclusier was on his way. SP was eventually able to continue through a scorching hot Sunday morning.

I drove close along the banks to gain shade from the thick trees. Twice I poured buckets of canal water over Loba who was still wearing her winter coat and panting in 30C and she dried off again in 10 minutes. Chauny was a small town where I found an Internet café and supermarkets. A house overlooked the canal next to the bridge. It had a snazzy repeating swastika design formed out of tiles in a band above the upper windows. A small, sleepy eye window was situated in the roof overlooking the canal, the bridge and the road junction and it was easy to imagine a Nazi look out, observing passers by. I wondered if a swastika motif was legal and how it was an unnerving choice of decoration.

The Chauny mooring was unshaded, I had no choice but to leave in search of a cool spot. An hour after I'd moored under large trees the hot spell broke into a thunder storm. It came down with a wrenching wind hurling leaves, twigs and seeds onto the decks. I closed the cabin on the weather, happy to be moored on the canal with no ugly waves or dangerous lee shore. The rain blattered visibility to the ground, thunder claps came close with lightning and the downpour was like an African monsoon. Shut inside the cabin, my thoughts travelled back to the River Gambia, wondering what my friends might be doing in the rains and hothouse heat of August. I pictured them hanging around on plastic garden chairs in the bar at Denton Bridge and heard their imaginary gossip:

*Fish Wife; Babacoo; Barman; and Sea Boy were talking about Bendt; Little Fella; Buba; Lady Sailor; the Dutch Couple; Condoron; Cap'n Tanears; and Belgian Sailor:*
*Like a wave of heat, Fish Wife swept into the midst of a relaxed, humid hour, "That man, you see how he stroke the boy and he stay many times on his boat up the river. Little Fella, he disturbed by that drunk, Bendt, patting his head, stroking his neck."*
*A road bridge carried the only land access to the capital city of Gambia, Banjul.*
*Babacoo, who repeatedly accidentally set fire to himself, liked a firebrand, "They go up river, maybe three, four days. His mother, she there and his sister. That family happy to meet him and he buy shoes, pens for school and pay school examination fees."*
*Once the site of an attempted coup, The bridge was known as a place where dubious people hung out.*

Barman looked at his bar, "Every day drinking. Beer, coffee, brandy, buying coca–cola for Little Fella. My cousin, make sandwich, she sell, it was very good for Denton Bridge?"

The bridge was guarded by a police station. A military post in a concrete shed stood nearby on rough ground.

Sea Boy couldn't stay still without asking for something, "Eh give me a cup of tea, Tom, he pay, I work with him today."

200m of sand track led off the road into mangrove swamp, past shacks and rusted out shipping containers to end at a slipway and a gravel floored, bamboo roof bar at the waters edge.

Barman ignored Sea Boy, "Those people have money, they want to buy those things. Europe is very rich. Some white men are very good people. That man, he drink many, many brandies! Sometimes he hardly open his eyes!"

Fish Wife was Senegalese, separated, with a three year old daughter and a one year old son. Sea Boy, an unusually cocky Gambian, once lived rough in London and did small jobs, "10 dallasi contracts", fetching kebabs for white men, or manhandling boats. Through missing front teeth he swore in a cockney accent, "He drunk, an' he lose his f*kkin' dinghy and had to swim to his f*kkin' boat. Every day he pissed, innit. Every day he say, 'Uuuur, I take a brandy, and a coke for the little Fella', ha, ha, ha! He drunk on brandy."

Fish Wife relied on tourists but there were few during the sweltering rainy season so she had no income and nobody to buy her a coffee. She often flew into a rage about injustices, "And the little Fella drown and now that man rot in prison!"

Bendt was a Scandinavian voyager in a small sailing boat. Little Fella was a ten year old Gambian and crewed with Bendt. Little Fella was the cousin of Buba who was a fisherman and joined Lady Sailor as crew. Barman was the universal barman, a devout Muslim, pleasant as could be and sober, but still liked to gossip, "Many times he lose his dinghy, when he drunk. Don't you remember when Lady Sailor and Buba were here at the bridge and we saw that Bendt's dinghy in the mangroves the next morning?"

Babacoo spoke with a smile, lived with a smile, despite the likelihood he was just about to set fire to himself again. As he spoke he looked up and down between the hat he was knitting and the bar where Fish Wife and Barman were, "And Lady Sailor went to get it." Lady Sailor was strong, he sailed alone from England to the Gambia.

Gambians, speaking Wolof, referred to others as "he", regardless of their gender. Sea Boy remembered the departure of Lady Sailor with her Gambian crew Buba, towards the Canary Islands and wished he too was back in Europe, "And he and Buba sail to the Canaries."

Babacoo also remembered the departure of Lady Sailor, "Yeah, almost two years back."

Fish Wife set a match to such nostalgia, "No! He come back, don't you know, even I see Buba in Serekunda."

A smiling Babacoo asked, "Why he come back here, I don't know why he leave Spain?"

Sea Boy spoke from his throat, his broken teeth gulping life like an ugly fish, "Little Fella was Buba's cousin, he didn't f*kin' drown. Tom say he see Little Fella and Buba in Kemoto, innit."

The boredom of the hot rainy season, with so few tourists or sailing boats, left nothing but gossip and after Bendt left the bridge without saying goodbye only rumours filled the vacancy.

Barman lifted a mug from a tub of water, dragging out the tea making, like a good story, "During the night, Bendt turned over his dinghy but he swim to his boat. Little Fella could not swim. It was a terrible thing."

Fish Wife gave her daughter a used tea bag to suck on, "And now that drunkard in prison for life. The whole bridge know he go in the prison."

Babacoo remembered a Dutch couple, who'd sailed to the bridge for the third time in an innovative self–designed and built sailing boat. He crocheted several loops of regard for the Dutch couple into his hat, "Those Dutch people, they were shocked to hear about it." Sea Boy saw Bendt sitting again in the bar with a brandy, "He worked on ships, he had big arms covered in tattoos; fish; mama water *(mermaid); anchor; things like that."*

Fish Wife stroked her hip, *"He have big knife, here."*

Sea Boy told of another sailor, named after the 'Condoron' – a Gambian leprechaun. Condoron had sailed from South Africa to Gambia in a self-built yacht. He was relentlessly and hilariously confrontational after growing up in the Whitby fish industry. *"F\*kkin' Condoron took that knife from Bendt's hip and he just joking innit."* Barman handed Sea Boy a mug of tea, *"They nearly fight with that knife. That was very dangerous, a very dangerous situation."*

Babacoo's hat and life grew another row of crochet, *"Those two, drunk and crazy with the knife between them."*

Fish Wife drew the knife, Bendt and Condoron together like a knot, *"If Bendt and Condoron fight, Condoron win, that drunkard Bendt have no power."*

Barman set a frying pan onto the gas ring, *"No wonder when the tourists come to the bridge they walk straight from the bus onto the boat and they never even look at us."*

Babacoo, still free of fire and smiling, changed black wool for green to make a stripe, *"All the hotels tell the tourists to look straight ahead at the bridge, they think Denton Bridge is a bad place. They don't want to buy from those bumsters."*

Sea Boy's throat complained through his missing teeth, *"They are bumsters over there! I'm not a bumster!"*

Barman dropped chunks of goat meat into the hot pan, *"Only Allah know what we are,"* *"I told the Dutch couple to tell Cap'n Tanears that boy was dead and Bendt he in prison."*

Cap'n Tanears was a tall, black bearded British sailor with an Indian father. He was on his third solo Atlantic voyage.

Sea boy laughed toothlessly, *"Cap'n Tanears he Bin Laden, innit."* Barman stirred sizzling chunks of goat meat, *"Cap'n Tanears is a good friend of Lady Sailor, so everybody who know Bendt know about it now."*

Belgian Sailor had sailed numerous times to Gambia, he often defended Lady Sailor against Condoron's relentless, anarchistic *humour, by saying, "Ee eees stupeed".*

*In her imagination Fish Wife stirred an imaginary pan of goats meat as her daughter sucked the tea bag, "Belgian Sailor said he would go to the jail to see Bendt there. That Bendt will die of malaria in the African prison."*

*Sea Boy supped his tea like a Londoner and felt himself part of the great flowing life of the bridge, "It's the prison on the road to town. You see the prisoners jogging along the beach, with the soldiers, innit."*

*Fish Wife peppered the rumour to taste, "Bendt in prison and he stay there forever. He die there and good riddance!"*

*Barman added rice, water and pepper to the pan, "Remember, only almighty Allah can judge."*

*Babacoo knitted against the rumour, "No, Bendt go to Matasutu tourist camp and he still there."*

*Fish Wife struck sparks out of the sweating air, "No! The boy drown and that drunk in jail, you listen to me, I tell you!"*

My thoughts cleared as the thunder storm left a clear blue sky and sunshine resumed. I opened the hatch to get out of the confines of the cabin and breath the rain washed air. I remembered how Bendt often tipped out of his dinghy while rowing to his yacht at night and how he always managed to swim to his boat and find the dinghy the following day. The young man's death and Bendt's imprisonment rumour reached me via the Dutch couple and thence to Cap'n Tanears via emails. It was even more tragic because the tipsy dinghy was the same "Blue Brick" that had so often dumped whosoever rowed it and had been sold to Bendt by me back in the Canary Islands.

After worrying about my far flung friends for several months and feeling unable to help, another email came with new information. It seemed Little Fella was not Buba's cousin, but another person. Even more of a relief was the news that Bendt had simply grown tired of the gossip at the bridge and left without saying goodbye. The old bugger had sailed away, free as a bird, and was now tipping out of the blue brick somewhere along the Brazilian coast. Around the same time as Bendt's departure, another boatman in another part of the River Gambia had gone to prison after he threw an intruder off his boat and the man drowned. So Bendt had left nothing but a rumour in his wake. Loba tugged me along the canal path until I let her off the lead. She ran ahead to greet some newly arrived fishermen.

Wednesday 14 June. SP entered the canal St Quentin and arrived at its town. The public quay was free but very insecure with streams of cars passing or stopped. No nearby cafés or shops to keep an eye, just a wide car park on the edge of the large town and two barges. I chose to enter the boat harbour, pay the mooring fees and earn them back by busking.

The next morning I earned more than the marina fee and felt optimistic. I was happy that I could play again later and make enough to buy food too, but the pedestrian police came and told me busking was forbidden so I knew I'd have to leave. St Quentin had been quite unfriendly, in a bar I was repeatedly asked, by a louche woman, if I was a Monsieur or a Madam, while a beaky old spiv with a handlebar moustache stared at me and sniggered rudely with the barman. In another bar I asked to use the loo but was refused because I had not ordered a drink. I was unfamiliar with city attitudes after so many villages and small towns. One café was happy to have me sit with a cup of coffee for nearly an hour while I wrote down my frustrations, but the milk was off.

The marina staff were friendly, even when I drew in breath at the price and electricity, showers and water were charged in addition to an already expensive night's mooring. I was offered a free shower and use of the water, but it was hardly free when a night's berth was already 10 euros. If busking was unhindered I would have stayed in St Quentin for several more days, even though hunting around for a pitch in competition with beggars and alcoholics was enervating. As usual The Pink Panther theme went down best.

At lunch time I walked down to the canal side to gain a second impression of the free moorings there. It was dire, with furtive characters standing about and cars trundling across a wide open space with a busy road right next to the canal. It would be impossible to leave the boat unattended for more than ten minutes. The marina with its fence and other vigilant boaters now looked cheap at 50 cents per hour, but I could not afford that security.

In the evening I phoned my mum and dad who told me they would be glad to bring Loba to the UK after I discovered it was illegal to import a dog on a private yacht (unless the dog had left on a yacht and not gone ashore anywhere outside the UK). Neither could I take her on the ferry as a foot passenger, unless she was inside a car. However she could travel on the Eurostar train, in a special compartment, through the Channel Tunnel, with me as a foot passenger. I wanted to get to Calais to sort it all out and also I imagined it would be very easy to set sail with Loba aboard and muddle into the UK without raising any suspicion along with the many other cruising yachts crossing to and fro.

After St Quentin I moored in a small village called Bellenglise. At the late hour of 10.30pm I took Loba for a stroll along the canal path under the amazing sky of a summer night. It was brimful of light and at past 11pm birds had finished singing. The chalk path shone mysteriously. Coming to a mound of radiant white chalk I marvelled to think how magical the Vale of the White Horse, in England, would appear on such a night.

In the morning I awoke at 5.30am to arrive at the designated 7am at the entrance to the Riqueval tunnel. The trees were thick with the sound of pigeons and the canal was full of mist. By 6.30am mist still filled the canal and I stood on the stern deck to gain visibility while performing a Tai Chi posture called "the Horse", which is like sitting on a horse but with no horse. The exercise releases tension and nourishes the pelvis and spine. Breaths swoop lower into the diaphragm with a feeling of opening and relief. After 3 km the tunnel and tugs appeared This was the longest navigable tunnel in France, at 6 km. Electric tugs supplied by overhead cables usually pulled dozens of barges and pleasure boats in a convoy, but SP made a lone transit behind the huge tug. For the next hour and 40 minutes a massive clanking tug yanked itself along, picking up a chain on the canal bed and feeding it through rollers. SP swung side to side and needed constant steering to avoid scraping the glistening black walls. There were four convoys each day, two heading north and two heading south. Inside the tunnel it was cold and damp.

Fluorescent strip lights converged and disappeared into a dark point ahead and gradually the same view closed behind as the tunnel mouth, a half circle of green brightness, closed with increasing distance.

Around the 2500m mark a graffiti artist had written in English, in neat white letters, "JUST ANOTHER MEDIUM SIZED BUCKET". Over the next 300m I wondered what the sentence could mean but found no sense in it, although it made me chuckle because I quite like buckets as definitively functional objects.

Canal art is either done under bridges, by local youths, or on lock gates and tunnel walls by Dutch boaters. In big cities graffiti can be really artistic, with faces and variations way beyond the hurried and unfinished tags of village kids.

A barge came out of the lock ahead, painted shiny green and cream, all new looking and named "ODIN". A northern god travelling south. A bubbly blond, smiled and called across the water as we passed. "You going home?", I called back in an exaggeratedly travel weary voice, "Yes. Been away four years!" A bearded man, excited to be in the canals, heading south at the helm of a barge, exclaimed, "Don't do it! You're going the wrong way!" Perhaps the wisdom of Odin's skipper was right and I should have turned the voyage southwards again, but I had known 'forever summer' and was looking forward to the good old turning of the seasons again. Passing below a motorway I saw a road sign indicating "Route du Soliel" – the highway to the south and the sun – I would have preferred a glimpse of a sign indicating "Hatfield and the North", on the Great North Road, the A1.

After being moved on by police in St Quentin, I expected a similar pattern in Cambrai. The boat harbour office was shut, so I left SP moored there and walked along the canal to find a pub called "The

Jolly Sailor". Someone had told me about a quay with free moorings. It needed checking out for depth and space, as well as security. I found an offshoot of the canal with yellow flowering lilly pads crowding one side and retired bargees cottages with painted barge propellers planted in gardens under the happy chittering of little birds on the other. On the opposite bank a line of barges had smaller boats knitted in amongst them. The Jolly Sailor stood by a disused steel swing bridge at the limit of navigation. A short buzz sounded each time a car passed over the metal grid of the bridge to and from the centre of Cambrai. Workshops and small industrial yards flourished in decay. A boy on a mini quad bike kicked up sparrow dust. Just right. I met an English woman, varnishing in dungarees, on a barge. Mary told me I might get SP up to the quay but the depth was uncertain and I must stay away from the lily padded side which was shallow. I shared a cup of tea with her and Steve, her partner who repaired barges.

I continued into town to play saxophone and later in a 'Mr Bricolage' hardware store, I found a cast iron barrel stove, just like one I'd seen a week earlier. I liked it very much and was delighted to see the price was only 27 euros. I sketched ideas to modify it for use as a heating stove. It needed a steel lid with a hinged opening and an aperture for the chimney to bolt to, as well as the feet being fixed in some way.

Back at the boat I slept after a two–day–vegetable–stew and then awoke at 10 minutes before 7pm. With a rush I realized the lock between here and the Jolly Sailor would close in minutes and I would have to remain in the boat harbour and probably pay for the night. I started the engine and untied to reach the lock with a couple of minutes to spare. Beyond the lock one side of the canal was occupied by fishermen and soon I turned off to slide slowly inwards between the line of black barges and yellow lilies up to the quay next to the Jolly Sailor. There was enough depth and my relief at finding a pleasant mooring for free was great. Mary appeared to loop my ropes onto bollards.

I'd irrevocably warmed to the barrel stove idea and I spent the evening drawing and measuring ways to fit it under the existing chimney on SP. I had already decided to fit another wood stove to keep SP dry throughout the UK winter. The cost of stoves was high and the saving this stove offered was massive. Mary and Steve clinched the matter when they told me they had the same type for ten years and still used it regularly.

In the morning I had only one thing in mind, that little barrel stove. While playing saxophone a stupid kid rode by too close on a bicycle and knocked it which could have hurt my mouth. My saxophone was not working well so I stopped for something to eat. I sat in the shade of a large stone doorway with a sandwich, rather than spend my earnings in a café.

Steve, the barge repair man offered to make the lid for the stove. He cut it out of 10mm steel, using a plasma cutter. The edges were perfectly smooth. I bought the stove and put the lid on top. It was bolted to the floor and worked very well. Steve really didn't charge me, well 10 euros, but that would barely cover the materials cost. My new cabin stove had cost a total of 37 euros. I lit a fire and it worked really well giving massive warmth and having sufficient depth to hold moderate sized bits of timber. Deeply satisfying.

I was vaguely aware of a serious problem with Loba's documentation regime for entering the UK but I was in denial. I had renewed her rabies inoculation in May, but noticed the previous one had expired a couple of months before. This meant she had technically begun a new rabies inoculation and would have to wait six months before having a blood test to measure antibodies response and a further month to qualify for importation to the UK. I wanted to go back to the UK by June when I planned to arrive at Calais. This 7 month situation would mean I could not import Loba until December. The northern French canals would be very cold during winter. The only alternative was to put Loba into UK quarantine kennels for months, which I found out would cost £2000. Quarantine was not an option, I could not put my little dog through half a year of separation.

The decision was made to go to Calais where the veterinarians would be familiar with the rules. Until I had reached Calais and spoken to the vets there I could not know if a two month break in her rabies vaccination was or was not significant.

Meanwhile there was still a couple of weeks to wait before two locks near St Omer, 100 km to the north, were opened again after maintenance closures. I tried to find out the long term berthing cost at the Cambrai boat harbour, but never found the capitanerie open. The Jolly Sailor mooring was ideal, but had no electricity supply for the winter.

A frail white haired woman lived, in the boat harbour, aboard an ex British Navy rescue vessel. I asked about living in the boat harbour. She said the electricity system was old and eccentric. Grappling with a huge long haired cat in her arms, we talked in pigeon French as she was not French either. A pigeon flew around inside the wheelhouse of her boat behind her as we talked. She too was old and eccentric. "A pigeon?" I asked, but she continued to speak of animals, boats, life, the past – not interestingly, but incoherently and oblivious of my words until I made my excuses to leave, the conversation having become a frustrating babble of French and Russian. When I left it was by sliding stubbornly away on my bike with the woman heedlessly talking still.

Another evening I saw her again and feeling a bit sorry for my rude departure, gave a second chance at talk. The conversation was fascinating – about her driving British pilots shot down over France in the 2nd world war, when she was fourteen, hundreds of kilometres to the ports in Brittany, helping them escape the Nazi occupation. I mentioned her to Mary and Steve and they told me she had escaped over a St Petersburg bridge by piling human corpses along either side across the span and crawling across the bridge with the sound of bullets thudding into the frozen bodies. Mary and Steve told me she used to take long cruises with her husband, to the English coast, then around Iberia and up through the French canals.

After ten days in Cambrai Loba and I set off optimistically towards Calais. The canal after Cambrai turned into a high capacity barge canal with 90 metre barges carrying up to 1500 tons. The banks were a continuous concrete wall and most pleasure boaters entered marinas off the main waterway to avoid the waves set up by the passing of those beasts. I turned in to a cut, previously used as a waiting basin before the locks were improved to double chambers and huge capacity, but at the entrance SP ran hard aground in mud. No amount of revving and writhing the rudder around would shift her, until, like an angel, a motor boat came around the corner, so fortunate because I had hardly seen any other pleasure boats all day and the thought of being dragged off the mud by a barge was too frightening to contemplate. A barge would be much too powerful and either rip out the cleats or damage the rudder. The motor boat pulled with all its might and gradually, gently, SP slid backwards through the shallows into deep water again. The two men gestured at the side canal I'd been aiming into and indicated it was shallow all the way through. I carried on along the main route and after 3 km the far end of the basin rejoined the canal and there was a sign indicating a depth of just 1 metre. The canal continued northwards in wide concrete banks with frequent road bridges crossing. At each bridge youths in shorts plunged into the water and stared challengingly as SP passed. I learned to ignore them completely, until at one bridge I tried another way of passing youths. England had lost the football world cup and France were still in it. At the stern of SP, two flags flew – the British red ensign and the French tricolour – so at one large group of swimming youths I held out the red ensign and looked disappointed. The crowd of boys and girls chuckled a bit and the girls sniggered in that intrinsically sarcastic way only teenage girls can. Then I held out the French flag and gave them the thumbs up at which they all burst out in cheers.

In the evening I stopped by a village and ate a huge mound of frites with mayonnaise. Then I came across a concert by local young musicians playing in a small marquee. I stood outside listening to the songs and the parents over–clapping at the sound of inexperienced musicians as green as new buds. The back of the marquee was open and I managed to see the wind players, all shiny saxophones, blowing cheeks with dead serious expressions and white shirts.

The next day I stayed and walked with Loba, making toy sailing boats out of polystyrene, plastic bags and sticks, setting on the busy water to be crushed by barges or swamped in their wakes. With a lump of white chalk I drew graffiti beneath a bridge, not words, but flowing interlocking shapes.

One place I had looked forward to seeing was the boat harbour at Courcelles–les–Lens. A UK sailor had crossed the English Channel and entered the French inland waterways with the intention of going all the way to the south of France on a dream voyage, but had stopped at Courcelles–les–Lens with no will to travel onwards. He wrote,

*"Many people have asked me why I didn't carry through the plan to go to the Med, and I'll tell you why in the simplest terms – I found that just doing what I felt like doing, from day to day, was far more satisfying than I had expected, and that I had so much fun and entertainment that I didn't want to do anything else. In effect, I stopped doing things which I'd planned to do, and did the things I wanted to do, that morning, when I awoke. And equally to the point, when I discovered that I didn't like something, I stopped – for me the stopping point was the charming little marina on the lake at Courcelles les Lens. It really is a lovely spot and just the right place to remember as the deepest I got into France on this occasion,"*

And he added philosophically,

*"If you want a moral to end this part of my tale, here is a suggestion for you: don't make too many wonderful plans. Life changes, situations alter, and if you don't get to do exactly what you want, make sure you do enjoy what you eventually end–up doing!"*

(Chris Gosling)

I found Courcelles–les–Lens just another marina with expensive overnight fees and to make it unbearable, after the sun had beaten down all day, the pontoons were unshaded, despite trees all around the lake. I did not stop and went back out onto the main water course again with a feeling of escape. I stopped at an abandoned factory wharf a little further on. After a longish walk into the village I sat down to write for a couple of hours on a café terrace. A crowd of locals were fairly drunk and one bridged the gap by buying me a glass of red wine. I left with three glasses of red wine inside me, merrily dissolving the sun, the disappointing marina at Courcelles–les–Lens and the interminable concrete canal embankments.

Back at SP I slept an evening siesta but was woken by the pitter-patter of bits of chewing gum, grass stems and small stones dropping onto the sun awning. Three blond haired small boys sat on the quay 3m above SP, looking innocent and sweet. I ignored them even when they tried to ask me questions regarding my gender. They went off to yell and clatter around somewhere in the disused factory. After a half hour the sound of pebbles plunging into the water angered me. After the seventh stone landed I grabbed a big stick and angry as a troll, clambered up the iron rungs of the quay wall. At the top I saw them in a group of three or four busily hurling stones in my direction and they turned and fled at the sight the big stick. I found it difficult to relax and sleep because they might have come back and could easily have dropped some of the really big stones heaped up nearby down onto SP in the night. They did not come back and that evening I was amused by the roaring cheers and honking car horns that went up as France won the world cup against Argentina. The bridge near where the stone throwing kids were was named Pont d'Assault.

The next day I arrived at the closed locks in time for their planned reopening the following day. A queue of barges lay in wait and I moored well back from them to take an evening stroll. In the morning I joined the queue by mooring with a couple of other British cruising boats. One boat gave me breakfast. The other were tempted to smuggle Loba back with them as they were planning on being in Kent by the following evening and they really loved her. The stress of these cruisers was incredible – on the one hand the weather window was just about to close down for weeks and on the other steering problems had to be fixed within hours of arrival at the coast prior to departure across the Channel. Boats contain the stress they leave with when they set out looking for endless pleasure.

The queuing arrangements for the locks were non existent, with the biggest barges gaining priority by default. VHF radio calls to the eclusiers resulted in the English getting more stressed by the nonsensical replies coming back through the hissing radio speaker. A Frenchman on a boat about half the size of SP went forward and tried to slip in to the lock with several huge barges but even he was repelled. At least the English could relax that a French yacht was unable to go through yet. Of course eventually we all piled into the lock, with a 1500 ton barge, two 300 ton barges, a 100 ton liveaboard barge, a 70 ton Dutch cruising barge, a 30 ton motor cruiser, SP at 2.5 tons and the French sailing yacht at about a quarter of a ton. We were all packed into the colossal lock chamber which took 40 minutes to empty its water.

Behind SP the lock sill appeared as a concrete step and grew and grew, higher and higher until it was more than 12m above the boats. Chaos ensued on exiting the lock as the propeller wash from the big barges came untrammelled at the small boats in the confines of the lock chamber. Outside the Ecluse de Flanders was the disused boat lift which the lock had replaced.

The next lock, the Ecluse de Fontinettes was soon ready and we did the same all over again. The distance from St Omer to Calais was now just 50 km and I paced the Dutch barge pressing onwards to reach Calais port by the evening. We swept along and shared the remaining two locks to arrive into Calais outer harbour where I moored SP on a buoy in the same place I had when I first sailed to Calais on Juggler in 1992 with my sailing partner Kresza. It all felt very familiar and I was filled with a feeling of soon–to–be–home–coming in the scintillating sea air of the harbour.

I had reached Calais hopefully anticipating a positive answer from the vet. The fact was explained by the vet that following her fresh rabies inoculation in May she was required to wait six months before qualifying for import to Britain. My choices were many but could be broken down into three – smuggle her to the UK – put her into six months quarantine in the UK – keep her outside the UK for six months.

Quarantine was out of the question because it would cost £2k and be like sending my friend to prison. Smuggling was equally untenable, not only because the risk of a heavy fine and forced removal of Loba into quarantine, but also possible confiscation of SP as a vessel involved in illegal importation.

Instead of being homeward bound across the Dover Straits I was stuck in France. My desire to return "home" to the UK after the long voyage was strong and I even noticed thoughts about letting Loba slip from my life to enable me to get back alone. When this idea arose I was horrified but instead of repressing it I added it to the list of possible choices, otherwise I'd feel resentful towards her as the sole reason for my being unable to go home. Some people I spoke to said, "Well, she is ONLY a dog." Implying Loba could be discarded and my reply was, "Well, we have come a long way together, 2000 km and Loba is my companion, not just a pet." It was me who took her away from Gran Canaria, took responsibility for her little waggly life, and now I was not prepared to cast her off like jetsam in a storm. No way.

My choice was to remain in France with Loba for six months.

Calais Marina had been cleaned up since I sailed there last. Over the past twelve years all the liveaboards had been hustled out and the place had no adventure, no dreams, only neat rows of modern regatta yachts. One night now cost a shocking 19 euros and the cheap option of laying against the quay wall, having to climb an iron ladder, with no services, but for half price, had been stopped. They simply did not want the impecunious to use the place. For a few hours I wondered about the logistics of smuggling Loba to the UK in Storm Petrel – I could enter some small river port where nobody would notice her arrival from France. Of course this is a smugglers mentality and exactly the type of yacht movement customs look–outs would notice.

I returned 35 km back down the Canal du Calais and went 8 km south on L'Aa to Watten. I had in mind a couple of small boats moored on a twist in the river bank that appeared homely with children's toys set up on the grass – and the boats had chimneys. I wanted to meet the people hoping they would welcome a stranger for a few weeks, or longer. At least I could pause there to think of how to make the next six months productive, rather than just a problem. There was a free river bank with strong bollards to moor to under shimmering trees and a string of liveaboard barges.

Watten was too small to be a very small town but busy, unlike the canal side villages in Burgundy and Champagne to the south. Watten had a frites kiosk, two large supermarkets, a small supermarket, two pharmacies, an opticians, domestic electrical store, newsagent, a couple of banks, a hardware store, half a dozen cafés and a restaurant. The railway station gave swift comfortable transport to anywhere. 40–50 barges per day made Storm Petrel dance sometimes but would surely break up winter ice. Surely the villagers and the liveaboard boats would welcome a sailor with a terrier into their midst.

In my diary I numbered the days before Loba could travel to the UK – day 182 soon became day 172 and almost suddenly, day 92 – like grains of sand toppling through an hourglass.

One day sitting on a bollard by the River L'Aa, beneath the big trees full of leafs, with months of exile ahead and 11,000 km behind, I knew what the Portuguese fado singers meant by saudade – I felt it, the distance in time and miles and a yearning to be home. I could live cheaply in France but winter would be really hard without an electricity supply to run a heater. The wood stove was warm enough for days and evenings but there would be a problem waking to a freezing cabin and having to build a fire, although the new stove could be shut down while I went out for several hours and opened on return to light up red within minutes. A stove gives raw warmth and autonomy away from marinas.

I soon made friends in Watten. Between 3 boats we purchased 12 cubic metres of logs for our stoves. Then I was given an electricity supply, so I could use a fan heater. I cut a step and faced it with planks with a silver birch bough as a handhold to get on and off Storm Petrel from the bank. Shovelling earth and chopping wood made me happy again.

Beneath those big trees I watched autumn arrive, the leaves turning yellow and brown and time falling through the hour glass of Watten.

Village life was friendly and relaxed. I got to know people by taking their portrait photographs and giving them away, became known and liked. Instead of spending days wandering and searching in malls and shopping streets I spent time aboard the boat and the other liveaboards welcomed and embraced my music, my boat, my dog – me.

Bridget and Michel had one of the sweetest little dogs I ever saw, called Teetoon. One evening aboard their barge we ate carbonara flamande – a Flemish dish stewed over several hours with Belgium brown beer. I played the saxophone, leading a mini parade around the large kitchen and living room like a scene out of the Dunkerque carnival.

Arno and Maite had a post box with the name of their boat, "LE NORD", celebrating the very idea of the north. Their daughter, Tara, liked to imagine herself as a princess called Jasmine. Arno worked with parquet flooring and Maite played guitar. In the late summer evenings we sat on the river bank under the trees around a fire, with bottles of brown beer, aperitifs of pastis and glasses of wine. My French improved almost enough to understand Arno's philosophy which seemed entirely based around some notion of 'vertical time'. Arno compared the vertical growth and progression of trees, fire and time.

Maite demonstrated the Dunkerque carnival again by prancing like a pony in a solo procession around the table, singing a marching tune and miming a trumpet while the delicious smoke of burning leaves and twigs went up, up and away in the luminous north night, into the vertical future.

## THE END

*Pontailler sur Saone*

*The bucolic wonder of central France*

*Bourg–et–Comin*

*Entering Balesmes tunnel, over 4km of black, echoing, dripping, underground canal.*

*Peniches at Bourg–et–Comin*

*Illus. Maps - Becky Gilbey*

# Epilogue
## Loba's Importation

By the second half of February the sunshine became more spring-like and I felt prepared enough to leave Watten and set-off towards Calais and the sea. Loba was officially entitled to enter Britain.

I cycled to the Champion supermarket to fill up a twenty litre diesel can and bought four kilos of good leeks from Chez Francine's, one bag for myself and the other to pay back Michel for a bag I owed him. Michel and Bridgette were out when I dropped off the leeks and I remembered they had gone to the St Pol carnaval. I was invited but declined as I do not enjoy Mardi Gras – all those men dressed as women and the riotous liberty in the air makes me nervous. I am not against freedom but when people who are normally constrained by repressive sexual mores are suddenly given free pratique to be drunken prostitutes and drag queens, and nothing but those figures, makes for a travesty of freedom rather than a celebration. I liked some aspects of Mardi Gras – the coming of spring, fecundity of the earth, warmer, lighter days and life alive – but tights, wigs and make-up do nothing to affirm those for a dogged old Hector.

On the first of March my parents came to collect Loba and we took the Euro tunnel to Dover. The journey began with a spaghetti map of access roads leading first to the massive shopping centre called Citè Europ to get a few bottles of wine and some camembert and baguettes to eat en route, then we found the Euro tunnel entrance with the pets arrival point to clear Loba. A two minute visit involved a wave of an electric wand over the embedded chip in her neck and we were free to go. After seven months waiting and preparation things suddenly seemed so simple. For the thirty minute train journey we sat in the car chomping camembert and baguette while ships plundered the waves somewhere above. Eventually I was dropped off at the Dover ferry terminal to buy a ferry ticket back to Calais where Storm Petrel was waiting to be sailed back to Britain.

## The Author

Born Huntingdon 1961. Sailed with parents in a GP14 dinghy, never liked it; too young to take control. This early experience gave her a deep sense of security offshore in later life. 1990 she sold her house and bought a small boat with a big dream to sail to Spain. The big voyage remained a dream throughout twelve years of cruising. Progressively audacious trips set out from the harbours and rivers of the East Coast of England, to arrive in France, Belgium; then the South Coast of Britain and eventually around Land's End into the Bristol Channel. She settled in Bristol for five years, graduated with a BA at UWE. Sociology taught her to organize large texts and sailing provided rich experiences. Bristol was the turning point which led to The Voyage of Storm Petrel.

Book 1. *Britain to Senegal Alone in a Boat.*
Book 2. *Gambia and Europe Alone in a Boat.*

17788488R00158

Printed in Great Britain
by Amazon